WILD MIAMI

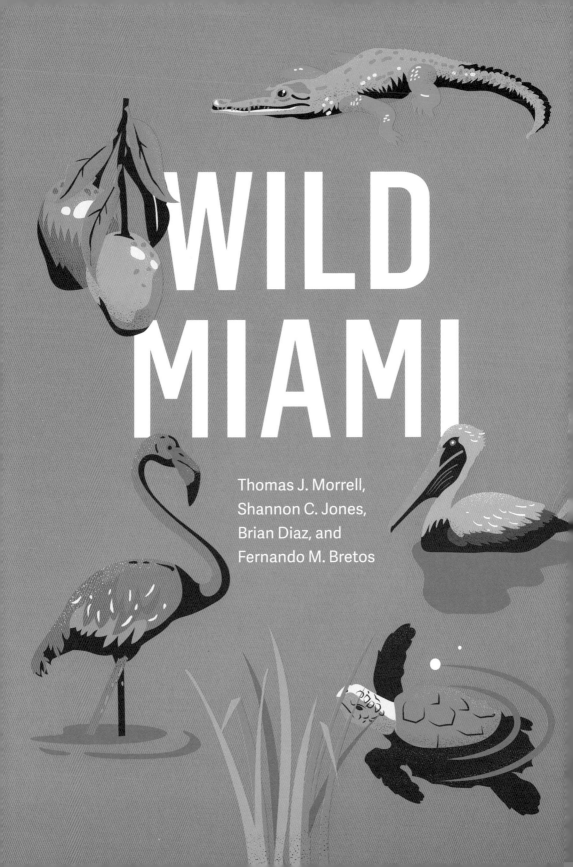

WILD
MIAMI

Thomas J. Morrell,
Shannon C. Jones,
Brian Diaz, and
Fernando M. Bretos

EXPLORE THE AMAZING NATURE IN AND AROUND SOUTH FLORIDA

TIMBER PRESS
PORTLAND, OR

From the ocean to the Everglades, to the
first Paleoindians and immigrants of all
races, genders, and ethnicities who helped
build this beautiful city, we'd like to recognize the Miamians who came before us
and helped mold this place into our home.
Forever 305.

Frontispiece: Queen Parrotfish
Copyright © 2022 by Thomas J. Morrell, Shannon C. Jones,
    Brian Diaz, and Fernando M. Bretos. All rights reserved.
Photo and illustration credits appear on page 366.

Published in 2022 by Timber Press, Inc.
The Haseltine Building
133 S.W. Second Avenue, Suite 450
Portland, Oregon 97204-3527
timberpress.com

Printed in China on paper from responsible sources
Text design by Anna Eshelman and Mary Velgos
Cover design by Adrianna Sutton and Kiko Rodriguez

ISBN 978-1-64326-074-7
A catalog record for this book is available from
the Library of Congress.

CONTENTS

INTRODUCTION

Part travel book, part nature guide, part conservation spotlight, this book aims to share a side of Miami that's often overlooked but aches to be discovered by locals and visitors alike. We hope you'll use it to learn about our history and ecology, find volunteer opportunities, identify species, and gain a better understanding of environmental sustainability.

We've divided the book up into three sections—history, field trips, and species—that aim to provide interesting and memorable information, shedding light on how humans and nature are connected within this amazing city. With twenty-five field trip locations and 305 species descriptions, we aim to show you the beautiful, natural aspects of the city's landscapes and highlight some of the wildlife you might encounter in your travels.

Conservation Connections found throughout the book give insight into what's being done by local organizations in the Miami environmental scene and how you can get involved. Whether highlighting the battle against sea level rise and efforts to protect our treasured pine rocklands, or just providing additional information on a particular species' general preservation status, these highlights are an introduction to the organizations leading South Florida's environmental charge.

This book is a culmination of years of experience and enthusiasm for nature, combined with a desire to create something truly useful for those with an interest in the natural world. It is our sincere hope you enjoy reading it as much as we did writing it.

► Staghorn Coral on Florida's Coral Reef

◄ Florida Burrowing Owl

MEET THE AUTHORS

The four authors of this book came together through a collective passion for the city of Miami and, more specifically, the hidden natural beauty it has to offer. With unique perspectives and fields of expertise, all four of us contributed knowledge, study, personal experiences, and environmental appreciation. Two of us are homegrown Miamians (from Hialeah and Miami Beach), and the other two are visitors from Pennsylvania and New Jersey who moved here and never left. We came together to share a part of the city people don't often get to see, but definitely should. Here's a little bit of background as to how we got where we are today.

Thomas J. Morrell

At some point in your life, somebody will ask you about your favorite superhero power. At that moment, you'll have to make a difficult choice— oftentimes publicly—as to which power suits you best. Despite the crowd favorites, or hundreds of other "better" options, the choice was always fairly easy for me. I remember being asked this question at ten years old, surrounded by my closest friends. Without hesitation, I confidently replied, "the ability to speak to fish!" This went over as smoothly as you might expect, but it was clear to me even at that young age that I wanted my life to be focused on the ocean. I mean, who wouldn't want to talk to a shark? That self-knowledge, among countless other experiences, helped pave the way for me as I began to focus on marine and environmental sciences. From interning in South Africa with great white sharks to working at the National Oceanic and Atmospheric Administration (NOAA) with fish larvae and migratory species, my passions center around nature, wildlife, and the environment. That, and also the hope of someday speaking to sharks.

Shannon C. Jones

When I was around seven years old, my parents brought me on my first trip to Orlando, Florida, where we went to Sea World and I instantly fell madly in love with dolphins. A few years later, I remember being in my fifth grade classroom drawing a picture of "what I wanted to be when I grew up." Although I couldn't spell the words marine biologist, I knew that was my path. First I studied psychology in Pennsylvania—not near the ocean. Then I studied animal behavior and cognition and went on to become a volunteer research assistant in Kona, Hawaii, learning about how tourism affected the resident dolphins. This inspired me to study marine conservation at University of Miami. My goal in life is to inspire others to feel a love of nature and a yearning to make changes that protect the world around us. I educate the public about marine life and conservation, specifically by raising awareness about threats to the ecosystems in which humans interact. Communication and outreach are important to me, because I believe it's vital to connect the science community with regular people, so we can all work together for a sustainable and healthy future.

Brian Diaz

As a child, I took every opportunity to watch Steve Irwin on television, staring wide-eyed as I vicariously met hundreds of wild animals through him. He introduced me to conservation and the threats facing the natural world. Today, conservation infuses every aspect of my life—it's my ever-present mission. Anywhere I go, my eyes naturally gravitate toward the color green. I have a deep-rooted fascination with plants (particularly native plants), and I understand my surroundings through the kinds of trees growing in the area. Owing to this and my shoulder-length hair, I am affectionately called Plant Jesus by friends, family, and colleagues, a nickname I always joke will fall out of favor the moment I get a haircut. But no matter how short or long my hair is, my love for plants and wildlife will always remain. It's a passion I share liberally, often distractedly stopping conversations midway to point out something that's in bloom or an interesting bird gliding overhead. My career centers on ecosystem preservation, essentially using native plants to rebuild nature where it has been lost and creating homes where wildlife can move in. I cannot imagine anything else I would rather be doing.

Fernando M. Bretos

Somehow, I always knew conservation was in my blood. As a child of Cuban parents growing up in Australia, I spent a lot of time outdoors with my family, and because my father always loved plants, we spent an inordinate amount of time at the Sydney Botanical Gardens. But it wasn't until I was a junior at Miami Beach Senior High School that I found my calling. Interestingly it came from English class. We were reading the English romantic poets and learning about how the Industrial Revolution created a romantic revolution, in which young artists like William Wordsworth and Percy Shelly became enamored by nature and its ability to cure the ills of industrialization. Buried within their poems was a longing to leave the gray contaminated skies of industrial England for idyllic woods. Their ideals sparked my passion, and I embarked on a mission to express it. I researched tropical rainforests in Panama and tiger sharks in western Australia, learning to make a career out of protecting the planet. Today, I have a dream job working as program officer at the Ocean Foundation, where I oversee projects to study marine migratory species, restore tropical coastal habitats, and use ocean diplomacy to encourage countries to protect shared marine resources.

WILD MIAMI

A History of 305

South Beach, Cuban coffee, the Wynwood Walls, and Ocean Drive. These all conjure an image of the trendy, modern-day Miami we've come to know and love. It's a city with a rich, diverse history built on migration. From the first Miamians who arrived at least 14,000 years ago to the most recent arrivals from Latin America, Europe, or even Manhattan, waves of visitors over the years have made Miami their home. Throughout the centuries, Miami has been a haven for those seeking a new beginning or fortune. While some crossed the Florida Straits from the Bahamas to build this city from pristine pine rocklands, others were forced to leave as new settlers arrived. Miami's origin story is one built on movement, war, innovation, and inspiration.

Miami's draw was not always its warm weather. When the first Paleoindians arrived in Florida, our mighty peninsula was just exiting the current ice age and its climate was colder and dryer. Since then, a warming trend commenced, which continues today at an accelerated pace. The size of the state was also dramatically different back then. In fact, not too long ago, Florida was twice as wide as today, its western half high and dry and bustling with woolly mammoths and giant sloths. Today, this half is submerged under the Gulf of Mexico. Going back even further—millions of years ago—all of Miami lay under the sea. This back-and-forth submersion and exposure explains why dinosaurs are nowhere to be found in Florida's fossil layers today. Instead, you can find shark teeth and shells embedded in a hard, white rock that was once an ancient coral reef and is now our limestone bedrock. This reminds us that Miami has always been at the beck and call of the ocean. It is our source of food, rain, peace of mind, and those stunning ocean-front views.

Water World

Ours is a history of water. We are surrounded by it. To the east lies the Atlantic Ocean and to our west the Everglades, the largest freshwater wetland in North America. These two bodies of water set off a convection cycle, and as a result, Miami is one of the rainiest cities in America. At sixty-two inches of average rainfall per year, our city receives almost twice as much rain as Seattle, Washington, a city famous for never-ending rain. Convection is also the source of our warm and sticky summer afternoons. Fortunately, our sandy soils and porous limestone bedrock allow much of the rain to drain rapidly. Ever wonder why Miami has so few rivers? Rainwater drains so fast

▲ The Florida Peninsula

here that there's essentially no need for them. Beneath the Miami cityscape is the Biscayne Aquifer, an enormous subterranean lake that gives us the excellent drinking water we enjoy. So, water and all of its forms is above us, around us, next to us, and even under us.

Miami's First People

Miami's human history is as rich as its natural history. The first documented civilization here was that of the Tequesta, a tribe that lived off natural resources of the sea and land. Due to a lack of topsoil, low nutrients, and near-impenetrable coral bedrock, agriculture in South Florida was a losing battle and therefore never practiced by the Tequesta. As hunters and gatherers, they stuck to harvesting naturally growing nuts, roots, and fruits and used resources from the sea such as mollusks, fish and even manatees. Archeological digs have revealed bones and shells at Tequesta sites that paint a picture of this lifestyle. Close your eyes and try to imagine what Biscayne Bay must have looked like back then: crystal clear waters teeming with fish and birds and underground springs bubbling freshwater into the saltwater bay.

The Tequesta lived at the mouths of our few rivers. During the hot summer, they would move to the barrier islands of Miami Beach and Key Biscayne where the mosquitoes were less of a nuisance. Today, you can visit a Tequesta archeological site right in downtown Miami at the Miami Circle National Historic Landmark. You can also see a Tequesta habitation mound just north of the Little River in El Portal; it's located at one of the highest points above sea level, suggesting the Tequesta recognized changing seas as a threat. As flat as Miami is, it's easy to discern the elevated knolls where the Tequesta once piled food remains in middens (mounds of shells and other artifacts).

▼ Statue of a Tequesta family on Brickell Avenue in Downtown Miami

▲ The Miami Circle is a National Historic Landmark and archeological site right in downtown Miami.

There's evidence the Tequesta, always sparse in population compared to the magnificent pre-Columbian civilizations of the American south or Meso-america, were pushed around by the more powerful Calusa who inhabited lands west and south of Miami. This and their lack of agriculture meant their population wasn't very large when the Spanish arrived in the early sixteenth century. It would soon disappear entirely due to the slave trade, forced relocations, and the spread of disease.

The first European to explore Florida was the Spanish conquistador Juan Ponce de León, who sighted the coast in 1513. As his sighting took place during Easter, or *Pascua Florida* as they call it in Spanish, the name Florida stuck. The first European settlement was at St. Augustine, about 300 miles north of Miami, where the soil was firmer and impenetrable mangroves weren't a concern. Founded in 1565 by Pedro Menéndez de Avilés, St. Augustine became an important Spanish colony for protecting Spanish galleons filled with pirated silver and gold from Peru and Mexico.

◄ Menéndez de Avilés, founder of St. Augustine

► St. Augustine was the first successful European colony in what would become the United States.

St. Augustine was always more of a defensive fortification, but it was critical to the Spanish in that it lay adjacent to the important Gulf Stream, the oceanic conveyor belt of warm, fast-moving ocean water that runs from just north of Venezuela all the way to Ireland via the Caribbean Sea and Gulf of Mexico. On its way it passes Colombia, turns north, and flows well off-shore from the Central American Caribbean coast before picking up speed at the Yucatan Straits. It then enters the Gulf of Mexico where half of its water splits off and passes by Florida into the Atlantic Ocean. Once off the coast of Florida, the water moves at about the speed of a brisk walk. Ponce de León himself was the first European to realize that ships could hitch a ride back home on this conveyor belt and save considerable time. Gold- and silver-laden galleons sailing from the mines of Colombia by way of Havana could stop off for provisions and fortifications before delivering their bounty to King Phillip II of Spain. A young Benjamin Franklin later took so much interest in what he called a "river in the ocean" that he lobbied hard in his position as the Deputy General Postmaster of the American colonies to use the Gulf Stream to increase the speed of the mail service from the east coast of America to Europe.

A Young History, Even for a Geologist

Florida, as we know it today, is quite young on a geological scale. Coming out of the ice age eleven millennia ago, rain levels increased and sea levels continued to rise until South Florida lay, like many other coastal areas, just above sea level. It remains at this level today. Miami averages only 6.5 feet in elevation, making rising ocean levels an increasingly worrisome threat.

▼ The Gulf Stream is an oceanic conveyor belt with an average velocity of four miles per hour, but it can reach speeds of more than five miles per hour near the surface.

Further inland, the vast Everglades wetland system is only 6,000 years old—quite extraordinary considering it spans the entire width of our state and is large enough to be seen from space. Heavy summer rains fall in the wetlands just north of Lake Okeechobee, Florida's largest lake, and are transported via the Kissimmee River directly to the lake, which, due to all that incoming water, overflows its banks and continues as a shallow river all the way south to Florida Bay, the southern terminus of the peninsula. Travelling over rugged,

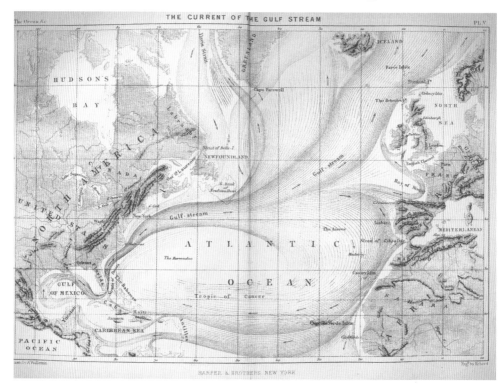

porous substrate makes the Everglades not only the widest river in the world, but also the slowest, moving at a speed of 0.00062 mile per hour. That's about fifty times slower than an applesnail (a common Everglades inhabitant). This enormous wetland is critical to our state's well-being. It not only provides freshwater for most of our urban areas and wildlife but also underpins the cycle of life here, supporting millions of birds, reptiles, and mammals. Unfortunately, all this water wasn't what the European settlers wanted to see, as it made settlement almost impossible.

Removing the Unwanted

Ever since Europeans first saw Florida, they set their sights on making it more like Europe: dry, temperate, agriculturally productive, and tame. This wasn't practical for the first European-Floridians who were struggling to feed themselves on a daily basis, but in the nineteenth century it became not only possible, but necessary. After Spain grew tired of American settlers entering their land, they ceded Florida to the United States as part of the Adams-Onís Treaty of 1819. This also meant the Spanish would no longer have to worry about the persistent confrontations with native Seminole warriors.

The Seminole, an offshoot of the Muscogee, also known as the Creek Tribe, originally from Georgia and Alabama, acquired their name from the anglicization of the Spanish word *cimarron*, which means runaway. Upon its possession of Florida, the new American nation decided it needed to rid its

▼ The Miami River was the Seminoles' home.

Florida territory of two stubborn elements: indigenous inhabitants and water. The two went hand in hand, as it wasn't until the young nation declared war on the Seminole and penetrated deep into their last hiding spot, the soggy Everglades, that the idea to drain the peninsula first dawned on them.

Seminole Wars

The United States needed not one, but three military conflicts, called the Seminole Wars (1816–1858) to remove the rebellious and elusive Seminole from Florida. Each of the three wars were highly unpopular, expensive, and deadly, with thousands of casualties on both sides. The First Seminole War was led by General (and later President) Andrew Jackson and led to the Seminole retreating deep into the Everglades. The Second Seminole War was intended to drive the Seminole out of Florida entirely but was unsuccessful. The Third (and final) Seminole War saw the end of Seminole Nation. Though 500 hardy individuals held out in the most inhospitable corners of the Everglades (a testament to their unflinching bond with their homeland) the majority of Seminole moved west along the Trail of Tears, one of the most infamously cruel episodes in American history, which saw the forced displacement of all major southeastern indigenous tribes to Oklahoma, where many of them still live today. Over 60,000 people died during this journey, many starving along the way. Throughout the wars, Miami, known then as Fort Dallas, served as a military base focused on purging the last of the Seminole. The origins of the name Miami remain a mystery, but most historians agree the name stems from the Mayaimi, a now-extinct tribe that inhabited the area near Lake Okeechobee.

▼ Seminoles sought cover from US soldiers within mangrove swamps.

Draining the Wetlands

During their forays into the Everglades, many Seminole War generals commented on the wateriness of South Florida, writing home with far-fetched ideas of draining the water for agriculture and habitation. The standing water had proven difficult to build on or harvest from, and the scourge of yellow fever and malaria from mosquitoes made permanent settlements south of Tampa impossible. Once the surviving Seminoles had been expelled from the state, Florida's new settlers turned their attention to removing as much water from the peninsula as possible, but, lacking modern machinery, there was no plausible way to pull this off.

In 1881, Hamilton Disston purchased four million acres of land for one million dollars (equal to about twenty-seven million dollars today). His original intention was to build canals that would drain the water, but he only ever managed to construct a few miles of them. Luckily for him, his project attracted so much speculative attention that population increases and a doubling of property values allowed him to recoup his money by selling off land by the acre. Decades later, Florida's nineteenth governor, Napoleon Bonaparte Broward, campaigned successfully on a promise to drain the state. He imposed a tax on all counties benefiting from drainage and managed to install two dredges that cut just six miles of canal before he had the state sell the land. In the end, wholesale draining of the Everglades wouldn't be successful until the next century. In the meantime, attempts to rid the area of water paved the way for another money maker: tourism.

Julia Tuttle, Henry Flagler, and The Brickells

◀ Governor Broward (1857–1910)

▶ Julia Tuttle (1849–1898)

Miami is the only major US city to be founded by a woman. In 1875, Julia "The Mother of Miami" Tuttle, a wealthy businesswoman from Cleveland, Ohio, came to Fort Dallas to visit a citrus grove owned by her father. At the time, Fort Dallas was a harsh backwater on the banks of the Miami River, but it must have made a positive impression. After her father died, she used her inheritance to purchase 640 acres of coastal land on the northern banks of the Miami River. After the devastating Great Freeze of 1894–95, which fortunately spared Miami, she began to sell parts of her tract and convinced railway tycoon and fellow Clevelander Henry Flagler to extend his great railroad to South Florida. Flagler eventually sent a team of speculators and, soon after, began building the Royal Palm Hotel as a terminus for his railroad on the land now called Brickell.

William and Mary Brickell were also instrumental in the foundation of Miami. The pair operated a trading post, exchanging goods with the remaining Seminoles and the Miccosukee, an offshoot Seminole tribe then living in the Everglades. The Brickells donated hundreds of acres to Flagler to extend his Florida East Coast Railway, which would eventually make its way all the way to Key West. On July 28, 1896, Miami went from a remote military base to an officially incorporated city of the United States. The Magic City was born!

A City Built on the Backs of Bahamians and African Americans

At the turn of the nineteenth century, there were few people willing to live in Miami and help build the city. The first Miami residents were Black laborers from the Bahamas. Initially they made the short crossing of the Florida Straits to use their seafaring talents salvaging shipwrecked vessels and repairing boats. As the city grew, more Bahamian laborers arrived to clear vegetation and build homes and hotels. The first Miami hotel was the Peacock Inn, which was built entirely by Black hands in 1882. Bahamians mostly settled in the current day Coconut Grove neighborhood, which lies south of downtown Miami. If you take a drive down Charles and Williams Avenues, you can see some of the old, British West Indian–style wood houses they built. As long-time island inhabitants, they knew how to build homes that suited Miami's climate and could withstand the strongest of hurricanes. In the early nineteenth century, African Americans, migrating from the rural South, joined the Bahamians to make up 40 percent of the city's population. Not only did they build the city with their own hands, but, when massive tropical cyclones such as the Great Miami Hurricane of 1926 and the Great Labor Day Hurricane of 1935 devastated the city, they rebuilt it.

The new Black Miamians settled in downtown Miami in what is now Overtown (called Colored Town at the time). Known as the Harlem of the South, Overtown was a cultural powerhouse, hosting music, sporting, and theater events featuring stars such as Nat King Cole and Muhammad Ali. When visiting Overtown today, make sure to visit the Lyric Theater, which has occupied the same building since 1913. Overtown, unfortunately, was the victim of a political agenda that would forever alter the town's layout. In 1961, the US Department of Transportation went in search of land for Interstate 95, a federal highway which would start in Miami near Vizcaya Gardens and

▲ Early Bahamian residents of Coconut Grove in front of the boat house that is now part of the Barnacle Historic State Park.

run 1,908 miles to the Canadian border in Maine. They chose the path of least political resistance, Overtown, as the site to build the overpass. This effectively cut the neighborhood in two with a concrete span, a specter of intolerance and exploitation that remains to this day. With no heed for the damage this caused, the city also built the I-395 connector through Overtown ten years later, this time quartering the neighborhood. Recent efforts to revitalize Overtown have made progress, but residents there and in nearby Liberty City are now facing another dilemma—getting priced out by developers searching for higher-elevation housing that's less vulnerable to sea level rise.

Harvesting the Everglades

Unable to effectively drain the Everglades in the early twentieth century, prospectors found a gold rush of another kind, hunting otters, alligators, and raccoons for valuable pelts. Wanting to squeeze additional money from the Everglades, the hunters also turned their guns on its plentiful and beautifully colored wading birds. Millions of birds were shot each year, mostly in the early spring when their plumage was brightest, for feathers to adorn women's hats. It's said that, once, Florida skies would go completely dark as countless birds flew overhead blocking the sun. Thanks to plume hunting, many species of wading birds almost went extinct.

A silver lining to this devastation was the creation of the National Audubon Society in 1905, which continues to protect American birds to this day. The carnage was also a major impetus for the creation of Pelican Island Sanctuary in 1903 and Everglades National Park in 1947.

The River of Grass

A woman founded Miami and another woman saved it. Marjory Stoneman Douglas, originally from Minneapolis, Minnesota, moved to Miami in 1915. Here, she started her career as a writer for the fledgling *Miami Herald*, then called the *Miami Evening Record*, which was founded by her father. Eight years later, she left the newspaper to write as a freelance journalist and hone her talents for scathing, yet poetic, independent writing in which she could express her passion for nature. While doing research for a book chapter about the Miami River, Douglas came to feel that South Florida's true

◄ Original cover of Marjory Stoneman Douglas's timeless classic

river was not the short and shallow Miami River but the Everglades, which she christened the River of Grass. Though it is a more complex ecosystem than a river, the Everglades does flow ever so slowly, covered in sawgrass and sitting atop a massive freshwater aquifer. Douglas's book, *The Everglades: River of Grass*, required five years of extensive ecological research and was published in 1947, the same year the Everglades became a national park. In it, she pointed to the unique nature of the wetland as a source of water, tranquility, livelihood, and wildlife and highlighted the threats it faces: cattle grazing, draining, and sugar cane production.

Marjory Stoneman Douglas lived a remarkably long life, passing away in 1998 at the age of 108. Her book has sold more than 500,000 copies and helped give this South Florida ecological marvel international recognition. In part or in whole, *River of Grass* is narrated by almost every schoolteacher in South Florida to young wide-eyed pupils realizing their city is buffered by one of the vastest, most unique wetlands on earth.

Miami Bustles with Tourism and Migration

▼ The iconic, modern-day Miami skyline is currently the third tallest in the United States, behind New York and Chicago.

The opening of the Royal Palm Hotel in 1897 initiated a phase of mass-scale tourism. While the hotel only stood for three decades (until the Great Miami Hurricane of 1926 caused enough damage that it needed to be demolished),

it and Flagler's railroad cemented Miami as a tourism destination. First to arrive were northern snowbirds, but eventually tourists from all over the world would start arriving. Only World War I, the Great Depression, World War II, and economic recessions in the 1970s and 1980s caused major pauses in the expansion of Miami tourism. While many of the early hotels have been destroyed or remodeled, several buildings still remain along Ocean Drive and Washington Avenue in Miami Beach. The Art Deco architecture alone is worth the visit. One example, the Miami Biltmore Hotel in Coral Gables, built in 1926, is a vestige of this period. Though it was abandoned for several decades, it has been restored and operates as a luxury hotel today.

In 1960, Miami had a population of 291,688, but that number soon began to grow. That year, Cubans fleeing the Cuban Revolution arrived in southeast Florida en masse. Subsequent waves of immigration further expanded Miami's population—Haitians and Nicaraguans in the 1980s and Colombians, Argentines, Central Americans, and Venezuelans in the years that followed. These migrations would lead to the city's incredible cultural diversity.

Miami Here and Now

Miami's metropolitan area, which includes areas in Miami-Dade, Broward, and Palm Beach Counties, now numbers over six million inhabitants and growing. Upon landing at Miami International Airport or driving in from I-95, you may be struck by the amount of concrete you see. Miami-Dade County lies on a thirty-mile-wide sliver of highly urbanized cityscape buffered by water on all sides. As a result, Miami has strict geographical limits. But don't let the concrete fool you into thinking there isn't a vast array of wildlife within and surrounding the city. Within our urban zone, and especially east and west of it, nature is everywhere. There are hundreds of city and county parks, green spaces, and undeveloped coastlines waiting to be explored. You just need to know where to look.

Clear Days and Sunny Rays

Miami's climate allows you to get outside and explore year-round. We typically don't have a harsh winter that traps you inside. In fact, winter is arguably the ideal time of year to enjoy outdoor activities, with temperatures generally around 70 degrees Fahrenheit during the day, as opposed to summer when it's usually hot, humid, and rainy.

Miami's location at 25 degrees north latitude puts it just south of the horse latitudes, which are located at roughly 30 degrees north and south of the equator and characterized by peaceful winds, minimal precipitation, and sunny days. The horse latitudes are named for the horses that were thrown overboard by crews on cargo ships who needed to conserve scarce

▲ With its gorgeous beach and pristine coastal environment, Crandon Park on Key Biscayne is the epitome of a beautiful subtropic habitat that invites you to be outside and enjoy it.

drinking water after being stalled by a lack of wind. The trade winds between the horse latitudes and the equator circle the globe in a constant westward direction and connect us to Africa and the Saharan Desert—importantly, they act as a carrier for the desert dust that blows across the Atlantic, bringing important nutrients for our coral reefs.

On the east coast, the trade winds come fresh off the ocean to envelop the city, leading to enviable air quality year-round. Winter is our dry season, with the period between November and April characterized by little rain and cool nights. Occasionally, a cold front descends from the north, plummeting temperatures to just above freezing, a reminder that though close to the tropics, Miami is still part of a massive temperate continent. Summer is our wet season, and the afternoons from May to October often experience the heavy summer rains common in tropical climates.

Diversity in Miami is emphasized in its habitats and native flora and fauna. The subtropical climate here on the southeast tip of Florida supports an incredibly high number of plant and animal species. There are few other places in the world where such a mix of temperate, tropical, marine, and aquatic organisms coexist.

Coasts in Crisis

Water is the defining feature of essentially all South Florida's ecosystems. It flows from freshwater wetlands to marine areas, intermixing with saltwater to form productive, brackish estuaries. In turn, ocean waters evaporate and form dense rain clouds, which bring freshwater back inland. Life is not possible without water, and this interconnected flow is incredibly fragile. South Florida's waterways have been altered over the past century and a half, affected by climate change-induced sea level rise, water quality, and pollution.

The Seas Are Rising

Miami's coastline is always changing. With today's atmospheric carbon dioxide level recently surpassing 400 parts per million, change is afoot again, and the consequences are not encouraging. Human activity is trapping

▼ With elevation averaging just over six feet above sea level, Miami is very susceptible to sea level rise.

Conservation Connection

Climate Leadership Engagement Opportunities

Recognizing the severe existential threat that climate change poses to Florida (and especially Miami), CLEO works to give communities across the state the tools they need to generate positive changes in the policies and social infrastructure necessary to mitigate and defend against the impacts of climate change.

Florida International University's Sea Level Rise Solution Center

With multiple locations in Miami-Dade County, this organization collaborates with experts around the world to develop sustainable responses to climate-change related threats. They are a reliable source for sea-level-rise education, communication, and research.

greenhouse gases like carbon dioxide and methane in our atmosphere, causing temperatures around the globe to rise. Our planet is heating up. Sea level has risen five to eight inches since 1900. Miami is low-lying and has historically relied on mangroves, beach dunes, corals, and seagrasses to create new land and break up wave energy. But a century of rapid urban development has relegated those habitats to fragments, replacing them with ineffective sea walls. Every autumn, during the king tides (the highest tides of the year), Miami experiences sunny day flooding—streets in low-lying areas, such as the southwest section of South Beach, which were once buffered by mangroves, are subjected to two feet of sea water on days when it doesn't even rain. The flooding can be so bad that, in 2016, somebody filmed an octopus swimming in the underground parking lot of a Miami Beach condo. But all is not lost. Many of the crucial habitats featured in this book are making a comeback through a combination of smart coastal engineering, volunteer restoration, and natural recruitment. Together, these habitats can act as green infrastructure that will help Miami withstand sea level rise and tropical storms.

A Bay in Bloom

Despite its immensity, Biscayne Bay has unfortunately not been able to escape human pressure. For years, there has been evidence that the bay's health is declining. Ecologically detrimental seagrass and coral die-offs are some of the more common outcomes, but in late 2020, something unthinkable finally happened. What started as a handful of isolated observations of

dead fish washing up on shore quickly snowballed into a massive fish kill. Droves of marine life started turning up dead in the bay. The culprit? A lack of oxygen in the water resulting from the presence of excessive nutrients from fertilizer runoff and leakages from septic tanks or broken sewer pipes. This hypercharged wastewater is carried directly to the bay via stormwater drains and underground seepage. It reduces water quality and spurs algal blooms—essentially an algae population explosion. As the algae dies and decomposes, it extracts heavy amounts of dissolved oxygen from the water in a process called eutrophication. With no oxygen in the water, animals that use gills to breathe die. This dramatic event was an environmental wake-up call for Miami and the rest of Florida.

Algal blooms also produce toxins in the water that make people and land-based animals sick, and they block sunlight for underwater vegetation like seagrasses. Because seagrasses are effective at water filtration, when they start to die off, the water only gets murkier and the damaging cycle continues (sediment runoff from erosion and careless construction has a similar clouding effect). Make no mistake, Biscayne Bay can die. The price for not acting swiftly and strongly will be the loss of Miami's marine lifeblood, the waters that have supported people for thousands of years and continue to do so to this day.

▲ The devastating fish kill and algal bloom in August of 2020 affected North Miami to Virginia Key.

► In 2019 and 2020 alone, more than 1.5 million gallons of "unauthorized discharges" of wastewater and sewage were released in Biscayne Bay.

Conservation Connection

Miami Waterkeeper

Perhaps Miami's most well-known water defender, this group was founded in 2010 with the goals of alerting residents about compromised water quality, protecting water-based habitats, and bolstering our strategies against sea level rise. They aren't a shy group, often bringing these issues to the direct attention of government entities and advocating for a change in the system. Their successes are many, and after the 2020 fish die-off, they launched a collaborative effort to save Biscayne Bay, helping secure governmental investment in restoration. Their 1000 Eyes on the Water program trains citizens to be vigilant about signs of declining water health and how to report what they see. They also conduct regular water quality monitoring throughout Miami's beaches to ensure they are safe to swim in.

Save the Water

This national program focuses on the issue of water pollution. Irresponsible practices in industry have contaminated waterways throughout the nation, introducing potent chemicals that not only directly harm ecosystems but people, too. One of their main projects is a study that aims to identify pollutants found in the water running through the Everglades, something which has yet to be comprehensively assessed.

The Pesky Plastic Problem

Plastic is ubiquitous in our everyday lives—it's hard to imagine living without it. But plastic is relatively new, only becoming a widely available material in the 1960s, when it was touted for its moldability and resilience. Today, a look around your home reveals it everywhere. It's in disposable items like bottles, wrappers, and party plates as well as more durable items like computer cases, sunglasses, children's toys, and clothing (polyester fabric). But the same ability to withstand the elements that makes plastic so useful also makes it a dangerous environmental pollutant. With so much plastic being produced every year, coupled with inefficiencies in the world's waste and recycling systems, it shouldn't be surprising that enormous amounts of the stuff makes its way into our ecosystems, particularly the oceans. There, it doesn't decompose like a fallen leaf or discarded banana peel would, as organisms have not evolved the ability to digest it. Rather, it breaks up, fragmenting into smaller and smaller pieces. The plastic doesn't disappear but rather disintegrates into what's called microplastic. Microplastics then find their way into the food web, with fish, marine birds, and sea turtles confusing them for a bite-sized snack. One recent report estimates that by 2050, there will be more plastic than fish in the ocean by weight. It's painfully clear that something must be done.

Though resolving the problem fully will require fundamental changes in the way humans use plastic, picking up litter from the environment goes a long way. Miami sees a lot of marine debris washing up onto its beaches. Thankfully, there are plenty of passionate groups working to help us clean up our act, providing volunteer opportunities to make our shorelines a cleaner, safer place for people and wildlife.

As an individual, you should never feel as though a problem is too big for you to make an impact. As we'll mention throughout this book, there are hundreds of ways for you to get involved, either through volunteering, or by performing smaller acts of environmentalism in your day-to-day life.

➤ As a coastal city, Miami is often one of the first to encounter the effects of climate change.

▼ Many local Miami organizations offer volunteer opportunities to help fight against plastic pollution.

Conservation Connection

Debris Free Ocean

The mission of this organization is to change our relationship with plastic at every level. You may have heard of the three Rs of waste management: Reduce, Reuse, and Recycle. Well, they actually use *six* Rs: Reduce, Reuse, Recycle, Rethink, Recapture, and Redesign, approaching the issue from multiple angles. Their recapture initiative involves hosting regular coastal cleanups around Miami, and they have robust educational programming to build awareness and get people excited to help and change their own plastic consumption habits.

FillABag

See a lot of marine debris at the beach but no cleanup events happening? Look around for a tall, white post with a diamond-shaped turquoise sign. Originating in Key Biscayne, the FillABag initiative is a gateway eco-activity designed to bring awareness to the issues of marine debris and plastic pollution. By installing thirty-nine (and counting!) wooden posts with reusable bags and buckets at local Florida beaches, FillABag invites individuals to turn an ordinary stroll into a meaningful clean up every day. Simply grab a FillABag bucket from the sign post and collect some trash along your walk. When you're done throw away the trash and return the bucket. Easy as that.

Surfrider Foundation

Active in coastal areas across the country, the Surfrider Foundation works to bring awareness and meaningful, positive change to the state of our oceans. In addition to activism and educational programming, they also host a variety of volunteer-based events, including beach cleanups. Miami has its very own Surfrider chapter with a special Butts off the Beach initiative that focuses on removing discarded cigarette butts from the environment (cigarette butts are one of those sneaky plastic sources that people thoughtlessly toss on the ground).

Clean Miami Beach

This relatively new group was founded in 2019. But by hosting weekly cleanups throughout Miami Beach, they have made quite an impact. As of mid-2021, Clean Miami Beach has engaged almost 3,000 volunteers to collect over 28,000 pounds of plastic trash. In addition to these impressive results, they also strive to educate the public and promote pro-environment ordinances within the city.

CAMINO 305 FIELD TRIPS

You are about to embark on Camino 305, a nature journey which will take you through some of the most exceptional parks and preserves in Miami and surrounding natural areas. These locations showcase South Florida's unique natural legacy and are entwined with its ecology and history. In naming this trail of field trips, we wanted to honor Miami's Hispanic heritage. If you're coming to Miami for a visit, it would be a good idea to brush up on your Spanish—Miami's people and culture have deep Hispanic roots, with the city and its Latin American influences being *dos lados de la misma moneda* (two sides of the same coin). The word *camino* translates to "trail," "walk," or "the way." We added some *sazón* (seasoning) to the trail's title by including Miami's famous 305 area code, often used in synonymy for the city itself. The two words come together to translate to "305 Walk" or "305 Way."

Because of its tropical and temperate ecological influences and varying topography, Miami is host to an incredible diversity of ecosystems and wildlife. It is a center for terrestrial and marine research, climate change analyses, and robust conservation and restoration efforts. What better way to show this remarkable nature than a trail featuring twenty-five of the coolest natural locations in South Florida? From national and local parks to tropical gardens and coral reefs, Camino 305 incorporates a little bit of everything.

What Exactly is Camino 305?

Camino 305 consists of fourteen locations running north-south from Dania Beach (just south of Fort Lauderdale) to Homestead (south of Miami) and encompassing a total distance of roughly sixty miles. Branching off this path are four extension trails that offer travelers another eleven locations, adventures that provide a fuller introduction to South Florida. Each of these extension trails highlights a different ecological aspect of Camino 305, including freshwater wetland, coastal, terrestrial, and aquatic habitats. At regular intervals along Camino 305, you will have the option to venture into one of the extension trails.

What to Expect

Now that you've seen the big picture, it's time to choose a destination. We've provided a general orientation for each field trip location with insider scoops, parking and access logistics, and some brief historical background (note that we list the presence of fees but not the amounts, as these are subject to change). We highlight the recreational activities and attractions each trip offers, as well as the ecosystems and species you're likely to encounter. Be safe out there, and enjoy Camino 305!

EXTENSION TRAILS

Barrier Island Extension

Between field trips 4 and 5, head to South Beach for a visit to Miami Beach Botanical Gardens (15). On your way back to the mainland between stops 5 and 6, head over to Virginia Key and Key Biscayne to visit Virginia Key Beach Park (16), Crandon Park (17), and Bill Baggs Cape Florida State Park (18).

Everglades Extension

Between stops 9 and 10, you can choose this extension to get a glimpse of the fresh-water wetlands through Shark Valley within Everglades National Park (19) and Loop Road in Big Cypress National Preserve (20).

Miami Gardens Extension

If you'd like to head to the coast for some green serenity between stops 9 and 10, visit Fairchild Tropical Botanic Garden (21), Matheson Hammock Park (22), and Deering Estate (23).

Florida's Coral Reef Extension

The southernmost extension. If you get to the entrance of Card Sound Road near the Last Chance Bar and Package store in South Dade wetlands and want to keep going, here's your chance to enjoy some ocean adventures with Biscayne National Park (24) and John Pennekamp Coral Reef State Park (25).

What is a Hammock?

You beach bum! We don't mean a long piece of cloth you tie between two palm trees to take an afternoon snooze. In the context of ecosystems, *hammock* refers to a relatively small island of hardwood forest set within a larger expanse of a different ecosystem. Think of a jungle-like patch of trees surrounded by a meadow or open pine forest. Though hammocks are found statewide, their plant composition is dependent on latitude. The further north you go, the more temperate trees (such as live oaks) you'll find. Here in South Florida, most hammocks will contain a mix of tropical and temperate species. Some, like the hammocks from Simpson Park, or those found in the Florida Keys, are almost completely tropical. The land's topography also helps differentiate hammock types. For example, Simpson Park, which occurs on an elevated limestone out-cropping, is what's known as a rockland hammock, while the prevalence of oaks and cabbage palms at Arch Creek Park make it a mesic hammock.

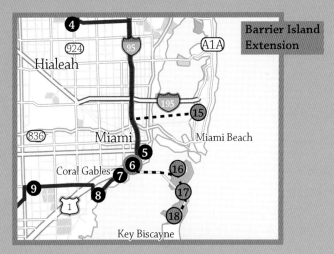

Barrier Island
Extension

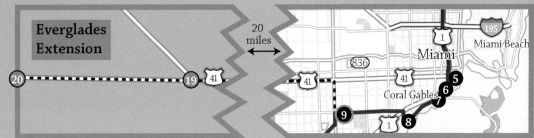

Everglades
Extension

20
miles

Miami Gardens
Extension

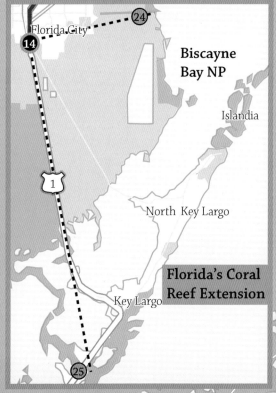

Biscayne
Bay NP

Florida's Coral
Reef Extension

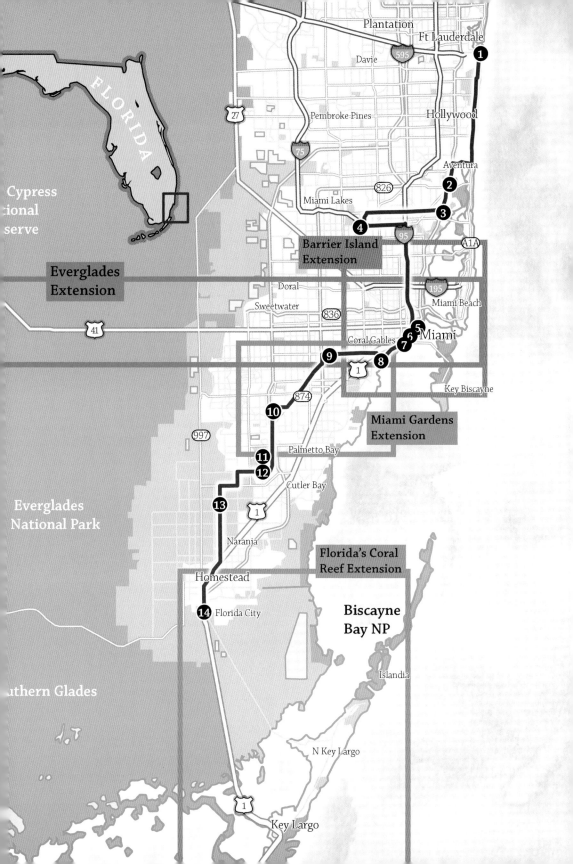

Dr. Von D. Mizell-Eula Johnson State Park

Located in Dania Beach, this park is home to some of the last pristine coastal habitats in Broward County.

STRANAHAN RIVER

BROWN PELICAN

WHISKEY CREEK

COMMON SNOOK

ATLANTIC OCEAN

SARGASSUM CRAB

N OCEAN DR

KEY

🚗🚗 Parking

Main Road

Smaller Road

Hiking & Biking Trails

▲ Boardwalks lead through the upland coastal hammocks to the beach.

Our Camino 305 trek begins well outside Miami at this incredible 2.5-mile stretch of beach bordered inland by mangrove forests and coastal uplands with no shortage of recreational opportunities. Long-time residents will remember that, until 2016, the park was called John U. Lloyd State Park. The reason behind its name change is steeped in South Florida's Civil Rights history, sharing similarities with the history of Virginia Key.

A Who's Who for the State Park

John U. Lloyd State Park opened in 1973, named after the Broward County Attorney who served for three and a half decades and was instrumental in getting the land designated as a park. The beach has a long history, trailing back hundreds of years to when the native Tequesta occupied the area, but its greatest historical significance happened a little over a decade before it gained status as a state park. In the early 1950s, Black residents in Broward had lost access to the only beach they had previously been allowed to visit. At the time, laws prohibited them from intermingling with white individuals at all other

WHERE: 6503 N Ocean Drive, Dania Beach, FL 33004
PARKING: Once you have entered the park, several parking lots can be found along North Ocean Drive, which runs along the park's length.
ENTRANCE FEE: Small fee per vehicle
DIFFICULTY, DISTANCE, ACCESS: Easy. Beaches are a short walk from the parking lots. There is a 0.5-mile-long nature trail that offers plenty of shade. ADA parking and shuttle transportation (including a chair lift) is available throughout the park. Paved roadways and sidewalks make it accessible by wheelchair.
FACILITIES: Restrooms, port-a-lets, showers, tables, pavilions, and concessions.
BEST TIME: Though the beaches can be enjoyed year-round, mind the lifeguard safety signs warning about spring and summer rip currents.

◄ The mangrove-lined Whiskey Creek. In years past, rumrunners used this passage to evade the coast guard. Today, it's popular with kayakers.

beaches. Public pressure eventually spurred the county to provide a replacement beach in 1954, the one currently in the state park. Unfortunately, this beach had little infrastructure and could only be reached by boat, making it difficult to enjoy. In 1961, Dr. Von D. Mizell, a Black physician and founding president of the Broward National Association for the Advancement of Colored People (NAACP), teamed up with the president of Fort Lauderdale NAACP, Eula Johnson, to protest the injustice. They led several wade-ins at the whites-only Las Olas Boulevard beach to compel the county to build a road to their beach. In 1962, they succeeded. Nearly five and a half decades later, the park was renamed to honor the Black struggle against our country's shameful enforcement of segregation.

Come One, Come All

Today, the state park is open and readily accessible to all. It's a true getaway, with a relaxed tropical atmosphere that makes you forget all the worries of the city. In addition to beachgoing (and there's plenty of space for that), boating and fishing are also popular pastimes. But the greatest value the park provides are its opportunities to explore nature on both land and sea. The park is part of the Great Florida Birding Trail, and a brief hike through the Barrier Island Nature Trail, which runs through a coastal hammock and mangrove forest, will give you the opportunity to add a wide variety of species to your life list (a nature enthusiast's record of every species they've ever seen), even outside of migration season. But don't stop there—take your adventurousness to the sea! Visitors can rent kayaks or book ecotours from the Whiskey Creek Hideout concession facility. Kayaking through the mangroves, you could encounter a Florida manatee, those gentle giants often seen floating at the water's surface. The three coral reefs offshore are also replete with marine life. The closest one is approximately 900 feet from shore and reachable only by strong swimmers, while the other two will require a boat. If you stick near the shore, don't fret the spring and summer accumulations of sargassum seaweed. Pick up a clump or two and discover the camouflaged fish and crabs living inside. This park is also one of Broward's most active sea turtle nesting beaches. Toward the end of the nesting season, nighttime tours are sometimes available to watch sea turtle hatchlings make their scramble into the ocean.

TRIP 2

Oleta River State Park

The Oleta River played an important role in Miami's history.

KEY

🚗 🚗 Parking

▦▦▦ Main Road

▬▬▬ Smaller Road

----- Hiking & Biking Trails

Whereas most of South Florida's natural waterways have been physically altered beyond recognition through dredging and flow diversion, the Oleta River has escaped this fate and remains as Miami's last free-flowing river. The river and its surrounding vegetation are all part of Oleta River State Park in North Miami, established in 1986. Many of the field trip sites in this book are relatively small, but at more than 1,000 acres, Oleta River State Park reigns supreme as Florida's largest urban park.

▲ The Oleta River is Miami's last wild river.

An Important Settlement Area and Corridor

A common theme among many of our field trip sites is they were historically home to the Tequesta tribe. The estuarine waters of the Oleta River, as well as the coastal uplands surrounding it, are their former territory. The river later became a strategic corridor for United States troops fighting in the Second Seminole War and would eventually become the City of North Miami Beach. Today, as part of the state park, the Oleta River is primarily used for recreation and as a harbor for wildlife.

Activities at Oleta River State Park

The most popular activities to do at Oleta River State Park are bicycling through the winding and hilly bike trails, kayaking, beachgoing, and nature watching. The bike trails are of varying difficulty and take you through a forest dominated by the invasive Australian pine. Though they're stifling the ecosystem, the pines do provide ample shade, keeping bicyclists shielded from the hot Florida sun. The park's long-term goal is to replace the pines with a diverse assemblage of native canopy trees.

If you want to tour the wide river on a kayak, canoe, or paddleboard, stop by the Oleta River Outdoor Center. Have your own kayak? You lucky duck! The park also has launching ramps designated for private access. A must-see destination on your paddling journey is Sandspur Island, a beach and hammock island south of the mainland. Luckily, the island doesn't have droves of prickly sandspurs growing on it, but it does have a raccoon welcoming party. These pudgy critters are accustomed to being near humans, so if you park your boat on the island, keep an eye on your belongings. Raccoons are cunning and persistent and will snatch your stuff at the first opportunity (no wonder they wear a bandit's mask). However, they'll usually scurry away if shooed. If you stick to the mainland, the park has reservable pavilions for outdoor gatherings and even fourteen small cabins for overnight stays.

The butterfly garden trails made by the nonprofit group Friends of Oleta River State Park have identification cards on the plants and educational signage. You're bound to find zebra longwings, hammock skippers, and orange Julias there. Coastal birds such as cormorants, pelicans, and egrets can also be found throughout the park, hanging around in the uplands, on the shore, or in the river.

WHERE: 3400 NE 163rd Street, North Miami Beach, FL 33160
PARKING: Street parking available at various locations around the park.
ENTRANCE FEE: Small per-vehicle fee
DIFFICULTY, DISTANCE, ACCESS: Easy. Kayaking is restricted to the river itself (no ocean access), and renting is not permitted during inclement weather. Several wheelchair accessible amenities, including beach wheelchairs, are available for rent.
FACILITIES: Restrooms at several locations within the park. Pavilions available for rent.
BEST TIME: Spring and summer when the water isn't as cold.
SPECIAL NOTES: Look out for mischievous raccoons if parking your kayak on Sandspur Island. They may steal unattended items.

◄ Dense mangrove and buttonwood fringes grow next to the popular dog park at East Greynolds.

East Greynolds Park

Following the Oleta River northward will take you to Maule Lake, which was a limestone quarry before it was a body of water. Directly west of Maule Lake is the county-owned East Greynolds Park. Managed by the county's Environmentally Endangered Lands (EEL) program, the park contains a mix of mangrove and hardwood hammock habitat. As a protected ecosystem, the mangroves have undergone restoration work, mostly to remove the invasive seaside mahoe trees that have taken hold here. In addition to having its own kayak rental center and launching ramp, the biggest draw to East Greynolds Park is the Northeast Regional Dog Park. This fenced, off-leash dog park is popular but spacious enough to not feel crowded.

TRIP 3

Arch Creek Park

This small, tucked-away park in North Miami is named for its limestone bridge situated atop a running stream.

WHERE: 1855 NE 135th Street, North Miami, FL 33181

PARKING: Parking near the museum is limited, so consider parking further along the roadway and accessing the trail system from its several entrances.

ENTRANCE FEE: None

DIFFICULTY, DISTANCE, ACCESS: Easy. Entrances to the hammock trail are near the parking spaces. Directional signs within the trails help direct visitors, and benches offer quiet spots to sit. The museum is ADA accessible. Large tree roots along the trails may make accessibility difficult.

FACILITIES: Restrooms at the museum.

BEST TIME: All year; look out for special events.

KEY

🚗🚗 Parking

▬▬▬ Main Road

▬▬▬ Smaller Road

┄┄┄ Hiking & Biking Trails

The limestone bridge at Arch Creek Park has been here for centuries, but with one important caveat: the original fell in 1973, a casualty of overuse or sabotage depending on who you ask. Today's bridge is a replica. It's a shame to have lost the original, as it carried the historical legacy of the Tequesta, who used the bridge to cross between Biscayne Bay and the Everglades. Thankfully, the entire park is now dedicated to preserving the natural and human history of the area and is listed in the United States National Register of Historic Places.

History Spanning Many Eras

The park's museum, located by the southern entrance, holds a collection of artifacts from different periods of Miami's history, from the time when giant mastodons roamed South Florida all the way to the pioneer age. As a general rule, something must have been buried for a minimum of fifty years before being designated as an artifact. Of particular importance to the park are the Tequesta artifacts discovered by archaeologists. Because the Tequesta stuck close to the coast, marine mollusks were a big part of their diet. Some mollusk shells were used to make tools, but most were discarded in mounds called shell middens. One of these middens is preserved within the park today. The Military Road, which is now the parking area, was built by the federal government during the Seminole Wars to facilitate mobility of troops and supplies. Fast forward through the centuries, and the running water of the creek was used by settlers to power an industrialized mill for processing coontie (a native plant that's been overharvested for its valuable starch). Today, the park is used for the enjoyment of nature and educational programming.

▼ This reproduction replaces the original, naturally occurring limestone bridge over Arch Creek, which had stood for many centuries until its collapse in 1973.

▲ Arch Creek Park offers shaded seating on hot summer days.

The Hardwood Hammock and Butterfly Garden

Arch Creek Park contains a cherished patch of hammock forest, punctuated by lower pockets of moist soils that support communities of wetland plants. Though the typical hammock fare is present (including gumbo limbo, pigeon plum, and cabbage palms), it is the old, large live oak trees that truly make the park special. With trunks several feet in diameter and sweeping branches decorated with airplants and resurrection ferns, the live oaks look like ancient guardians of the smaller plants growing beneath them. The walking trails through the hammock are leisurely, and the benches found within encourage visitors to sit for a moment to take in the scenery. One particular open area with three benches is called the Hammock Rest Area, perfect if you visit with a small group. A butterfly garden near the main entrance, along with nectar and host plants growing around the park, attract plenty of these colorful fliers. Wild lime is also common along the edges of the hammock trails. If you observe one for a few minutes, you're bound to see the kite-like wings and yellow and black stripes of a giant swallowtail, North America's largest species of butterfly.

Events

Miami EcoAdventures offers educational programming at Arch Creek Park and is one of the few places in Miami that offers nighttime tours through the trails, increasing your odds of spotting some of our nocturnal wildlife like opossums, raccoons, and owls. Night events usually culminate in a marshmallow roast around the park's large, open fire pit. Daytime guided hikes are also offered, in addition to occasional novice archery classes and archaeology programs.

Amelia Earhart Park

With lots of room for activities, this family-oriented spot boasts diverse amenities that appeal to the entire age spectrum.

BIKE TRAILS

IBIS

FL-924 TOLL

PEREGRINE FALCON LAKE

NW 42ND AVE

BOX TURTLE

ANHINGA LAKE

SABAL PALM

E 65 TH ST

KEY

Parking
Main Road
Smaller Road
Hiking & Biking Trails

▲ The tranquil lakes at Amelia Earhart Park

This 515-acre greenspace is a welcome break from the concrete that makes up much of Hialeah. The park has large open fields, an abundance of trees, pavilions, and lakes offering opportunities for recreation and relaxation. It is a microcosm of Miami, culturally and ecologically. People of diverse backgrounds come to enjoy its spaciousness while the flora and fauna, both native and non-native, seem to strike a temporary truce for the sake of keeping the hearty vibe of the park.

The Unfortunate Last Voyage

You're probably familiar with intrepid aerial explorer Amelia Earhart, who broke several aviation records and milestones, including being the first female aviator to fly across the Atlantic Ocean alone in 1932. In 1937, Earhart attempted to circumnavigate the world, determined to be the first woman to do so. This voyage is infamously known as her last, for she disappeared somewhere over the Pacific on her way to

WHERE: 401 E 65th Street, Hialeah, FL 33013
PARKING: Free weekday parking and paid parking on weekends and holidays.
ENTRANCE FEE: None
DIFFICULTY, DISTANCE, ACCESS: This is a larger park; reference a map beforehand. Bicycle trails are of varying difficulty. Paved walkways accessible for wheelchairs are found throughout.
FACILITIES: Restrooms, pavilions, and a dog park.
BEST TIME: All year; particularly popular for hosting birthday parties.

Howland Island. The mystery of her fate remains unsolved. Miami-Municipal Airport, now known as the Miami-Opa Locka Executive Airport, which is just north of what is now Amelia Earhart Park, was one of her stopping points. In the late 1930s, the land that makes up the park was undeveloped. It officially opened in 1980 and was named in her honor to commemorate her bravery and her legacy.

A Blend of Nature and Urbanization

Many come to Amelia Earhart Park, colloquially shortened to Amelia, to enjoy a balance between the beauty of nature and the safety of an open urban park. It's a reach to call the park a natural area, as the bulk of it consists of expansive lawn dotted by hundreds of large specimen trees. However, it's a mistake to overlook the nature here. Most of these trees are native species, including oak, mahogany, gumbo limbo, and cabbage palm trees. Cypresses and pond apples grow along the edges of the park's artificial lakes, along with a variety of native, semiaquatic wildflowers.

Unfortunately, the park hasn't escaped the pernicious encroachment of invasive species, which have the effect of disrupting natural ecology. Native ibises intermingle with non-native Egyptian geese and Muscovy ducks. South American green and black iguanas bask in the sunlight by the

▼ Urban Paradise Guild is restoring native pine rockland habitat in the park

Conservation Connection

Urban Paradise Guild

UPG is a local nonprofit organization that works to rebuild natural habitats throughout Miami-Dade County. In addition to leading projects at Vizcaya Museum and Gardens and Arch Creek East Preserve, they also have an active pineland enhancement project at Amelia Earhart Park. Since 2019, UPG has recruited volunteers to plant native South Florida slash pines along the southern border of the park. Around each pine, they plant native wildflowers and butterfly host plants so the space can also function as a pollination corridor. UPG employs dynamic, practical strategies to conduct their work, and the results speak for themselves. The pines are growing beautifully, on their way toward becoming a unique type of forest within the park. The organization has no shortage of volunteer opportunities. Check them out and get your hands dirty!

water and entire sections of the park are littered with tall Australian pine trees. Despite conservationists' qualms, those shady spaces between the trees do give these invaded corners a cool, open, almost whimsical quality. Additionally, the park's mountain bike trails seem to have been created when every invasive plant species in Miami held a meeting and decided to make a forest together. And yet, somehow the state-protected Florida box turtle and a variety of birds, fish, and other reptiles all call Amelia Earhart Park home. Signs even warn of the potential presence of alligators (though you're not very likely to find one).

Just about any outdoor activity you can think of is possible at Amelia Earhart Park. Among the appealing amenities are the popular bicycle trails, with tracks of varying difficulty and creative names such as Trick-or-Treat, Chupacabra, and Plymouth Rock. There was a time when Hialeah (a Seminole word meaning "beautiful prairie") was a predominantly agricultural area. The Bill Graham Farm Village hearkens to this time, teaching the public through small agricultural plots that replicate historical ones. There is also a petting zoo and a large, barn-style facility for hosting social events. The tables and shaded pavilions scattered throughout the park are popular for hosting birthday parties, a nostalgic memory for many who grew up in Hialeah. For your adrenaline needs, Amelia is also home to the Miami Watersports Complex, where folks can rent a wakeboard or water skis to test their skills, speed, and ramp-jumping abilities on a powered zipline across Peregrine Falcon Lake. To top it all off, the park is dog friendly. A large, fenced in area called the Bark Park has plenty of space for furry family members, even designating areas for small dogs and large dogs.

TRIP 5

Simpson Park

Only eight acres and inconspicuously nestled within the urban infrastructure of Miami's Brickell neighborhood, this dense hardwood hammock nevertheless carries the legacy of one of Miami's biological treasures.

OLD GROWTH FOREST

FLORIDA BITTERBUSH

SW 15TH RD

GRAY FOX

PARADISE TREE

ENTRANCE AND RECREATION CENTER

SW 17TH RD

S MIAMI AVE

KEY

Parking
Main Road
Smaller Road
Hiking & Biking Trails

▲ Entrance to Simpson Park and Educational Center

Predominantly a hardwood hammock forest, Simpson Park joins Alice Wainwright Park and Vizcaya Museum and Gardens as the last remaining fragments of the once-majestic Brickell Hammock, which formerly ran from the Miami River to Coconut Grove. Though the Brickell Hammock has been all but lost, these three parks keep the memory of it alive.

As Yoda once said, "judge me by my size, do you? And well you should not." Though it is small, Simpson Park contains dozens of native plant species, many of them exceedingly rare. It has even been said the park might contain the highest concentration of floral diversity (most number of plant species per unit area) of any forest in the United States. As a place for education and peaceful reflection, this park can't be beat.

A Push to Preserve

Simpson Park has been around for more than a century; the City of Miami purchased the land from Mary Brickell in 1914 thanks to the public's desire to preserve the land as a park. Initially called Jungle Park, its name was changed in the 1930s to honor botanist Charles Torrey Simpson. Known as "The Sage of Biscayne Bay," he was one of Miami's first conservationists. Even 100 years ago, many people understood the intrinsic value of the Brickell Hammock. Despite public calls for more land to be preserved, the city's acquisition of the beautiful hammock remained

WHERE: 5 SW 17th Road, Miami, FL 33129
PARKING: Free parking at park entrance and along South Miami Avenue.
ENTRANCE FEE: None
DIFFICULTY, DISTANCE, ACCESS: Easy. Trails are short and paved with crushed shells. Facilities are ADA accessible.
FACILITIES: Restrooms.
BEST TIME: The evergreen tropical hardwood forest remains verdant year-round.
SPECIAL NOTE: Ask the park staff to direct you to the Gulf licaria trees. This rare species is a must-see.

limited. Over the years, the ancient hardwood forest gave way to buildings and roads, and Simpson park was neglected. In 2008 this jewel of a park was unearthed again, and a strong effort began to revamp the park's accessibility and ecology. There is now a visitor center, well-maintained walking paths, and educational signage. Park staff regularly conduct restoration work to minimize the impact of invasive species.

The Jewel, Explored

Simpson Park contains ninety-six species of native hardwood trees, under-story shrubs, and herbaceous plants—and another sixty-six non-native ones. As in other rockland hammocks, you'll encounter plenty of strangler figs, pigeon plums, gumbo limbos, and stoppers. So densely foliated is the park, that it blocks out much of the surrounding urban noise. Standing at its center, you may almost forget the regular battalions of cars navigating Miami's concrete jungle just outside. Benches are placed throughout, including next to its meditative koi pond. You'll know you've achieved absolute stillness if a shy gray fox passes by unaware of your presence.

When you first step onto the park's trails from the main building, look to your left and you'll immediately see a very tall tree. This is a paradise tree, a common component of tropical hardwood hammocks, and the sheer size of this specimen sets it apart. At fifty-five feet tall, it's one of the largest in the country, a national cochampion in its species. It takes a long time for a tree to get this big, and the paradise tree isn't the park's only giant. Between these large trees is a jungle-like web of smaller understory plants. The forest has been growing for so long that in late 2018, the Old-Growth Forest Network (OGFN) officially designated it as an old-growth forest, the first in Miami, joining 128 such sites across the country. To qualify, a forest must have developed into its fully mature state. And though much of Simpson Park has been the result of restoration work, it also contains original trees.

▶ The koi pond is arguably the most peaceful and reflective spot within Simpson Park.

Among the more commonplace plants grow some that are quite rare. Meet the West Indian cherry tree, Miami's only native species in the genus *Prunus*, which also includes edible cherries, plums, and peaches. If you crush one of its newer leaves in your hand and hold it to your nose, you'll be rewarded with the sweet smell of cherry candy. Florida bitterbush, a critically imperiled native tree not often seen outside this area of Miami, lines many of the park's walking trails, and its seasonally abundant production of fruit attracts many birds. Most special of all is Gulf licaria, which is not only an extremely rare tree in South Florida, but is historically only recorded in the Brickell Hammock. Identifiable by its spear-shaped leaves with wavy margins, it was previously thought to have been locally extinct. Fortunately , it was rediscovered in recent years by former park manager Juan Fernandez.

Conservation Connection

Headquartered in Little Havana, Citizens for a Better South Florida aims to spur environmental action through education. They believe that when people are aware of local issues, they will become motivated to help solve them. Their programming includes teaching elementary-age students at the Little Havana Leadership Learning Center, hosting tree plantings, beach cleanups, and bioblitzes (an attempt to record as many species as possible living within a certain area), and helping create vegetable gardens and food forests within Miami's underserved communities. They've led volunteer and educational events at parks throughout Miami, including Virginia Key and Simpson Park. They often work with another local, education-based organization called Dream In Green, whose focus is teaching the public about power and water conservation.

TRIP 6

Alice C. Wainwright Park

The rockland hammock here joins the forest at Simpson Park as one of the last remaining portions of the historical Brickell Hammock.

BRICKELL AVE

COMMON PEAFOWL

RICKENBACKER CAUSEWAY

SE 32ND RD

GULF LICARIA

OLD GROWTH FOREST

FLORIDA MANATEE

BISCAYNE BAY

KEY

Parking

Main Road

Smaller Road

Hiking & Biking Trails

The northern end of Alice C. Wainwright Park abuts the world-famous Brickell Avenue, now an international banking hub. The park's name celebrates Alice C. Wainwright, who, in 1961, became the first woman to serve as a City of Miami Commissioner. She was also a staunch, careerlong advocate for environmental issues. Her many achievements include drafting the charter for the Friends of the Everglades (a nonprofit whose mission is to protect the natural character of the Everglades) and helping secure the Big Cypress region as a national preserve. With such a legacy, it's only right that a park containing such rare biological treasures be named after her.

Rare Hammock Plants

Though the park has many fun amenities, a tour through the hammock, designated and protected as a Natural Forest Community, is a must-do for nature lovers. Like Simpson Park, the hammock at Alice C. Wainwright Park was inaugurated into the Old-Growth Forest Network in 2018, and it contains many of the same

WHERE: 2845 Brickell Avenue, Miami, FL 33129
PARKING: Limited parking spaces are available just outside the park.
ENTRANCE FEE: None
DIFFICULTY, DISTANCE, ACCESS: Easy and accessible, though the hammock trail may sometimes be closed. Mind your footing if approaching the limestone outcroppings. Paved areas and facilities are wheelchair accessible, but rocks interspersed across the lawn can make mobility difficult.
FACILITIES: Restrooms and pavilions.
BEST TIME: The beautiful view from the park's ocean edge is enjoyable year-round.

▼ This small but well-aged patch of trees represents a once-opulent tropical forest.

threatened and endangered plants, including West Indian cherry, Florida bitterbush, and Gulf licaria. At three and a half times the size of Simpson, Wainwright Park also has an additional 50 plant species, for a total of 228. In Wainwright, the shelves of limestone that characteristically underlie rockland hammock ecosystems also create large, impressive, jutting out-croppings. We explore these a little more when we reach the South Bayshore Drive Rock Ridge outcroppings (page 69).

▲ The gorgeous waterfront view at Alice C. Wainwright Park

An Eye-Widening View

The ocean edge of Wainwright Park consists of a large, grassy lawn peppered with coconut palms and water-facing benches. Located on the northern tip of Coconut Grove and overlooking Biscayne Bay, the openness of that section of the park is complemented by the azure water of Key Biscayne on the hori-zon, making for a stellar view and a relaxed atmosphere. Once you take that first look, you'll want to bring friends and family. With a basketball court, a playground, built in exercise equipment, and shelters perfect for small social gatherings, you're sure to have a fun time.

TRIP 7

Vizcaya Museum and Gardens

A hop and a skip west from Alice C. Wainwright Park are the primary hardwood hammock forests located on the doorstep to these luxurious grounds.

KEY

🚗 🚗 Parking

Main Road

Smaller Road

Hiking & Biking Trails

Here, you might wonder for a moment if you've been magically transported to a far-off land, perhaps muttering "We're not in Miami anymore." The neatly tended grounds framing the ornate architecture of a stone villa make the place seem more fitting for Renaissance-era Venice. That was kind of the point, as the structure was designed to blend local materials with classic Italian design. The pale stone that makes up the building's walls, outdoor flooring, and archways are Cuban and Florida limestone. The old, undisturbed rockland hammock and mangrove forests surrounding Vizcaya are important habitats for wildlife and have been used for conservation and education since Miami-Dade County acquired the land in 1952.

Vizcaya's Conservation Areas

Charles and James Deering were brothers who owned a family-run agricultural equipment company. James, the younger of the two, built the Vizcaya estate and was an avid conservationist. He purchased land from Miami pioneer Mary Brickell and launched the construction of his dream Italian villa, consisting of seventy rooms overlooking Biscayne Bay, in 1912. Five years later, the famous manicured garden was constructed. Keeping the original coastal hammock in place provided a buffer and a perfect blend of native

▼ The Venetian Vizcaya villa is built with local limestone.

and ornamental gardens that continues to attract scores of tourists every day. The hammock at Vizcaya is the third and final remaining fragment of the original Brickell Hammock. Taking a hike through the shaded trails, you'll find large specimens like the redberry stopper. The state of Florida considers this tree endangered—its natural range is limited to mainland coastal areas bordering the northern portion of Biscayne Bay and the Florida Keys from Elliott Key to Key Largo. Though it's known for its very slow rate of growth—even more so when it's growing in a shady hammock—the hammock at Vizcaya possesses astonishingly tall redberry stopper specimens, with trunks much thicker than you'll find anywhere else. Since it takes such a long time for a redberry stopper to grow this large, these trees are something of a clock, measuring the old age of this forest.

▼ Guests can explore Vizcaya through pathways between manicured gardens.

WHERE: 3251 South Miami Avenue, Miami, FL 33129
PARKING: Free parking within the main lot and across the street at Vizcaya Village.
ENTRANCE FEE: Tickets are only available online; varying prices for adults and kids, but free for children 5 and under
DIFFICULTY, DISTANCE, ACCESS: The limestone villa has several stairways, but is also wheelchair accessible.
FACILITIES: Restrooms.
BEST TIME: The grounds remain beautiful and open all year, though renovation work is often occurring.

▲ The vast grounds at Vizcaya offer pathways through beautiful old specimens of native Miami trees.

◄ Queen butterflies are a common Vizcaya visitor.

Plenty of Photo Ops

You may not want to go to Vizcaya with a group of Instagram influencers. Anywhere you go on the estate, there is an ideal backdrop for a photo. The villa, the gardens, the forests, and the back porch facing Biscayne Bay are all beautiful locations. Whether they're amateurs or professionals, you'll always see someone holding a camera here. The grounds at Vizcaya are a particularly popular place to take quinceañera photos. If you see a girl wearing a brightly colored, voluminous dress, it's most likely for this traditional Hispanic celebration of a young woman's fifteenth birthday. That, or you really did travel back in time to Renaissance Italy.

TRIP 8

The Barnacle Historic State Park

At only five acres, this is one of Florida's smallest parks, but it contains the state's oldest house, still in its original location.

WHERE: 3485 Main Highway, Miami, FL 33133
PARKING: Metered parking for motor vehicles is available throughout Coconut Grove near the entrance to the park.
ENTRANCE FEE: Small per-person walk-in fee
DIFFICULTY, DISTANCE, ACCESS: Easy; 95 percent of the trail is concrete, brick or pavers. This state park carries an unwaveringly relaxed atmosphere. Wheelchair accessible amenities are available.
FACILITIES: Restrooms and a museum.
BEST TIME: Open all year, but look out for special events like the Haunted Ballet.

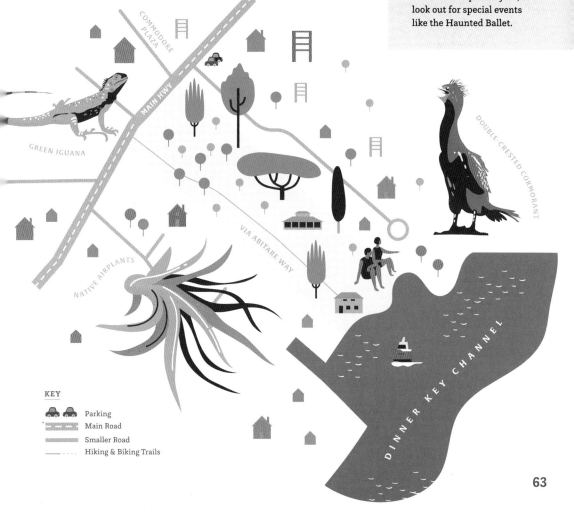

KEY

🚗🚗   Parking

Main Road

Smaller Road

Hiking & Biking Trails

Located on the laid-back coast of south Coconut Grove, what Barnacle Historic State Park lacks in size, it makes up for with a tremendous amount of charm. Based on the name, you might believe the property is encrusted with millions of armored crustaceans, but that's not the case at all. The name comes from the bungalow (a type of house with a broad porch), which was built on the property five years before the city of Miami was even officially founded. Built in 1891 (largely with South Florida slash pine lumber) by Miami pioneer and cofounder of Coconut Grove Ralph Middleton Munroe (no relation to Monroe County, which was named after the fifth President of the United States, James Monroe), the house earned its affectionate name for the trapezoidal shape of its roof, which Munroe believed resembled a barnacle. He loved the design so much that when he needed to add a second floor to the home's original single story, he did so by raising the whole house up and building beneath it. Still in its original location and currently listed in the National Register of Historic Places, the Barnacle holds the prestigious title of oldest house in the county. The grounds were donated to the state park system in 1973 by Munroe's descendants.

▲ For a house nearly 150 years old, The Barnacle looks essentially new. Its crustaceous roof is a Miami icon.

Nature As It Was

Munroe bought the original forty-acre plot of land in 1886. His deep appreciation of the lush hammock forests on the property meant he kept construction to a minimum. Prior to building the bungalow, he had a small boathouse

▲ The boathouse predates the main home by four years. Ralph Munroe lived in it before the house was built, never too far from his boat-building workstation.

where he could launch his sailboat, but beyond that, he refused to create anything larger than a small vehicle trail through the trees, which is now a pedestrian path. Visitors today can enjoy the same trees, many of which are quite large due to their old age. Though it's a small parcel, the hammock ecosystem provides support for rare wildlife, including native airplants and the atala butterfly.

Pull up a Chair, Get on a Boat, or Party Like It's the 1920s

This park is an excellent place for relaxation; visitors can take a leisurely stroll through the hammock trail to view wildlife, relax on one of the comfortable rocking chairs placed on the back porch, or admire passing sailboats from the grounds' ocean side. At the water's edge you can see replicas of Munroe's two favorite sailboats—a fitting tribute for someone who made his fortune in yacht design.

In addition to regularly scheduled tours through the grounds, the park also hosts special events. The theatrically inclined may enjoy one of the productions by Miami's Shakespeare in the Park. For a spooky experience, the annual Haunted Ballet takes place every October and consists of a ghost tour and performative dances. You can learn about upcoming events from the Florida State Parks website or the calendar posted by the nonprofit Barnacle Society.

A. D. (Doug) Barnes Park

This park is a well-kept urban oasis, especially popular among those in the birding community.

BALD EAGLE

N WATERWAY DRIVE

SW 72 ND AVE

FLORIDA SLASH PINE

N LAKE DR

SW 70 TH AVE

PAINTED BUNTING

SW 40 TH ST

KEY

Parking

Main Road

Smaller Road

Hiking & Biking Trails

▲ The lakeside pavilions are perfect for watching herons, ducks, and ibises.

Possessing many of the same fun, family-oriented amenities as Amelia Earhart Park in Hialeah, this park also boasts healthy stands of imperiled natural habitats, particularly rockland hammock and pine rocklands. Whether you're looking for a quiet lunch-break getaway, a venue for a weekend birthday party, or a place to encounter rare plants and wildlife, this park has got you covered. Named in honor of Miami's first Parks and Recreation Director, A. D. Barnes Park is a great example of what an urban park should strive to be: a place where nature and people can coexist.

WHERE: 3401 SW 72nd Avenue, Miami, FL 33155
PARKING: Free parking lot.
ENTRANCE FEE: None
DIFFICULTY, DISTANCE, ACCESS: Easy. Hammock and pineland trails are short and leisurely. Facilities and paved nature trails are ADA accessible.
FACILITIES: Restrooms and lakeside and terrestrial pavilions.
BEST TIME: The peak southbound bird migration occurs in September, while the northbound migration occurs in early spring.

Pine Rockland Trails

A keen nature observer will immediately notice the tall South Florida slash pines standing proud at the park's entrance. Few urban parks in Miami can boast having a functioning pine rockland ecosystem, let alone fifteen acres of it. Though it doesn't compare to the thousands of acres that once surrounded Miami along the Miami Rock Ridge, it's enough to attract a variety of unique critters. On your visit, you'll first want to stop by the Sense of Wonder Nature Center to get the lay of the land. Unless you're squeamish, take a peek at their collection of reptiles. The venomous snakes that live here serve the county fire department's antivenom unit. Next, step outdoors and begin exploring the trails.

You may want to bring a pair of binoculars, as A. D. Barnes Park is famous within the birding community for a diversity of songbirds and birds of prey. What's better than one pair of eyes? Ten pairs of eyes! Even better if they're all enthusiastically searching for the same thing. This is the fun of joining one of the Tropical Audubon Society's birdwatching tours at the park.

For the botanically inclined, the Dade Chapter of the Florida Native Plant Society sometimes leads field trips here. On these trips you could be lucky enough to find critically endangered plants like crenulate lead-plant and pineland lantana. So robust is the ecosystem here, some claim to have spotted white-tailed deer, a species usually only found near the Everglades.

▲ Avid birders should check out the accessible and biodiverse pine rockland trails.

Amenities and Overnight Lodging

There's no shortage of fun activities at A. D. Barnes Park. Social and family events can be held at one of the many outdoor tables or shaded pavilions, children can enjoy the playgrounds, and anglers looking for tranquility can spend some quiet time enjoying the park's lake. One of the county's premier guided nature-programming operators, Miami EcoAdventures, offers educational tours that focus on Miami's history and ecology, both terrestrial and marine. They also run a variety of outdoor activities and camps for children.

Not many urban parks in Miami allow people to stay overnight, but A. D. Barnes Park is special. Through Leisure Access Camp, you can reserve one of the two rentable cabins nestled within the pine rockland, each capable of housing about twenty people. Staying here overnight is a great way to get a sense of the nocturnal wildlife that lives within the park. You may spot a mischievous raccoon or hear a hooting barred owl. With some luck, you may even see a stealthy gray fox.

TRIP 10

South Bayshore Drive Rock Ridge Outcroppings

The Miami Rock Ridge is our region's defining geological formation.

EASTERN GRAY SQUIRREL

US HWY 1

BAYSHORE DRIVE

SOUTHERN CURLY-TAILED LIZARD

NORTHERN MOCKINGBIRD

KEY

Parking*
Main Road
Smaller Road
Hiking & Biking Trails

* Bayshore Drive is busy, so park on a small side street to view safely or drive the road slowly and take in the sights from your car.

WHERE: Along the north side of South Bayshore Drive in Coconut Grove, including under the Brickell Metrorail Station, and at Alice C. Wainwright Park.
ENTRANCE FEE: None
PARKING: Free street parking.
DIFFICULTY, DISTANCE, ACCESS: Outcroppings are easily visible from the street.
FACILITIES: None.
BEST TIME: The elevated limestone rock is a permanent feature of the land and can be seen any time of year.

In this pancake-flat city the Miami Rock Ridge's exposed limestone outcroppings stand out, but the covered parts of the Ridge are just as important. This line of uncovered rock formed more than 100,000 years ago from the calcium carbonate remains of ancient corals, shells, and other organisms. Look closely at an outcrop and you can see prehistoric reef creatures and old coral skeletons embedded in the rocks. Limestone is extremely hard, yet permeable to water; the jagged edges, holes, and missing chunks in the outcroppings are the result of naturally (slightly) acidic rainwater eroding the limestone over many years, forming a landscape known as karst.

Starting from northern Miami-Dade County and moving south toward the Florida Keys, the Ridge parallels Biscayne Bay and eventually curves westward into Everglades National Park. Though its twenty-five-foot height is paltry compared to elevations in other states, were it not for the Ridge's slight lift above sea level, Miami may never have been habitable. A wholly flat landscape would have likely made the entirety of South Florida a wetland, essentially one big Everglades region. The Miami Rock Ridge hosts a wide variety of flora and fauna. Before urban development, it formed the basis for huge expanses of pine rockland and rockland hammock forest.

The best places to see the exposed outcroppings are in Coconut Grove, particularly along South Bayshore Drive. You'll find that houses on the northern end of the street stand several feet higher than those on the southern side, almost as if built on a hill. Other places to see pronounced exposure points of the Ridge are Alice Wainwright Park and underneath the Brickell Metrorail station.

▼ The Miami Rock Ridge is an ancient coral reef. These exposed limestone outcroppings are the closest thing Miami has to a mountain range.

The Miami Circle

Limestone also forms the basis of what is perhaps the most significant archeological site in Miami. Discovered in downtown in 1998 during a preliminary archeological survey for a development project, the Miami Circle represents the city's earliest human history. Our local analog to the famed moai statues of Easter Island or the sarsens and lintels of Stonehenge, the circle is nonetheless impressive, particularly given its geometric precision. This perfectly circular, thirty-eight-foot-diameter carving in the limestone bedrock seems to have once been the foundation for a Tequesta-made structure, which means it may have been constructed millennia ago.

After the Circle's discovery, there was strong public opposition toward allowing the developers to continue their project. Plans were made to remove the circle from the limestone to relocate it, but a legal battle ensued.

The site was eventually purchased from the developer by the state, ensuring it would stay where it was meant to be. The circle was then reburied and the site opened as a small public park, eventually being registered as a National Historic Landmark. Though nobody can say with absolute certainty what the Miami Circle's purpose was, it's likely to have been a ceremonial site, a place for the Tequesta to exercise their culture.

Sitting on one of the limestone benches bordering the now-buried Miami Circle, you can contemplate the past, present, and future. As Miami strives to achieve balance between the unwavering pace of development and the struggle against climate change and biodiversity loss, it's hard not to wonder what the future has in store.

TRIP 11
Zoo Miami

One of the most popular attractions in the area, Zoo Miami is world-class, a place where visitors can enjoy an immense variety of animal species from across the world while also engaging in powerful lessons about conservation.

KEY

Parking
Main Road
Smaller Road
Hiking & Biking Trails

▲ Brave visitors can crawl through the croc tube in the zoo's Everglades exhibit.

Though it once focused only on exotic animals, Zoo Miami has extended itself to include (and teach about) South Florida native species. Called the Miami MetroZoo from 1980 to 2010, it opened in the wake of the Crandon Park Zoo closing with just 38 exhibits and has expanded and diversified over the years to house 100 major exhibits and 500 animal species.

Wondrous Forms and Colors

The zoo is divided into several stations, each highlighting different continents, including Asia, Australia, and Africa. Some of the animals found in particular stations have overlapping native ranges, giving visitors a sense of their natural associations in the wild. In this free-range zoo, the dozens of species vary from familiar

WHERE: 12400 SW 152nd Street, Miami, FL 33177
PARKING: Free parking in the lot.
ENTRANCE FEE: Varying fees for adults and kids, but free for children 2 and under
DIFFICULTY, DISTANCE, ACCESS: Walkways are paved and wide, very easy to traverse. You can also rent a Safari Cycle to pedal your way around. Shaded rest areas can be found throughout the park. Zoo Miami allows service animals, has wheelchair and electric convenience vehicles for rent, and has ADA-accessible facilities and amenities.
FACILITIES: Restrooms, restaurants, and wheelchair rentals.
BEST TIME: Some of the animals within the park may be less active in the cooler winter months or in the hotter summer months.
SPECIAL NOTES: Many animals at Zoo Miami cannot be seen anywhere else in South Florida, presenting a great opportunity to see some rare species.

elephants, lions, and tigers to lesser-known harpy eagles, tapirs, and howler monkeys. The zoo even offers feedings and encounters with some of the animals. Particularly memorable is the tall wooden platform where you can feed lettuce leaves to eager giraffes. Their hilariously long tongues are surprisingly mobile, and will wrap around a leaf before snatching it out of your hand.

▲ The zoo has a resident Florida panther, an extraordinarily rare species in the wild.

The Richmond Tract

Though exotic animals are its mainstay, Zoo Miami has recently done significant work building awareness toward preserving Miami's native pine rocklands. Though they once covered 185,000 acres in Miami-Dade County, the pine rocklands now occupy less than 2 percent of their original range outside of Everglades National Park. Of the parcels that remain, the largest is the 850-acre Richmond Tract, which abuts Zoo Miami.

▲ One of the zoo's newer exhibits highlights the globally unique Everglades.

Many Miami residents are not aware of this globally unique ecosystem, something the zoo has tried to remedy recently by opening a new pine rockland exhibit featuring a variety of native species. Touring this area of the park may provide you your only chance to ever see a Florida panther. In addition to housing animal representatives of the pine rocklands, they also engage in direct conservation by maintaining their own parcel of pine rockland forest in conjunction with Miami-Dade County and partner conservation organizations.

Here's an example of why it is valuable to maintain the Richmond Tract in perpetuity: a previously undescribed species of trapdoor spider was discovered in the zoo's rockland forest. Considering how much of Miami has been explored and traversed, you'd never expect new species to still turn up. It begs the questions: What more is out there waiting to be found? And will we be able to discover them before they disappear?

Going Beyond the Zoo

Zoo Miami does a lot to extend its work beyond the boundaries of the park. Their aim is to be a place where people can not only see animals but also do positive conservation work. Partnering with organizations like the Everglades Foundation, they engage in educational programming with schools. Regular news watchers are sure to be familiar with the zoo's communication director, Ron Magill, who frequently makes television appearances talking about local environmental issues as well as exciting goings-on at the zoo. This facility also offers conservation grants and scholarships, funding research and work that directly protects wild animals.

TRIP 12

Larry and Penny Thompson Memorial Park

This park contains 270 acres of the Richmond Tract, the largest remaining piece of pine rockland in Miami-Dade County.

KEY

🚗🚗 Parking

Main Road

Smaller Road

Hiking & Biking Trails

▲ The large lake offers a safe swimming spot for beachgoers. In summer, visitors can enjoy speeding down the winding waterslide found at the end of the beach.

Larry Thompson was a humor writer for the Miami Herald. He and his wife Gladys (nicknamed Penny), who was an aviator, strongly promoted the establishment of parks in Miami-Dade County, ascribing much value to accessibility of greenspaces. Opened in 1977, the park was named after them posthumously and their legacy was immortalized in a park exhibit that describes their accomplished lives.

Camping in the Rocklands

The pine rocklands at Larry and Penny Thompson Park are its main feature. A tall canopy of slash pine grows over an understory of saw palmetto, cabbage palm, and many more native plants—almost 400 plant species are growing in the park, including the endangered Miami endemic pineland lantana. Back when the pine

WHERE: 12451 SW 184th Street, Miami, FL 33177
PARKING: Free for general public and campers alike.
ENTRANCE FEE: Beach access has varying fees for adults, seniors, and children; campgrounds have different rates depending on length of stay
DIFFICULTY, DISTANCE, ACCESS: Easy. Paved roads and clearly marked trails make the park easily navigable. However, the trails themselves aren't paved and may pose difficulty for wheelchairs.
FACILITIES: Restrooms, shelters, and campgrounds.
BEST TIME: Fall and winter are the best camping months, with the cooler temperatures keeping the mosquitoes at bay. The beaches are best enjoyed in spring and summer.

◄ Pine rocklands once dominated Miami's landscape. Today, the pineland at Larry and Penny Thompson Park is one of the healthiest examples of this globally imperiled ecosystem.

rocklands were a contiguous ecosystem, they provided enough habitat to support a wide animal diversity. Though many of these species have become locally extinct (meaning the species is still alive, just not here), there is still plenty of wildlife to see at the park. The three-mile Larry and Penny Thompson Loop will take you through the pinelands and along the park's large lake, where you are most likely to encounter bird life.

This park is special for allowing overnight camping, a rare amenity in such a beautiful example of a pine rockland forest. Spending the night at the park gives you a unique opportunity to spot the rare Florida bonneted bat. Once common, it is one of the many species whose population has been greatly reduced due to the destruction of Miami-Dade's pinelands.

 ## Conservation Connection

One of South Florida's premier conservation organizations for terrestrial ecosystems, the Institute for Regional Conservation (IRC) provides a wealth of open-access (available to anybody) plant data and also engages in direct conservation work. Its extensive survey data is available online in their Floristic Inventory of South Florida. You can use it to search for a particular species and pull up a map of every conservation area where it has been observed. Or you can click on one of the several hundred conservation areas in South Florida and get a list of plant species that have been found in that specific area. For people interested in native landscaping, IRC has their Natives for Your Neighborhood website. Typing in your zip code on the site produces a list of native plants, with detailed information on each, that were historically found there, a launching point for creating miniature pockets of native habitat at home. Finally, IRC has several active restoration projects in coastal uplands and pine rocklands.

TRIP 13

Castellow Hammock Preserve and Nature Center

Bring sturdy footwear and get ready to do some butterfly spotting at this Miami oasis.

RUBY-THROATED HUMMINGBIRD

STRANGLER FIG

GRAY FOX

SW 162 ND AVE

SW 157 TH AVE

BUTTERFLY GARDEN

FLORIDA TREE SNAIL

KEY

Parking

Main Road

Smaller Road

Hiking & Biking Trails

WHERE: 22301 SW 162nd Avenue, Miami, FL 33170
PARKING: Parking outside the gate adds a quarter mile to your hike.
ENTRANCE FEE: None
DIFFICULTY, DISTANCE, ACCESS: Moderate. The trail that winds through the bulk of the park is clearly visible, but largely composed of exposed tree roots and limestone rock. Wear sturdy footwear. The nature center is ADA accessible, but the trails are not.
FACILITIES: Restrooms.
BEST TIME: Fall and winter, as mosquitoes tend to congregate in the rainy season.

The 112 acres of Castellow Hammock Preserve and Nature Center contain rockland hammock, an educational nature center, and a native pollinator garden. They are surrounded by the Redlands, Miami-Dade's agricultural area named for the layer of red clay soils that sits atop the limestone bedrock.

The Trails

Be sure to bring sneakers or hiking boots if you plan on touring the trails at Castellow Hammock. While most forest trails around Miami are paved or consist of level dirt paths, the ones here are majorly composed of exposed limestone. The jagged edges of the rock will tear up flimsy footwear (you do not want to be caught in sandals here), making the trek along this short trail somewhat slower. Large solution holes, the result of limestone dissolving in rainwater over many years, are found close to the main path. The short trail takes you through the heart of the

▼ This gap in the rock is called a solution hole. It formed after many years of rain weathering away the limestone. Strangler figs have formed a living "bridge" across it.

▲ The charming entrance to Castellow Hammock's nature center pays homage to its pollinator garden, which is often busy with nectar-hungry butterflies and hummingbirds.

hammock, amid dense assemblages of gumbo limbo, false tamarind, and mastic trees. Look on the false tamarinds for Florida tree snails, one of Miami's characteristic animals. Colorful birds called painted buntings also make seasonal rounds here. Females are jade green and yellow, and males are an extravagant mix of blue, red, yellow, and green; their bright colors make them a special treat for patient birdwatchers.

The Nature Center and Butterfly Garden

The nature center has educational exhibits and a classroom space that hosts school groups, teaching them about the ecosystem of the park. The butterfly garden on the park's west side grows native plants to attract pollinators and is a good place to watch for the several dozen species of butterflies who live here. Ruby-throated hummingbirds also make use of the garden, happily sipping nectar from the tubular firebush flowers.

South Dade Wetlands and Southern Glades Wildlife and Environmental Area

An expansive and open habitat, the South Dade Wetlands are unique among Camino 305 field trips in that they do not possess a specific park address.

SPOTTED SUNFISH

CARD SOUND RD

US HWY 1

MUHLY GRASS

ROSEATE SPOONBILL

KEY

🚗🚗 Parking

▬▬▬ Main Road

▨▨▨ Smaller Road

‒‒‒‒ Hiking & Biking Trails

▲ Thanks to its specialized neck vertebrae and height of more than four feet, a great blue heron can strike prey at a distance.

Though perhaps only the most intrepid and experienced naturalists should explore deep into the South Dade Wetlands, everyone should at least be aware of their purpose and importance. This little-known area of southeast Miami-Dade County was an important strategic acquisition for conservation groups looking to preserve the landscape and the species that live here. Its 34,000 acres contain a mixed assemblage of fresh and saltwater habitats that include marl prairies dominated by muhly grass, sawgrass prairies, patches of cypress, and mangrove forests. Unfortunately, interspersed among these native ecosystems are dense, monocultural stands of invasive species, including melaleuca, Brazilian pepper, and shoebutton ardisia.

EELs and Rivers

The Miami-Dade County Environmentally Endangered Lands (EEL) and the state's Save Our Rivers (SOR) programs share similar goals and origins. SOR was created in 1981 by the state legislature. Funded by state tax revenue, the program grants power to the South Florida Water Management District to purchase land that carries a high value for conserving our natural waterways. EEL was formed in 1990, funded by a voter-approved, two-year property tax. The funds collected by the program allowed the county to purchase parcels of rare natural habitat, protecting them from development. Of particular concern were the globally imperiled pine rocklands, of which EEL now manages more than 400 acres (a drop in the bucket compared to the roughly 24,000 acres of habitat EEL has successfully acquired in coordination with other programs).

WHERE: No exact address. The Last Chance Bar and Package (35800 South Dixie Highway, Homestead, FL 33034) is a good address to use as a starting point before heading down Card Sound Road.
PARKING: Free street parking.
ENTRANCE FEE: None
DIFFICULTY, DISTANCE, ACCESS: The part of Card Sound Road that runs through the South Dade Wetlands is approximately 10 miles long. This is open wilderness, so take proper care if you plan to traverse it.
FACILITIES: None—be sure to use the restroom beforehand.
BEST TIME: All year, as different animals can be seen with the changing water levels.

SOR and EEL pooled their resources to secure the South Dade Wetlands. Most people think the entirety of the Everglades exists within the national park, but there are connected wetlands outside its boundaries—nature doesn't often respect the borders humans make on paper. The South Dade Wetlands are important because they form a bridge between the national park and the southern waters of Biscayne Bay. Everglades restoration mainly involves restoring its historic flow, with water passing through the land and emptying into the sea. Without the acquisition and management of the South Dade Wetlands, this flow of freshwater would have been significantly decreased, disrupting not only wetland ecosystems but also marine habitats found near the outflow points. The South Dade Wetlands also form part of the remaining range of the iconic Florida panther and a handful of other federally listed animals.

The world would greatly benefit from enacting more programs like SOR and EEL. We can see their effectiveness at protecting wilderness areas here in South Florida and hold out hope that soon people will back such endeavors on a global scale.

▲ Dwindling Florida panther populations rely heavily on South Florida wetlands.

A Visitor-Friendly Neighbor

Though the South Dade Wetlands are incredibly important for conservation, there aren't exactly any public trails through them. The two-lane Card Sound Road, which runs to and from North Key Largo, bisects the area and is essentially the only infrastructure that allows access—and even there, it has low barriers on either side. But just west of the wetlands is the Southern Glades Wildlife and Environmental Area, which was also acquired by the state's SOR program. Though it doesn't have a visitor center, this area is easier to access for a variety of recreational activities. including bicycling, fishing, boating, and nature viewing. Ecologically, it has a very similar character to the South Dade Wetlands. By visiting the Southern Glades, you can get a solid idea of what its conservation-oriented neighbor is about.

TRIP 15 BARRIER ISLAND EXTENSION

Miami Beach Botanical Garden

Our smallest field trip site, this intimate, tropical garden is a sustainable urban oasis in the middle of South Beach.

WHERE: 2000 Convention Center Drive, Miami Beach, FL 33139

PARKING: Metered parking available along 19th Street and in the adjacent parking lot between Meridian Avenue and Convention Center Drive at standard City of Miami Beach rates; parking garages on 17th and 18th Streets offer lower hourly rates.

ENTRANCE FEE: Small per-person fee

DIFFICULTY, DISTANCE, ACCESS: Easy. It's a relatively small garden with walkways kept open and clear. Walkways and facilities are ADA compliant.

FACILITIES: Restrooms, gift shop, plant nursery, and compost hub.

BEST TIME: All year; depending on when you visit, different plants will be blooming.

KEY

- Parking
- Main Road
- Smaller Road
- Hiking & Biking Trails

Based on the incredible amount of floral biodiversity within the Miami Beach Botanical Garden (both native and non-native ornamental), you would never believe it's just 2.6 acres. A gleaming emerald that's somewhat hidden from view, the garden provides much-needed greenspace for Miami Beach residents, relieving them from the stresses of asphalt roads and concrete buildings. It is full of colors, textures, and smells. Find a spot you like and just breathe easy for a while.

▲ The gardens within this lush, urban oasis have a diversity of forms and colors.

Meditation and Festivities

Though it opened in 1962 as a city park called the Garden Center, the Miami Beach Botanical Garden began to take its present-day form in 1996, when the nonprofit Miami Beach Garden Conservancy was created. One of their goals was to revamp the garden, which had deteriorated over the years, into something more lively and inviting. In 2011, the South Florida landscape architect Raymond Jungles designed and implemented what would become a massive renovation, reshaping the garden into what it is today.

Walking in on gleaming, white-limestone footpaths, visitors immediately have a variety of scenic choices to make. The garden is a mosaic of eleven smaller microgardens, each featuring different plants and gardening styles. There's a Japanese garden with a small pond, tall bamboo, and a crimson wooden bridge. The Banyan Lawn is overlooked by a massive seagrape and strangler fig, century-old trees that are absolutely magnificent to view in person. There's even an edible garden containing various tropical fruits and herbs. The lemon bay rum tree growing here has leaves whose heavenly sweet smell is to die for. And this just scratches the surface of what's there. Explore further and you'll find attractive water features,

▲ This part of the garden is inspired by Japanese landscape techniques. The crimson bridge sits over a tranquil and shaded pond.

blooms of all colors of the rainbow, and a white unicorn statue hidden among the foliage.

Despite their unique qualities, if there's one thing that permeates each and every one of these microgardens, it's the element of tranquility. Generally uncrowded on weekday mornings and afternoons, the garden's serenity will surround you anywhere you sit, whether it's on one of the lawn chairs, benches, or right beneath the canopy of a tree. If you're yearning for something more interactive, the garden hosts regular group yoga. The garden's tranquility contrasts pleasantly with the liveliness of its Garden After Dark events, which feature jazz performances, movie screenings, and dance parties.

Native Wildlife in the Garden

One very special section of the garden is the Native Garden, which exclusively holds species indigenous to South Florida. As a general rule, native plants attract native wildlife, and this spot is no exception. The plants here have grown much as they would in nature, creating a beautiful and natural aesthetic. Branches of different hammock-associated trees and shrubs coalesce to provide excellent shade, while understory shrubs fringed by a variety of native wildflowers attract birds and pollinators. Our favorite feature of the Native Garden is the pine rockland demonstration plot. Here, you'll find exceedingly rare pine rockland species like Mexican alvaradoa and crenulate lead-plant growing between several medium-sized South Florida slash pines. Educational signage examines the plight of the pine rockland forests, inspiring visitors to take action in protecting this important facet of Miami's natural legacy. Though butterflies can be found throughout the

Conservation Connection

In 2017, the Miami Beach Botanical Garden excitedly anticipated welcoming the rare atala butterfly. A handful of caterpillars had pupated on some of the garden's coontie cycads, hanging from the leaves like Christmas ornaments. The butterflies finally emerged, gleefully flaunting their bright red abdomens and iridescent blue and black wings—and the very next day, South Florida was hit by Hurricane Irma. In addition to damaging the plants, Irma's heavy wind and rain unfortunately swept away the small atala colony. The following year, our own Brian Diaz teamed up with head gardener Sanna O'Sullivan to introduce roughly 150 atala caterpillars to the garden. These had been rescued with permission from the Montgomery Botanical Center, where, ironically, atalas pose a severe threat to their collection of critically endangered cycads. In a happy convergence, the Botanical Garden butterflies arrived at the same time that the City of Miami Beach was planting hundreds of native coonties in the surrounding area, including the convention center adjacent to the Garden. Conditions were perfect for an explosion in the atala population. From that initial handful of caterpillars, the garden now supports a concentrated population of a species once thought to be extinct. We're talking about hundreds of butterflies. The lesson is clear: the more we South Floridians landscape our homes and public lands with native plants required by native wildlife, the better off our endangered animals will be.

Miami Beach Botanical Garden, they are particularly concentrated in this corner that emphasizes native plants. Monarchs, sulphurs, and populous clusters of zebra longwings are just a few of the species you may come across here.

Wildlife happily makes use of the rest of the garden, too. By the freshwater pond at the garden's center, you can often spot a variety of wading birds, including a resident green heron that likes to cause quite the commotion when bothered by other birds. Basking turtles and graceful koi fish live in the water. Hawks stoically patrol the grounds from the high tree branches. Perhaps the most unusual avian visitor was a limpkin that visited in 2020—these rare birds are usually only found in freshwater natural areas. Under the cover of darkness, nocturnal opossums and raccoons make their nightly rounds searching for food, watched over by a charmingly cute screech owl that was introduced into the gardens in 2020.

BARRIER ISLAND EXTENSION

Virginia Key Beach Park

Few parks in Miami exemplify the cohesion between wildlife and humans as Virginia Key does.

WHERE: 4020 Virginia Beach Drive, Miami, FL 33149

PARKING: Free parking throughout the park.

ENTRANCE FEE: Small fee per vehicle, but pedestrians and cyclists enter for free

DIFFICULTY, DISTANCE, ACCESS: Beaches are readily accessible from the parking lots. Most of the bicycle trails are designed for more experienced cyclists, but there are beginner trails. Pavilions and facilities are wheelchair accessible.

FACILITIES: Restrooms, pavilions, and bicycle and kayak rentals.

BEST TIME: The beaches are best enjoyed on warmer spring and summer days; just be careful around the staked sea turtle nests and be mindful of rip currents.

SPECIAL NOTE: Can you find all the inspirational signs placed within the Historic Virginia Key Beach Park hammock trails? Which is your favorite?

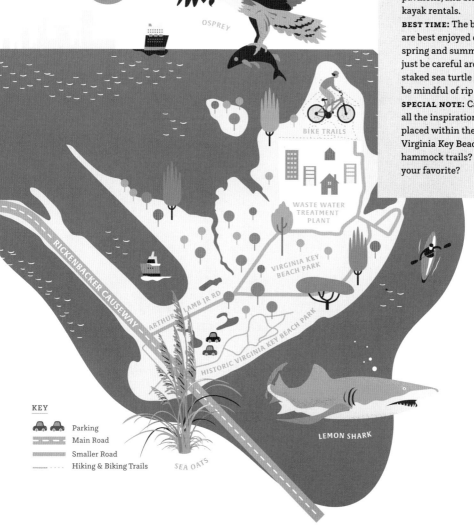

OSPREY

BIKE TRAILS

WASTE WATER TREATMENT PLANT

VIRGINIA KEY BEACH PARK

RICKENBACKER CAUSEWAY

ARTHUR LAMB JR RD

HISTORIC VIRGINIA KEY BEACH PARK

LEMON SHARK

SEA OATS

KEY

🚗 🚗 Parking

Main Road

Smaller Road

Hiking & Biking Trails

Virginia Key is a barrier island—a type of protective sandy island off the coast of a mainland—located just off of Downtown Miami. A significant portion of its 850 acres are composed of sandy beaches, coastal uplands, and mangroves, and it's all surrounded by seagrass meadows growing in shallow waters. In 2010, the City of Miami passed a master plan that would maintain Virginia Key as a place where the public can visit during the day, but where wildlife can reign undisturbed at night. The island remains uninhabited by people, but it supports a variety of coastal and marine habitats as well as popular beaches, bicycle trails, water sports, and major outdoor events. With its many protected areas that give us a glimpse of past Miami frozen in time, Virginia Key offers a perfect balance between ecology and recreation. This coastal oasis offers a rare view of a more natural environment in Miami, juxtaposed with the image of modern downtown and Fisher Island in the backdrop. You can reach Virginia Key by driving the Rickenbacker Causeway from Miami, a long bridge that also connects to the sister island, Key Biscayne.

A Tale of Two Parks

The island of Virginia Key is divided into two City of Miami run parks—Virginia Key and Historic Virginia Key Beach Park—each offering a unique history and opportunity for recreation. In Virginia Key, the extensive network of mountain bike trails on the North Point section of the park, maintained by the Virginia Key Bicycle Club, are very popular. With their steep slopes, narrow stretches, and rocky terrain, many of these bicycle trails aren't appropriate for the casual rider, but thanks to a handful of flatter, beginner-level trails, there's something for everyone to enjoy. Didn't bring your bike? No problem! The Virginia Key Outdoor Center has all the equipment you could want for a

▼ Virginia Key supports a rain-fed freshwater wetland surrounded by restored beach dunes and maritime hammocks.

thrilling day at the park. You can rent mountain bikes, kayaks, paddleboards, and more. If you'd rather stick to slower-paced activities, there are plenty of beach and nature trails to enjoy.

Historic Virginia Key Beach Park is great for family gatherings, whether in the form of a lazy beach day or a large birthday celebration under one of the several rentable pavilions. Part of what makes this park different is the open field space, perfect for events like the annual Miami Vegandale Food and Drink Festival or Love Burn, Miami's unique version of the Burning Man festival.

There's plenty to explore in this leisurely park, including a nine-hole disc golf course, a miniature train and antique carousel children can ride, and serene nature trails that offer inspiration in the form of regularly placed signs inscribed with insightful quotes from famous authors and historical figures. Across the park's entrance is an elaborate preserved sandcastle, built in 2015 by Turkish Airlines. Standing at forty-five feet tall, it once held the world record for largest sandcastle and looks fit for a beach-going monarch. Or perhaps a pair of regal crabs?

An Island with a Deep Significance for Miami's Black Residents

▼ Virginia Key Beach is an important location in the history of Miami's civil rights movement.

In 1835, a powerful hurricane passed through South Florida, bringing wind and waves so strong they severed a huge piece of land off what we know today as Miami Beach. This island was named Virginia Key in 1849. Despite its violent beginning, the island was mostly quiet over the next century. Its most important period would occur in 1945. Back then, what is now called Fisher Island was owned by a man named Dana A. Dorsey, Miami's first Black millionaire. The beaches on the island were reserved for the

"We must learn to live together as brothers or perish together as fools."
- Dr. Martin Luther King Jr.

city's Black residents, as they were not allowed at any other beach during that time. Dorsey was compelled to sell the island to entrepreneur Carl G. Fisher in 1919, which spelled the end of the Black beach. The injustice of being left with no opportunities for coastal recreation led a group of Black Miami residents to stage a wade-in protest at the nearby whites-only Haulover Beach. This protest, led by Black Miami attorney Lawson Thomas, was an intentional breach of the Jim Crow laws that prohibited Black individuals from using white-tourist beaches. Though seven of the protestors were arrested, the move put pressure on Miami-Dade officials. Later that year, they commissioned Virginia Key Beach as Miami's first permanent Black beach. Accessible only by boat, the island became a refuge.

The Haulover Beach wade-in took place two decades before the American Civil Rights Movement. Once segregation ended, more easily accessible beaches became more popular, and Virginia Key was left relatively quiet. The park's condition declined over the years, but in 2008, restoration efforts began to protect its historic and natural spaces.

▲ Soft, white sands border this outflow from a stand of mangroves. This section of the beach is called the Cove.

A Thriving Hub for Nature

The feature that unites both parks, and which is largely responsible for making them so attractive to local Miamians, is their vibrant plant and animal life. As a coastal barrier island, Virginia Key hosts a rich mosaic of coastal ecosystems, including extensive beach dunes and coastal strands, canopied maritime hammocks, thick mangrove forests, and isolated brackish and freshwater wetlands. This diversity of habitats invites a range of native fauna. On any given day, egrets, herons, ospreys, and ibises can be found wading in the shallows of the shore or perched high above, keeping a lookout for prey. Through a combination of luck and a talented naturalist's eye,

Conservation Connection

In the decades when the island was closed and without maintenance, disturbance events like the mass depositing of dredge material from the Port of Miami gave invasive species ample opportunity to take over. When the two parks reopened in 2008, Australian pines, Brazilian pepper, and beach naupaka abounded. What followed was an incredibly successful campaign led by local nonprofits, the City of Miami, and Miami-Dade County to remove the invasive exotics and rebuild native habitat. The Museum Volunteers for the Environment (MUVE) program under the Phillip and Patricia Frost Museum of Science, initiated by our own Fernando Bretos, has actively led the charge to restore ecosystems at North Point since 2013. MUVE has recruited thousands of volunteers to plant tens of thousands of native plants, restoring land previously stifled by a monoculture of Australian pine. Their crowning achievement was restoring the beach's dunes, the coastal hammocks, and the freshwater wetland. With much restoration still to be done, MUVE continues to host monthly volunteer events.

At Historic Virginia Key Beach Park, a local nonprofit called TREEmendous Miami has worked for a decade and a half to restore the park's maritime hammocks and other coastal uplands. By recruiting volunteers to get their hands in the ground, they not only strive to rebuild the park's habitats (and rebuild they have, planting more than 13,000 trees and shrubs at Virginia Key) but to build the community's love and appreciation for the benefits provided by trees and healthy native ecosystems. Led by a passionate and knowledgeable team, TREEmendous also plants native trees at the Florida International University Nature Preserve and in economically disadvantaged communities. They take their slogan of "caring for the environment has never been more important" with them wherever they go.

you can also spot much rarer creatures like manatees, dolphins, loggerhead sea turtles, and American crocodiles. Explore the park's beaches or the Mabel Miller Trail and you're bound to encounter something exciting.

Virginia Key North Point and a few other local areas are home to one very special plant resident. The beach peanut (Okenia hypogaea), also known as burrowing four o'clock, is found exclusively along open, sunny areas of foredunes. These plants aren't related to edible peanuts but do grow in a similar style, developing their fruits underground just like their namesake. Decades of coastal development, combined with its relatively narrow habitat preferences have thrust this species toward an unfortunate state-endangered status. Enjoy their vivid purple blooms from afar, and please take care not to step on them.

Crandon Park

Natural habitats and recreation areas occupy the top third of the barrier island known as Key Biscayne.

FLORIDA SANDHILL CRANE

BEAR CUT BRIDGE

RICKENBACKER CAUSEWAY

FOSSILIZED REEF

FLORIDA PRAIRIE CLOVER

BEACH CLUSTERVINE

LOGGERHEAD SEA TURTLE

KEY

Parking

Main Road

Smaller Road

Hiking & Biking Trails

WHERE: 6747 Crandon Boulevard, Key Biscayne, FL 33149

PARKING: Large, metered parking lot.

ENTRANCE FEE: None

DIFFICULTY, DISTANCE, ACCESS: Nature center and trails are accessible via the north entrance; botanical garden from the south entrance. Taken together, the Bear Cut and Osprey nature trails are a little less than a mile in length. Wheelchairs can be reserved for free, the nature center is ADA compliant, and there are plenty of paved walkways.

FACILITIES: Restrooms, pavilions, playgrounds, nature center, cafes, tennis courts, marina, and golf course.

BEST TIME: Spring and summer, but be ready for afternoon rain showers.

SPECIAL NOTE: Don't get spooked if you see a crocodile casually walking on the road; just give it ample space and marvel at it.

▲ The northern end of this pathway through Crandon's coastal strands leads to Bear Cut and a fossil reef.

The southernmost third of Key Biscayne is a state park called Bill Baggs Cape Florida State Park, the middle section is primarily residential, and the northern third consists largely of this county-administered urban park and protected natural area. With extensive beaches and near-pristine coastal habitats, including mangroves and coastal hammocks, tennis and golf courts, and plenty of open space for events, Crandon Park accommodates nature lovers as well as those looking for weekend recreation with an idyllic back-drop. You could explore this park's 800 acres more than a dozen times and still not see everything it has to offer.

Coconuts and Causeways

Prior to being established as a county park, the land was owned by indus-trialist William John Matheson, who operated what was then the largest coconut plantation on the island. Though the coconut palm once supported this lucrative business, it is now, to the surprise of many, classified as an invasive species; as seemingly fitting and ubiquitous as they are in the Miami landscape, they aren't native to here. A decade after Matheson's death in 1930, his children opted to donate the land to Miami-Dade County with the stipulation that the county must maintain it as a publicly accessible park. Then why is it called Crandon Park instead of Matheson Park? Well, the

reason Virginia Key and Key Biscayne are easily accessible today is because of a push by former chairman of the county commission Charles Crandon to build the Rickenbacker Causeway. Without the causeway, the islands would only be reachable by boat. Crandon Park is named in his honor.

▲ The Crandon botanical garden retains much of the old zoo's infrastructure.

We Sold a Zoo

Abandoned ruins are interesting places. The skeletal structures of decrepit buildings reveal the passage of time, sparking the imagination. Take a walk in the southeastern portion of Crandon Park, and you'll come across large, empty cages, some decorated with paintings of naturescapes and animals. This is the once-popular Crandon Park Zoo, Miami's first.

The zoo had humble beginnings, housing just six animals when it opened in 1948. Over the years, hundreds more were added, making it a must-see destination for locals and tourists. But it didn't take long for people to realize that maintaining a zoo in a hurricane-prone, coastal park was a flawed concept. In 1965, more than a quarter of the zoo's 1,000 animals perished in the category 3 Hurricane Betsy, calling into question the ethics of the place. Public outcry intensified as people became aware of the animals' treatment and paltry housing. When the safer, free-range Miami Metrozoo (now Zoo Miami) opened in 1980, the Crandon Park Zoo closed down. Today, many of the original animal enclosures still stand, eerily empty. Now it's a botanical park where you can enjoy a relaxed walk through the grounds admiring the thriving population of extravagant peacocks. There is also a handful of one very special species, the Florida sandhill crane. These tall gray birds, identifiable by their cap of red feathers and dinosaur-like stature, were introduced into the park years back and are now thriving.

► As water temperature increases during the summer months, it's not uncommon to see a build up of sargassum along the shoreline.

Dedicated To Nature Education

The folks at Crandon Park take an active approach to teaching the public about South Florida's ecology and environmental issues. The seat of their environmental education efforts is the Marjory Stoneman Douglas Biscayne Nature Center. The Nature Center benefits from being surrounded by extensive coastal habitats, a natural classroom that extends beyond the center's limestone walls. They teach through exploration of the surrounding land and firsthand encounters with plant and animal life, creating links to Miami's broader ecology and environmental issues. Children can gain lifelong memories and lessons about environmental stewardship by attending the center's summer camps and field trip programs, while anyone can put these lessons into practice by volunteering at beach cleanups and restoration events.

Biological Beach Marvels

At high tide, the beach at Crandon Park looks like any other. The shoreline is separated from the upland dune and coastal strand plant communities by a couple dozen feet of sand. At low tide, however, the beach turns into something else entirely. Extensive sandflats and pockets of seagrass beneath the shallow water become exposed to the air. Miniature tidal pools form, attracting hungry gulls, egrets, and sandpipers. People are also attracted to the sandflats and can sometimes be seen far out on the edge of the mud with a rod and reel. Many different kinds of critters reveal themselves, with small fish, crabs, and shrimp being careful to stick close to the patches of seagrass. Lucky observers may come across queen conchs, small stingrays, and nurse sharks. Once the tide comes in and covers them back up, the seagrass beds attract a plethora of ocean life. For avid explorers, we recommend revisiting the park at varying times of day to get a full appreciation for the waxings and wanings of the ecosystem.

◄ Two miles of picturesque beaches make Crandon Park a popular destination for residents and tourists alike.

Bear Cut and The Fossil Reef

Bear Cut Bridge, named for the inlet it crosses, is the only way to reach Key Biscayne by land. The inlet is characterized by fast-moving tidal flows from the open ocean into Biscayne Bay and vice versa. Bear Cut is named for the black bears who once lived here and would cross back and forth to feed in the lush coastal forests at low tide. The bears have since disappeared (humans decided it would be impossible for us all to coexist), but what rests immortal on the north side of Bear Cut is a type of habitat found in few other parts of the world. Under the waves is a fossilized reef, where prehistoric coral, mangrove roots, and other organisms lie petrified, frozen in time. Like the sandflats, these stretches of fossil rock are exposed at low tide, form-ing tidal pools and making them another great place to search for small (still-living) marine critters.

Rare Plants and Butterflies

Because it covers so much land, Crandon Park is able to support a diverse array of flora, harboring more than 200 species of native plants. Among these are species not often seen in Miami, including the federally listed Florida prairie clover and beach clustervine, as well as the state-endangered Biscayne prickly ash. The relatively small populations of these species make them vulnerable to strong disturbance events, and even today their survival isn't guaranteed. In 1992, category 5 Hurricane Andrew devastated the area's vegetation. Strong restoration efforts helped the ecosystem recover, but it's a harder road back for rarer plants. Luckily, the conservation team at Fairchild Tropical Botanic Garden monitors all federally listed species in Crandon annually. Their science-driven conservation efforts help ensure the rare species' long-term persistence in the park.

Two plants growing in the park offer a prime opportunity to reintroduce one of the country's rarest butterflies. Once one of the most common insects in South Florida, the federally endangered Miami blue butterfly now has just a few pocket populations in the Florida Keys. Its caterpillars feed primarily on blackbead and nickerbean, which are abundant at Crandon Park and other adjacent natural areas. Because of this, we maintain hope that the Miami blue will one day be reintroduced to the area.

BARRIER ISLAND EXTENSION

Bill Baggs Cape Florida State Park

On the southeast tip of Key Biscayne, a 95-foot-tall lighthouse stands as a shining symbol.

FIELD TRIP 18

WHERE: 1200 Crandon Boulevard, Key Biscayne, FL 33149

PARKING: Free parking throughout the park.

ENTRANCE FEE: Small fee per vehicle, smaller fee for pedestrians and cyclists

DIFFICULTY, DISTANCE, ACCESS: All parts of the park are easily reachable from parking lots. Facilities and amenities are ADA accessible. Beach and swimming wheelchairs can be reserved for free.

FACILITIES: Restrooms, showers, restaurants, pavilions, lighthouse tours, and bicycle and kayak rentals.

BEST TIME: Spring and summer.

SPECIAL NOTE: On a clear day, you can spot Stiltsville from the edge of the park.

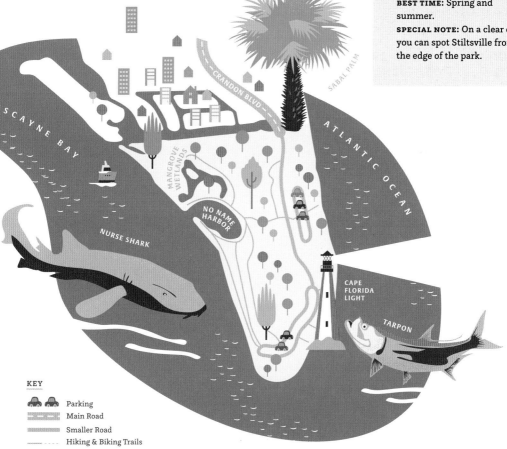

BISCAYNE BAY

CRANDON BLVD

SABAL PALM

ATLANTIC OCEAN

MANGROVE WETLANDS

NO NAME HARBOR

NURSE SHARK

CAPE FLORIDA LIGHT

TARPON

KEY

Parking

Main Road

Smaller Road

Hiking & Biking Trails

Referred to as the Cape Florida Light, the lighthouse was built in 1825 to warn nighttime sailors of the treacherous shallow waters they were approaching. Though decommissioned, the lighthouse remains as the park's stalwart sentinel. It has braved the ravages of history, witnessing wars, including an explosion during a battle with the Seminoles, the full strength of powerful hurricanes, and the degrading effects of time. Today, it is Miami-Dade's oldest standing structure. We encourage visitors to take a moment to climb the lighthouse's spiral steps and ponder the concept of resilience. As Miami faces the existential threats of climate change and sea level rise, it must follow the example given by the Cape Florida Light: only by bolstering our resilience to these environmental problems can we hope to remain standing.

▲ Built in 1825, the Cape Florida Light is the oldest standing structure in Miami.

A Tumultuous History with a Silver Lining

Since this region of Key Biscayne was named Cape of Florida by the early sixteenth century Spanish explorer Juan Ponce de León, it has been the center of several periods of civil unrest and acted as safe ground for the persecuted. In the early 1820s, the Cape of Florida was a gateway to freedom, a place where Black Seminoles secretly congregated to await safe passage to the British-owned Bahamas. For this reason, the region is now registered as a National Underground Railroad Network to Freedom site. But the installation of the Cape Florida Light effectively cut off this escape route. During the Second Seminole War (1835–1842) the lighthouse experienced such extensive damage during a battle that it had to be rebuilt. Two decades later, the heat of the American Civil War also found its way to the Cape of Florida and the lighthouse was damaged again.

Fast forward 100 years to the 1960s—the verdant green of the Cape is under threat again, this time by plans for development. William Calhoun Baggs (or Bill Baggs), the editor for the Miami News, campaigned to keep the park as a protected area. His efforts led to the state purchasing the land in 1966, naming it a state park in Baggs' honor the following year. But even though it was protected, it was still in danger. Years of degradation, in which

▲ Boardwalks allow for great views of Cape of Florida while keeping visitors respectfully off the dunes.

developers cut down trees and filled in wetlands, had destroyed native habitats and opened the door to a severe invasion of Australian pine trees.

In 1992, with a massive display of destructive force, Hurricane Andrew toppled nearly every Australian pine within the park. Left standing was a singular native strangler fig tree, a humble symbol of hope for what the park could be. The opportunity to rebuild the ecosystem was recognized by the land managers, and the park today is almost wholly the product of ecological restoration work.

A Variety of Ecosystems

Bill Baggs State Park's 400 acres now house a variety of coastal ecosystems, including maritime hammocks, beach dunes, coastal strands, and mangrove forests, composed of an impressive assemblage of more than 300 species of native plants. This diversity of flora translates to a diversity of fauna, with the park being one of the best places to observe passing migratory birds and year-round populations of native butterflies, mammals, reptiles, and marine animals. It's this biological richness that makes Bill Baggs State Park a popular destination for Miamians. Many come to enjoy the splendid, mile-long beach on the park's eastern edge, while others hike through the nature trails, kayak through the mangroves, or fish along the western seawall. Walking the three-mile Robin's Birding Trail and Lighthouse Loop will give you a full sense of the park's natural areas. It would seem two centuries of conflict within the area has culminated in a peace between people and nature. Bill Baggs State Park should serve as an example of what a community stands to gain by opting for stewardship over skyscrapers.

Shark Valley at Everglades National Park

The Everglades are the defining ecosystem of South Florida.

HWY 41

SAWGRASS

WOOD STORK

AMERICAN ALLIGATOR

KEY

Parking

Main Road

Smaller Road

Hiking & Biking Trails

▲ Once used to observe dry-season fires, the watchtower now offers park visitors a spectacular view of the River of Grass.

Any definition of this region would be wholly incomplete without the gold and green expanse of sawgrass marsh that has been here for five millennia. The first person to have laid eyes on it may well have believed it to be endless, for it's hard to wrap your mind around 3,000,000 acres of open prairie. The Everglades are a product of water spilling over from Lake Okeechobee (the tenth largest US lake), which itself is fed by a complex system of naturally occurring wetlands. A wide sheet of excess water from the lake begins its steady flow south across land that possesses the tiniest of inclines, slowly making its way to the ocean across the southwestern end of the Florida peninsula. This flow of water is the reason why you'll often hear the Everglades being called the River of Grass. Though drainage of the Everglades, particularly over the last century, has reduced its area by half, there is still plenty of it to marvel at. Shark Valley is one of the best places to get a sense of the true Everglades experience.

Seasonal Habitats

Shark Valley puts you in the center of the sawgrass prairie, the most characteristic ecosystem of the Everglades. It's a biodiverse and productive place, and you'll have no shortage

WHERE: 36000 SW 8th Street, Miami, FL 33194

PARKING: Park in the lot at Shark Valley Visitor Center or on the side of US-41 near the park entrance.

ENTRANCE FEE: A per-vehicle fee and lower fee for pedestrians and cyclists

DIFFICULTY, DISTANCE, ACCESS: The 15-mile bicycle trail can be physically demanding. Trolly tours are available and are fitted with a ramp for wheelchair accessibility.

FACILITIES: Restrooms, visitor center, and bicycle rentals.

BEST TIME: The dry season makes the park more traversable, but a greater diversity of wildlife can be seen during the wet season.

SPECIAL NOTE: This park can occasionally flood if there is too much rain. If you're planning a trip in the rainy season (May–September), double-check for any notices on their website.

of wildlife to gawk at. The types of wildlife you encounter will depend on the time of year you visit. Is it the wet season or the dry season? Depending on the month, there may be no water at all, or there may be so much water that the park needs to close. Different water levels attract different wildlife species. In the wet season, the most common species you'll come across are American alligators and a wide variety of wading birds like the statuesque great blue heron and colorful roseate spoonbill. During the dry season, seeing a flock of stocky wood storks slowly walking across the sawgrass will make you think you've entered an African savanna.

On this fifteen-mile bike path, you're sure to see an alligator, or twenty.

Shark Valley offers some of the closest alligator encounters you'll find in South Florida—it's common to see them resting on the edges of the roads. Park rules require visitors to retain several feet of distance from the alligators—a precaution that should be common sense around wild animals. As long as you maintain a wide berth, you've no need to fear, since the alligators typically do not go out of their way to bother people. During the day, they are extremely docile, resting like statues in the sun, soaking up its warmth.

If you visit during the wet season, you might notice mats of spongy material growing in the water. This is called periphyton and is composed of algae, microbes, and small animals. The periphyton is incredibly important as it forms the base of the entire wetland food web. Small fish and invertebrates eat the periphyton, birds and bigger fish eat them, and so on all the way up to the alligators.

The Shark Valley Bike Trail

When you first arrive at Shark Valley, you'll park at the visitor center, which has educational signs teaching about the biology, ecology, and fragility of the Everglades ecosystem. Most people come to the park to ride their bicycles across the fifteen-mile loop that starts and finishes at the visitor center. You can either bring your own bike from home or rent one at the park for an hourly rate. If you maintain a steady pace, it will take a couple hours to complete. Because the trail is so long, you'll have lots of space to yourself, away from any crowd. We invite you to stop for a moment and just listen to the peaceful silence of the prairie; it should come as a welcome escape from honking cars and construction sites. At the halfway point of the trail is the Shark Valley Observation Tower, a forty-five-foot-tall structure you can climb via a circular ramp to get a bird's eye view of the park, allowing you to take in the many miles of prairie all at once. If you're not much of a cyclist, the park also offers educational tram tours that allow you to see everything without needing to break a sweat.

 ## Conservation Connection

What inspires people to want to become environmental stewards? Everybody's story is unique, but one powerful common thread is that they were taught from an early age to appreciate nature's beauty and importance. It's hard to care about something if you know nothing about it, and by the time we reach adulthood, many of our worldviews have already become fixed. Enter the Every Kid in the Everglades Program, which brings elementary age students into Everglades National Park to learn about the ecosystem's history, ecology, and conservation issues. These lessons are taught through ingeniously designed, hands-on activities and ecosystem tours that provide plenty of "wow!" and "aha!" moments that kids can carry into adulthood. And forget four walls, the Everglades itself is the classroom (in particular Shark Valley and the Royal Palm Visitor Center).

EVERGLADES EXTENSION

Big Cypress National Preserve

This more than worthwhile adventure requires leaving Miami to travel about 50 miles west along US 41.

KEY
Parking
Main Road
Smaller Road
Hiking & Biking Trails

▲ The National Preserve's dense cypress forest hosts American alligators.

Can you guess what you'll find at Big Cypress? Yes, big cypresses! And with 729,000 acres, lots of them. Florida has two native species in its freshwater swamps, the bald cypress and pond cypress. Some of the trees at Big Cypress predate the European discovery of the Americas by more than 150 years. Their longevity is unmatched by any other Florida organism, plant or animal. Big Cypress National Preserve is not part of Everglades National Park, but it's connected to it and has federal protections of its own that focus on its rich ecology (which houses some of South Florida's rarest). Most come to Big Cypress to witness the pristine, thriving natural environment and take a casual drive down Loop Road (County Road 94) which is a beautiful, twenty-four-mile stretch of serene dirt road right off Tamiami Trail.

A New Kind of Land Management

Before Florida was colonized, the region now called Big Cypress was inhabited by a South Florida Tribe known as the Calusa. A powerful tribe, 50,000 strong at its height, the Calusa once occupied the entirety of southwest

WHERE: 33100 Tamiami Trail East, Ochopee, FL 34141
PARKING: Big Cypress National Preserve is a big place; most activities have associated parking lots, including the visitor center, nature trails, and campgrounds.
ENTRANCE FEE: None, but certain activities may require paid permit.
DIFFICULTY, DISTANCE, ACCESS: Depends. The nature trails are not very demanding, but you'll need to be well-equipped for an overnight camping trip. Some trails have wooden docks, making them wheelchair accessible. Facilities are ADA compliant.
FACILITIES: Visitor centers with restrooms, eating areas, and ranger-guided activities.
BEST TIME: The character of Big Cypress changes with the wet and dry season; visiting at different times of year will present new kinds of wildlife.

Florida. Like the Tequesta in Miami, their civilization was weakened by disease and violence brought by the Spanish, eventually collapsing in the eighteenth century. The Seminole tribe would later call this region home, until they too were driven from it.

In the 1960s, plans to build a massive airport on the land sparked a years-long legal conflict between the developers and various community groups hoping to keep the land as is. The result was the creation of the country's first national preserve. Today, there are only nineteen such places throughout the United States. A national preserve differs from a national park in that it allows for activities like hunting, cattle grazing, and (at least in the case of Big Cypress) oil exploration. Though not without its controversies, the national preserve designation protects the land from full-scale development while allowing native residents to continue their traditional cultural practices.

▲ Big Cypress's Loop Road offers visitors the opportunity to tour a portion of Florida's wilderness from the comfort and convenience of a vehicle.

Where to Explore?

Big Cypress is a remarkably big place, so if you're a first-time visitor, you may want to make the Oasis Visitor Center your first stop. The small museum and the regularly scheduled Big Cypress educational videos are good ways to gain some background knowledge of the area. A fenced-in pond located in front of the center usually has a few alligators and provides an opportunity to watch them from a safe distance. From there, it's a short drive to Kirby Storter Roadside Park. The park is surrounded by marl prairies, pineland, and a mixed cypress and pond apple swamp with a mile-long boardwalk running through it that lets you see the swamp up close. The trees here are replete with airplants, native epiphytes (plants that grow on other plants) that anchor themselves on the tree branches. From here, you're not too far from Loop Road. On the Loop Road drive, you're likely to see a range of wildlife including wading birds, turkeys, songbirds, snakes, alligators, turtles, and freshwater fish such as the Florida gar. Black bears, river otters, bobcats, fox squirrels, and the extraordinarily elusive Florida panther also live in the preserve, but they are shy and much rarer to spot.

TRIP 21

Fairchild Tropical Botanic Garden

A must-see for any nature enthusiast, this popular Miami destination hosts thousands of native and ornamental plant species and wildlife.

WHERE: 10901 Old Cutler Road, Miami, FL 33156

PARKING: Designated parking area, including handicap spaces; during some events, additional disabled parking is designated in the Lowlands Parking Field.

ENTRANCE FEE: Varying fees for adults, seniors, and kids, but free for children 5 and under

DIFFICULTY, DISTANCE, ACCESS: You could probably see the whole park in a couple hours, but we recommend taking your time and observing the scenery up close. The Garden is fully ADA accessible; wheelchairs can be reserved for free and fit onto the trams.

FACILITIES: Restrooms and cafes.

BEST TIME: The wide variety of plants bloom in different seasons; visit the website for annual events within the facility.

FIELD TRIP 21

KEY

- Parking
- Main Road
- Smaller Road
- Hiking & Biking Trails

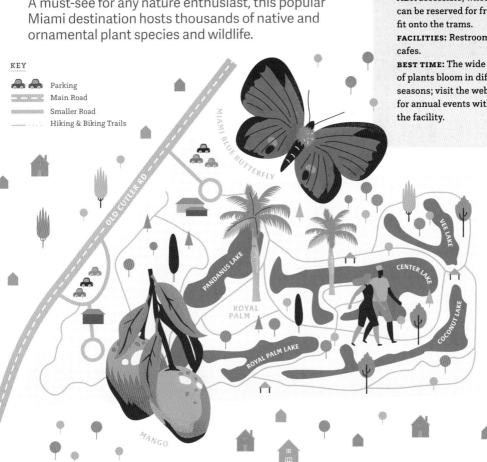

MIAMI BLUE BUTTERFLY

OLD CUTLER RD

PANDANUS LAKE

ROYAL PALM

ROYAL PALM LAKE

VEE LAKE

CENTER LAKE

COCONUT LAKE

MANGO

109

People from all over come to enjoy the beautiful aesthetic of the many hundreds of tropical plants contained within the garden's eighty-three acres. From tiny orchids to behemoth baobab trees, the gardens represent the breadth of the world's tropics. Named for David Fairchild, an enthusiastic botanist who, in the early to mid 1900s, introduced thousands of species and varieties of plants to America, including the mangos revered by Miamians, cotton that serves the textile industry, and cherry blossom trees that are now a symbol of our nation's capital, the gardens were founded by Robert Hiester Montgomery, a retired accountant and friend of Fairchild, and opened to the public in 1938. Today, the grounds offer opportunities to learn, relax, and above all revel in the magical and often strange world of plants.

▲ Every section of Fairchild's grounds offers unique botanical treasures, vistas, and seasonal additions.

▼ These inviting benches sit beneath deep-red gumbo limbos and statuesque live oaks.

The Question Is, What Isn't There to Do?

Fairchild is constantly hosting events, some regular and others annual. Regular programming includes guided tours of the gardens, virtual plant sales, and a variety of plant-related courses. From plant propagation techniques to artforms that focus on botanical subjects, you can take advantage of the wide range of available expertise. The Ramble festival hosts local conservation organizations and vendors, and if you've got a sweet tooth, be sure to visit during the annual Chocolate Garden festival, which features the delicious and crafty creations of several local chocolatiers. There's also the incredibly

popular NightGarden. From November to January, the garden becomes a luminous wonderland, with string lights creating the illusion that all the plants are bioluminescent. Finally, there's the Fairchild Challenge, an annual science competition for pre-K through grade twelve students, which encourages learning through direct engagement with a project.

These programs and festivals only scratch the surface of what the gardens host—the folks at Fairchild are busy bees! On regular days, visitors have much to explore. The Wings of the Tropics exhibit features butterfly species from across the tropics in a protected conservancy, and several sections of the garden are dedicated to Florida's native plants. Because different plants bloom at different times of the year, the character of the park is constantly changing.

Conservation Connection

Fairchild has a robust conservation team that focuses on the protection of the many threatened and endangered species in South Florida. Between their Million Orchids Project and their nursery at Montgomery Botanical Center, they grow state and federally listed plants of all kinds for reintroduction in natural areas. Perhaps their most well-known conservation program is Connect to Protect, which was founded in response to the continuing loss of Miami's pine rocklands. Connect to Protect's goal is to build pockets of this pineland habitat throughout the county by distributing native pine rockland plants to registered participants. The hope is that these micro-habitats will connect the remaining fragments of natural pine rockland forests, helping their plant and animal populations grow strong and healthy. This program is an excellent place for beginners to start landscaping with natives at home.

Matheson Hammock Park

Opened in 1930, this was Miami-Dade's
first county park.

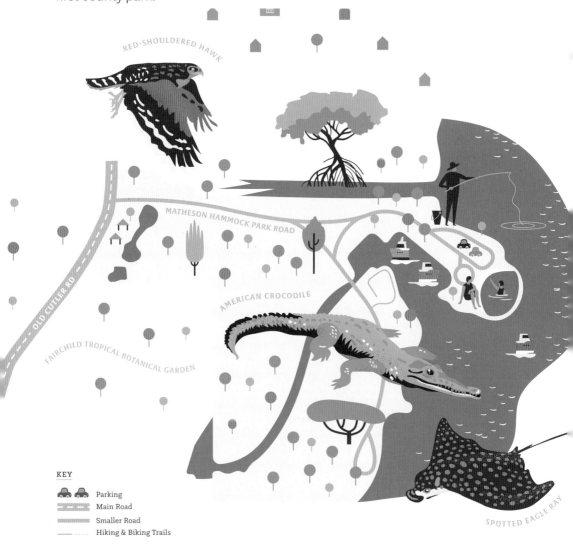

RED-SHOULDERED HAWK

MATHESON HAMMOCK PARK ROAD

OLD CUTLER RD

AMERICAN CROCODILE

FAIRCHILD TROPICAL BOTANICAL GARDEN

SPOTTED EAGLE RAY

KEY

Parking
Main Road
Smaller Road
Hiking & Biking Trails

▲ The famous atoll beach at Matheson Hammock is great for swimming.

Just east of Fairchild Tropical Botanic Garden, this coastal park offers plenty of opportunities for recreation in nature. You can explore the hiking trails winding through the lush tropical hammock forest, lazily enjoy the beach with a stellar view of Biscayne Bay, or embark on an adventurous fishing trip from the park's marina. At 630 acres, it not only offers a spacious daytrip but also contains the largest remaining tract of rockland hammock forest in the county.

A Generous Donation

Wealthy industrialist William J. Matheson had a deep appreciation for nature and understood the value of green spaces. Shortly before his death in 1930, he donated eighty-five acres of pristine hardwood hammock to the county on the condition it be made accessible as a public park. A few years later, the county was able to expand the park's boundaries by purchasing over 400 additional acres of adjacent native forest. We can't be certain of what would have happened to this rare, verdant forest were it not for this donation, but we do know that the natural areas within Matheson Hammock Park carry an important natural legacy, and they should continue to be preserved in perpetuity.

WHERE: 9610 Old Cutler Road, Coral Gables, FL 33156
PARKING: Metered, pay-by-phone parking.
ENTRANCE FEE: Small fee per vehicle
DIFFICULTY, DISTANCE, ACCESS: Not directly connected to the ocean, the shallow atoll beach is one of the safer outdoor swimming areas for children. ADA accessible facilities and nature trails.
FACILITIES: Restrooms, kayak and windsurfer rentals, marina, and restaurants.
BEST TIME: Warmer spring and summer months.

In the Heart of the Jungle

Technically a tropical hardwood hammock is not a true jungle. Ecologically speaking, hammocks are relatively small pockets of canopied forest that punctuate a different type of ecosystem. Jungles are much larger expanses of trees, shrubs, and vines—but we won't blame you for marveling at the healthy vigor of the forests within Matheson Hammock Park and thinking of them as jungly. The half-mile Matheson Hammock Trail is one of the few opportunities you'll ever have to visit the heart of a rockland hammock forest.

▲ The park's entrance sign sports the khaki and green color combo characteristic of Miami-Dade County park signs.

A Unique Kind of Swimming Pool

If you walk a short distance past the Matheson Hammock Marina, you'll reach the eastern, coastal end of the park, where you'll encounter the park's saltwater atoll pool, which resembles a coral atoll (a ring-shaped coral reef system that encircles a lagoon). The man-made, circular pool of water is adjacent to, but disconnected from the ocean by a berm of sand and limestone. It's a perfect swimming place for families with small children, as the shallow and still water makes it one of Miami's safest beaches. Next to the atoll beach is the Adventure Sports center, where you can rent kayaks, paddleboards, and even kitesurfing equipment if you're a thrill seeker.

Conservation Connection

Through the lens of climate change resilience, Miami's mangrove forests are arguably its most valuable asset. Extensive development has already destroyed many of Florida's mangrove ecosystems, and now a new, potentially catastrophic threat has arrived. Though it looks similar to our native black mangrove, the non-native white-flowering black mangrove (Lumnitzera racemosa) comes from eastern Africa and coastal Asia, and, if given the chance, will stifle the native trees. Planted in a mangrove-adjacent section of Fairchild Gardens in the 1960s, it escaped cultivation and grew from a handful of specimen plants to thousands of seedlings. The year 2008 was the "oh snap!" moment when biologists realized the plant was invasive. Conservationists from Fairchild Gardens responded swiftly. Since 2009, they have led the charge, working alongside partners like Miami-Dade Natural Areas Management (NAM) in an extraordinary effort to completely eradicate the invasive tree. Volunteers help in the annual Lumnitzera Blitzera, where they are trained to identify and remove the tree (and are rewarded with free passes to the Fairchild Chocolate Festival). The efforts have been remarkably successful, reducing lumnitzera to 5 percent of its 2008 population, but the hope is to eventually mark that percent at zero.

TRIP 23 MIAMI GARDENS EXTENSION

The Deering Estate at Cutler

Travel back to 1920s Miami at a spot where the Miami Rock Ridge and the swampy Everglades run into Biscayne Bay.

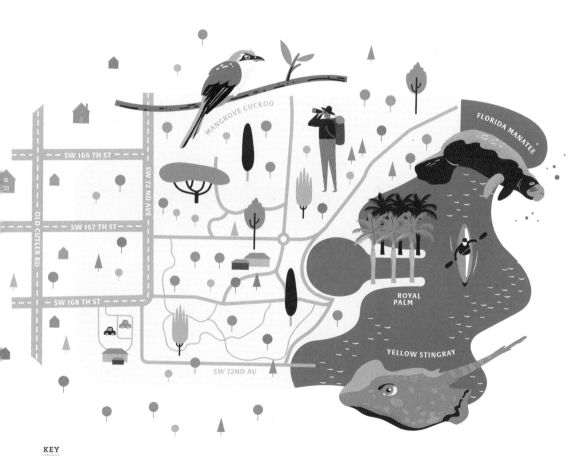

MANGROVE CUCKOO

FLORIDA MANATEE

ROYAL PALM

YELLOW STINGRAY

SW 166 TH ST

SW 72 ND AVE

OLD CUTLER RD

SW 167 TH ST

SW 168 TH ST

SW 72ND AV

KEY

Parking

Main Road

Smaller Road

Hiking & Biking Trails

Charles Deering, brother of James Deering (who built and lived at the Vizcaya Villa), was also engaged in the arts, philanthropy, and conservation, and his roughly 450-acre estate is now listed in the National Registry of Historic Places. Like James, he also appreciated his land's pristine habitats, opting to preserve and enhance the native flora on and around the property by recruiting the famed Florida botanists David Fairchild and John Kunkle Small. A fortunate thing, as the hammocks surrounding this estate are one of the the largest untouched tracts of this ecosystem left in the county. Walking through the grounds today is like walking through a snapshot of the 1920s. The estate is now owned by the State of Florida and managed by Miami-Dade County; the Environmentally Endangered Lands program maintains its natural areas.

Beyond-Impressive Biodiversity

Back when the Tequesta inhabited this area, living off the abundant sea life that thrived along the coast, freshwater from the Everglades cut through the

▼ The Charles Deering Estate was home to Mr. Deering until his death in 1927.

limestone of the Miami Rock Ridge before entering Biscayne Bay. Though that historic flow was diverted long ago, several of the original ecosystems still thrive here, including hammock forest, pine rockland, and mangrove swamp. The adjacent marine areas support seagrass beds that are home to fish, manatees, stingrays, sharks, marine birds, and a variety of invertebrates. The plant diversity of the grounds is beyond staggering, with 800 recorded species—about half of all the plant species recorded in Miami-Dade County—89 of these are listed as threatened or endangered. Diverse flora will, of course, beget diverse fauna. As part of the Florida Great Birding Trail, the Deering Estate boasts more than 170 species of birds observed on the property.

Exploring the Estate

The Deering Estate's biodiversity creates ample opportunity for exploration. Tours through the grounds will give you a basic lay of the land, while renting a kayak will let you tackle the marine angle. Special nighttime kayak and cruise tours give a unique nocturnal perspective of the park. The Deering Estate also hosts educational programs for grade school students that explore the area's human and natural history. No indoor classroom can match this living classroom where students can become immersed in the subject matter. Other fun events include ghost tours, film screenings, and concerts. Particularly popular is the annual Deering Seafood Festival, which takes place on the estate's back lawn, right next to the bay.

▼ The estate stretches into Biscayne Bay. Keep an eye out for manatees here.

Biscayne National Park and Stiltsville

Miami is sandwiched between not one but two national parks, Everglades National Park and Biscayne National Park.

KEY

- 🚗🚗 Parking
- ▬ ▬ ▬ Main Road
- ▓▓▓▓ Smaller Road
- — - - - Hiking & Biking Trails

▲ This lighthouse at Boca Chita Key in Biscayne National Park is ornamental.

Most national parks are terrestrial, but Biscayne is unique in that most of the area it encompasses is marine. In fact, approximately 257 of its 270 square miles are ocean, a full 95 percent. Here, landlubbers have ample opportunity to acquaint themselves with the sea, whether through swimming, fishing, boat tours, snorkeling, or scuba diving.

Key Biscayne, Biscayne Bay, Biscayne Boulevard. What's a Biscayne? The word has two possible origins, both rooted in Spanish history and geography. The first suggests it's related to the Bay of Biscay, the body of water north of Spain and west of France. The second proposes the name honors early Spanish explorer, Sebastián Vizcaíno, who had lived in the northern Basque region of Spain. Wherever its name came from, one thing is certain: Biscayne Bay is the crown jewel of Miami's marine ecosystem. Its riches can only be fully comprehended by diving right in.

WHERE: 9700 SW 328th Street, Homestead, FL 33033
PARKING: Park at the visitor center lot.
ENTRANCE FEE: None
DIFFICULTY, DISTANCE, ACCESS: You won't get very far in Biscayne National Park without a boat. Whether on a kayak, personal motorized boat, or a tour cruise, this park is for the water bound.
FACILITIES: Restrooms throughout the park; campgrounds reachable only by boat.
BEST TIME: Camping is best in cooler fall and winter months, whereas in-water activities like snorkeling are better suited for warmer spring and summer months.

To Be or Not to Be a Park?

The City of Miami was officially inaugurated in 1896, and it grew slowly at first. When it began experiencing its development boom, buildings started appearing everywhere. The land surrounding Biscayne Bay was no exception. In 1968, the threat of development spurred lawmakers to designate part of the bay as a national monument. When its boundaries were increased in 1980, it gained sufficient area to be redesignated as a national park. Since then, the park has been a place for ecological and historical protection and recreation. The only settlement it had supported was the former City of Islandia, comprising Elliott Key and a few other surrounding keys, which had only the most basic infrastructure and never more than a few dozen residents, mostly park employees. Islandia's status as a city was invalidated in 2012, primarily because it never followed formal municipal procedures.

Stiltsville

If you trail back to Bill Baggs State Park on Key Biscayne and stand somewhere along its western edge looking out to sea, you might notice the outlines of some odd structures seemingly plopped in the middle of the bay. A handy pair of binoculars (or a very clear day) will reveal the structures to be an array of buildings. Standing on long, wooden legs and completely surrounded by Biscayne Bay are six wooden houses collectively called Stiltsville. The first was built in the 1930s as a bait and beer shop, and, at one point, twenty-seven of these stilt houses stood in the bay. Their most famous function was as a getaway for Miami's well-to-do, who retreated to several exclusive clubs that operated within the buildings. Over the years, fires and hurricanes destroyed most of Stiltsville, and the six remaining houses now fall within the marine boundaries of Biscayne National Park, where they are maintained by the Stiltsville Trust. Access requires a federal permit, but one of the trust's goals is to expand the site's use as an educational space. The middle of the ocean is a precarious place for buildings, but we hope the whimsical Stiltsville maintains its well-earned sea legs as a functioning feature of Miami history.

▼ In 2003, a nonprofit organization called the Stiltsville Trust was established to help maintain and preserve the houses as a way to showcase the marine environment within the park.

▲ Biscayne Bay hosts a variety of top predators like the hefty bull shark. These striped sergeant majors don't seem to mind it though.

You're Going to Need a Boat

Biscayne National Park contains only a tiny sliver of land within its boundaries. Elliot Key is the most well-known, but it, and most of the rest of the park, is accessible only by boat. Don't have one of your own? No problem! The Biscayne National Park Institute, a nonprofit partner of the national park, is a one-stop shop for any water-bound educational program you can think of. Through them, you can book a cruise tour, a guided snorkeling, scuba, or kayak adventure, or an overnight camping trip.

Wildlife Haven

South Florida is one of the only places in the world where a coral reef exists right next to a busy metropolitan area. The rich marine life that attracts anglers and nature explorers to Biscayne Bay is the result of three healthy ecosystems, namely mangrove swamp, seagrass meadows, and coral reef. Though they're often studied in isolation, you can't get a full picture of Biscayne Bay without understanding how these habitats are related.

Let's use marine fish as an example. In order for a fish to reach adulthood within an ecosystem, it requires the big three habitats. Adult fish lay their eggs within the mangrove forest because this "nursery" offers protection for their fry (baby fish). Once in adolescence, these fish migrate to the seagrass beds and eventually move to the coral reefs, where they may spend most of their adult lives before they complete the cycle by heading back to the mangroves. Destroy any one of the big three, and the entire interconnected cycle will be severely disrupted.

Biscayne National Park is also a refuge for many migratory bird species and sixteen federally threatened and endangered plants and animals, including the American crocodile and Schaus' swallowtail butterfly.

TRIP 25 — FLORIDA'S CORAL REEF EXTENSION

John Pennekamp Coral Reef State Park

A short drive south to the Florida Keys will first bring you to Key Largo, where you can find the doorstep to this aquatic park.

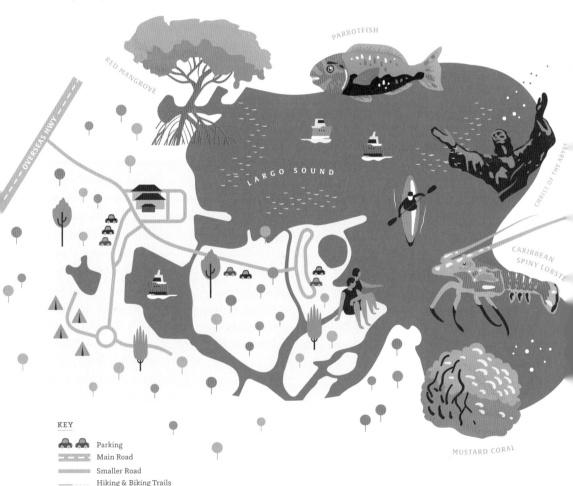

PARROTFISH

RED MANGROVE

OVERSEAS HWY

LARGO SOUND

CHRIST OF THE ABYSS

CARIBBEAN SPINY LOBSTER

MUSTARD CORAL

KEY

🚗 🚗 Parking
Main Road
Smaller Road
Hiking & Biking Trails

▲ Florida's Coral Reef is the third longest barrier reef in the world.

Established in 1963, John Pennekamp Coral Reef State Park carries a special significance as the first US marine park and preserve and is the only Florida Keys destination included in this book. The true splendor of Florida's Coral Reef, including its multitudinous colors and diversity of life, is readily accessible from this state park. Visitors can enjoy a variety of activities, including kayaking, fishing, beachgoing, snorkeling, and the popular glass-bottom boat tours, which give you a full view of the underwater reef from a dry perch on a boat.

In Honor of John Pennekamp

When plans were being made to establish Everglades National Park, conservationists pushed to include the coral reefs in the northern keys. There was a growing concern that the common practice of collecting corals and other

WHERE: 102601 Overseas Highway, Key Largo, FL 33037
PARKING: Lots within the park.
ENTRANCE FEE: Small per-vehicle fee, smaller fee for pedestrians and cyclists
DIFFICULTY, DISTANCE, ACCESS: Easy, but you may encounter some narrower channels if kayaking through the mangroves. Facilities are ADA accessible and beach wheelchairs are available without cost.
FACILITIES: Restrooms, aquarium, concessions, and kayak rentals.
BEST TIME: Most activities here are water associated and best enjoyed in spring and summer.

organisms that lived on the reef was chipping away at the vital, slow-growing ecosystem. Laws in place at the time were too weak to defend the corals, so what better protection than the full backing of the federal government? Unfortunately, the reefs weren't included in the final boundary of the national park.

Enter Dr. Gilbert Voss and John D. Pennekamp. Voss was a researcher at the University of Miami who recruited Pennekamp, then a news editor for the *Miami Herald*, to continue the fight for the reef's protection. Pennekamp carried hefty conservation clout as he was instrumental in getting the Everglades designated as a national park. Bolstered by Voss' scientific research, Pennekamp wrote extensively about the issues facing the reef. In 1960, the idea had gained enough support for the state to officially declare the area a permanent preserve. Originally christened as the Key Largo Coral Reef Preserve, it was redesignated as a state park in 1963 and renamed to honor Pennekamp.

Exploring the Reef

The reef at John Pennekamp State Park is just one section of Florida's Coral Reef, the third largest barrier reef on the planet. Composed of approximately eighty species of coral and stretching for 70 miles, it should be no surprise that hundreds of species of marine animals—from fish to cetaceans (whales and dolphins) to reptiles—make their home here. As a visitor, you can spend ages kayaking through its mangroves, fishing for your dinner in one of the designated areas, or feeding your brain on a tour of the museum. The reefs at Pennekamp contain forty-six of the eighty coral species native to South Florida's waters, an incredible slice of biodiversity. Though the closest

▲ A diver meets a shark on the resplendent reef. Snorkeling and diving are two of the park's primary appeals.

▼ The Christ of the Abyss stands submerged in the depths.

encounters require jumping into the water with snorkel or scuba gear, those less inclined to get in the water are in luck; the popular *Spirit of Pennekamp* is a tour boat with thick glass panels as its bottom. Acting like a large, floating dive mask, this boat allows you to view life below while staying dry.

If you decide to snorkel or scuba dive, be sure to ask how to find one of the park's more interesting submerged features. Standing at the bottom of twenty-five feet of water is a bronze statue of Jesus Christ, head and arms turned upward toward the surface in a stance that can either be described as praising glory or pleading supplication. Cast in Italy and placed in the park in 1965, *The Christ of the Abyss* is the third (and final) statue of its kind. The original, identical statue is found in the Mediterranean Sea, and the second one is off the coast of Grenada in the Caribbean.

Why Not Stay the Night?

John Pennekamp State Park is also camper-friendly, with campgrounds that allow for a unique nighttime view of the park. Few things are as relaxing as sitting by the ocean at night, hearing the gentle breaking of the waves. Stay comfy and cozy in an RV or brave the elements (and potentially plenty of mosquitoes) in a tent. Either way, get your spots quick, as there's very limited space.

 Conservation Connection

Coral reefs are majestic but fragile living temples. Coral polyps (the animals that build the reefs) are an ancient group. The first species appears in the fossil record approximately 535 million years ago—so they have survived every global mass extinction event in Earth's history (five in total). But there's one thing they may not be able to make it through: human pressure. Voss and Pennekamp's work to save the reef was an insightful venture that recognized the fragility of the ecosystem. Today, coral reefs are one of the most at-risk ecosystems in the world. They face warming ocean temperatures and acidification due to climate change, physical disruption, ocean pollution, and illegal harvesting, and once they are damaged, they are slow to recover. Organizations around the world, such as South Florida's Coral Restoration Foundation and University of Miami's Rescue a Reef, are hard at work developing effective strategies to protect corals while also engaging in direct restoration work. You can help corals by volunteering with or donating to these or similar groups, minding your proximity to the actual reef (even the smallest of nudges can have a negative impact), and supporting sustainable fisheries that don't damage reefs.

305 SPECIES TO KNOW

Terrestrial   134

Choosing 305 species to represent Miami was no easy task. We contemplated ecological importance, cultural association, invasive status, conservation concerns, and even local recognition. For reference, Zoo Miami alone hosts more than 700 different species, so whittling down the list was definitely an undertaking. Telling our "plant guy" Brian Diaz that he could choose only sixty-six plant species for this book was equivalent to requesting his first-born child. Everyone had to make sacrifices.

In general, biodiversity increases as you move from the poles toward the equator—an effect known as a latitudinal gradient. With its tropical climate, South Florida has higher biodiversity than more northern portions of the United States, so choosing the best representatives from all areas of natural Miami had to be a balanced effort. To make the process more manageable, we put species into seven categories—plants, insects and arachnids,

▶ Red mangroves provide habitat above and below the waterline.

▼ Laughing gulls perch near the ocean.

marine and freshwater fish, reptiles and amphibians, invertebrates, birds, and mammals—doing our best to represent each group with the most relevant species. Though we couldn't include everything, this list is an excellent sample of what nature in Miami has to offer.

Residential Status

Miami is an incredibly diverse city that hosts multiple cultures and ethnicities from around the world—this is true for its wildlife too. As the world became smaller by means of transportation and accessibility, new species made their homes here. A large percentage of South Florida's current plants and animals migrated here from the Caribbean and Central and South America. Some of these organisms continued to evolve here as a result of

Miami's unique subtropical and peninsular climate. Over the years, as more species were introduced, both intentionally and accidentally, through ballast water, transportation miscues, or natural occurrences, a high percentage have established themselves in this welcoming environment.

Given that much of South Florida's flora and fauna came from the tropics via hurricanes or ocean currents, some have argued that most Miami species are non-native. For our purposes, native species in the United States are commonly defined as being present here prior to European colonization, gradually adapting over thousands of years. This allowed the ecosystem a chance to adapt to each newcomer. Thanks to human activity, recent introductions have occurred in a much shorter time frame, often adding multiple new species in the span of just a few years.

Once introduced, non-native species either survive in the new habitat, adapting to factors such as climate, urban development, predation, available space, and native competition—or they don't. If they do survive and are able to reproduce without human intervention, maintaining a population over time, they fall into two categories: If the new population fits into the ecosystem without displacing native species, it's defined as *naturalized* (for example, the cattle egret), but if the new species continues expanding its population, disrupting native species and ecosystems along the way, it is considered *invasive* (for example, the Australian pine).

We don't believe that plants or animals should be considered good or evil. Even the invasive species negatively impacting Florida's ecosystems are not doing so out of malice. Like all living things, they are simply trying to survive. In their native ranges, these species may be contained by predators or geography, but in their new environment, those checks and balances don't exist, allowing them to spread prolifically. With invasive species, human intervention is often needed to protect ecosystems, habitats, and even entire regions, which could be forever altered for the worse (worse for native species and worse for us humans).

When we were creating this list, we took native ranges into consideration, collectively agreeing it should be a primary piece of information for each of the species listed. Within the header for each species, we noted whether it qualified as non-native or invasive, and used the attached summaries to explore the origins of its introduction and the impact it has had on South Florida. If a species is listed as native to the 305, it's likely to be the focus of conservation efforts aimed at preserving Florida's natural ecosystems.

Conservation Status

Unfortunately, there are a number of species in this guide currently in desperate need of conservation. Human impact, whether through habitat loss, pollution, competition from invasive species, or other human-caused pressures, has devastated a large portion of species local to Miami and South Florida, some to the point of extinction. The Florida Fish and Wildlife

Conservation Commission (FWC) maintains Florida's Endangered and Threatened Species List, which we've used to classify the species in this book as either extinct (no longer in existence), endangered (could go extinct in the foreseeable future if trends continue), or threatened (likely to become endangered in the near future). Neither endangered nor threatened are definitive classifications, as any species can absolutely rebound, especially if humans take the proper conservation measures. Our goal is to highlight species in need of our assistance so we can collectively work together as a community to save them before it's too late.

Habitat Preference

Each of our 305 species were assigned to one of three habitats: coastal, freshwater wetlands, or terrestrial. While some species do cross between multiple habitats, a majority spend most of their time in one. For cases in which species did split habitats, we've listed them in whichever habitat would give you the best chance of an encounter. In this guide, the term *coastal* refers to South Florida's beaches, dunes, and marine environments. *Freshwater wetland* includes the vast stretches of marshes such as those found in the Everglades, which consist of large, flooded areas dominated by grasses and sedges. *Terrestrial* mainly refers to dryer upland areas such as scrub habitats, hardwood hammocks, and rocklands.

Helpful Anatomy Terms

We all know about ears, tails, and scales, but can you point out a lateral line? How about a bird's mantle? Some critters, like fish and birds, are best identified by specific bits of anatomy whose names you probably don't hear every day. On marine animals the same body feature might look different between fish, sharks, rays, marine mammals, and others. Though we couldn't include features for all species, we think this primer should give you a good leg up (fin up?) on telling a snook from a snapper and a grackle from a gallinule.

crown

breast

primaries

secondaries

mantle

dorsal fin

caudal fin

anal fin

pectoral fin

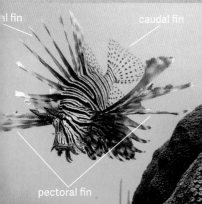

al fin

caudal fin

pectoral fin

dorsal fin

melon

pectoral fin

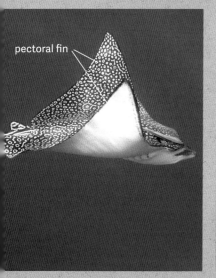

pectoral fin

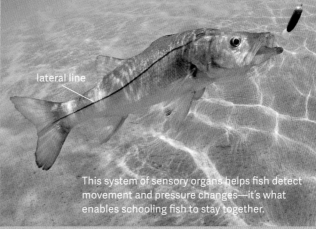

lateral line

This system of sensory organs helps fish detect movement and pressure changes—it's what enables schooling fish to stay together.

Terrestrial

Let's begin by looking at our terrestrial ecosystems, found in areas that are elevated above sea level. Land topography is one of the strongest factors to affect the type of ecosystems that can become established within a certain area. The boundless expanses of freshwater wetlands that comprise the Everglades, for example, may not have formed were it not for the fixed flatness of the land between Lake Okeechobee and the southern tip of the state. The flatness allows water to distribute over the landscape and flow as a wide sheet rather than as channeled rivers. Historically, most of Miami-Dade County was composed of these low-lying freshwater wetlands, but there have always been pockets where the ground's limestone base bulged upward or where soil or sand had accumulated, creating zones that are higher and dryer than what surrounds them. These support plant species that aren't able to live in persistently wet ground—trees and shrubs that would otherwise drown. The most substantial stretch of raised land in our watery landscape is the Miami Rock Ridge, a massive limestone outcrop that extends approximately seventy miles. It's basically a large plain of rock with a very thin layer of soil on top, and it supports two of Miami's most biodiverse ecosystems: the pine rocklands and the tropical hardwood rockland hammocks.

▼ Tailless whip scorpion

Before its development boom, about 11 percent of Miami-Dade County (and most of the rock ridge) was composed of pine rockland, which covered almost 200,000 acres. The only large tree in this ecosystem is the South Florida slash pine—it's the understory, the plants that grow between the pines, that make this habitat a biological marvel. Sharp, dense saw palmetto forms much of the understory, an obstacle for early explorers attempting to walk through the rocklands without a machete.

Several hundred species of shrubs and herbaceous plants grow among the pines and saw palmettos. This understory is a fire-dependent habitat, which means it relies on naturally occurring wildfires to prevent large hardwood trees from encroaching and competing for resources.

The hammocks and pine rocklands have unfortunately experienced heavy destruction, particularly since Miami's development boom started in the 1920s and 30s. The elevated land they grow on is extraordinarily valuable, providing some of the best building opportunities in South Florida. Logging has been intense over the years, and 98 percent of the rocklands outside Everglades National Park are now gone. These ecosystems once supported thriving populations of Florida panthers, eastern indigo snakes, and gopher tortoises, and the fragments that now remain preserve the slighter pulse of Miami's unique terrestrial ecosystems. Most of our surviving pine rocklands exist within parks and preserves, many of them quite healthy thanks to the outstanding efforts of land managers and conservationists.

Heavy losses have not stopped the pine rocklands and hammocks from being biodiversity champions. Let's take a walk through the forest and find what charismatic creatures roam here.

▼ Corn snake

Mammals

Brazilian Free-Tailed Bat

Tadarida brasiliensis

`NATIVE`

WHERE TO FIND THEM:
Camino 305 Field Trips 1–23

With a wingspan of twelve inches, the Brazilian free-tailed bat, or Mexican free-tailed bat, is the smallest and most common free-tailed bat found throughout Florida. They have wrinkled cheeks, long tails, and a color that varies between dark brown and a grayish brown. Commonly seen near human development, they are often found roosting in man-made structures such as attics, sheds, and bridges, but can also live in natural cave habitats. Because they are nocturnal, you'll find them roosting during the day. If you spot one, keep looking around for more—they sleep in colonies of thousands, often emerging all at once at dusk to hunt and forage.

 Fun Fact

Bat poop, called guano, is super useful for humans. Rich in phosphorus, it's an excellent plant fertilizer and was even an ingredient in gunpowder during the Civil War.

Although pop culture gives bats a bad or scary reputation, they are hugely beneficial to agriculture and general human comfort, gobbling up countless pesky moths, beetles, and other flying insects.

Florida Bonneted Bat

Eumops floridanus

NATIVE ENDANGERED

WHERE TO FIND THEM: Camino 305 Field Trips 11 and 12

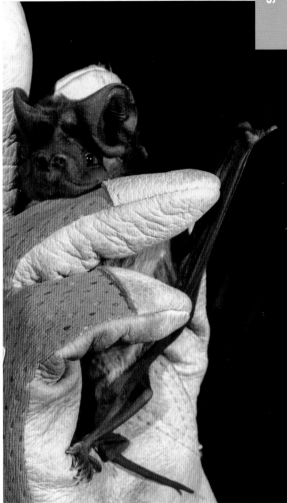

The Florida bonneted bat, also known as the Florida mastiff bat, is both federally and state protected and is listed as critically endangered on the International Union for Conservation of Nature (IUCN) Red List. A South Florida endemic species, its restricted range and small population makes it the rarest bat in the country. Although it's the largest species of bat in Florida, with a wingspan of twenty inches, very little historic data is available on these mysterious flyers. Only a handful of their roosts have ever been documented, but researchers have been exploring the role of artificial roosts to help with conservation efforts. They have short, funnel-like ears that fold over their head like a bonnet, and their fur varies in color from a brownish cinnamon to gray. Unlike other species of bats that can be found together, sometimes by the thousands, the roosts of the Florida bonneted bat are more intimate, hosting fewer than 100 individuals.

Bonneted bats only give birth to about two offspring a year, which means their population is slow to grow, but their biggest threat currently is habitat loss, particularly the already scant pine rocklands. A combination of human development and natural disasters, specifically the toppling of older trees with large roosting cavities, have decimated their natural habitat. At the same time, because they eat mainly flying insects, pesticides have made it difficult for the bats to find adequate food.

Bobcat

Lynx rufus

NATIVE

WHERE TO FIND THEM: Camino 305 Field Trips 19 and 20

What is smaller than a Florida panther but larger than a housecat? Enter the bobcat. More common than Florida panthers, bobcats roam across Florida and the majority of North America. However, as a result of their shyness, sneakiness, and preference for hiding out during the day in swamps, forests, and dense shrub thickets, spotting one of these cats isn't very easy. About the size of a coyote, bobcats are usually yellowish-brown, with black spots and a white belly. They have a distinct short and fluffy white tail and their ears are tufted, which means they have extra hairs growing from the tips. Scientists aren't sure what the tufts are for—some think they help keep debris out while others believe they help the cat hear. These carnivorous animals usually hunt at night and dine on small mammals and birds. Like panthers, bobcats are territorial, marking their home range with ground scrapings and strategic urination. Despite their small stature, the breadth of their territory can be up to six square miles.

Feral Cat

Felis catus

INVASIVE

WHERE TO FIND THEM: All Camino 305 Field Trips

How did our domestic feline companions find themselves in a book about wildlife? House cats might be cute and cuddly, but they are wreaking havoc on our native habitats and wild species. Often seen in parking lots, yards, and street corners (sometimes by the dozens), there are many more of these carnivorous kitties than their larger counterparts, and their negative impact on the environment unfortunately may be irreversible.

Feral and free-ranging cats are one of the most devastating invasive mammals in South Florida. Descendants of the African wild cat, they were domesticated about 4,000 years ago and spread around the globe with humans, making them decidedly non-native. Studies estimate that each one of these sneaky hunters kills roughly 100 birds and other native creatures each year, making them a huge threat to migrating songbirds, second only to habitat loss.

Unfortunately, we cannot just adopt all the cats into our homes in order to stop the carnage. There is a difference between feral, stray, and free-ranging cats. Stray and free-ranging cats are socialized with people. Free-range cats are animal companions that live or spend part of their day outdoors, while strays could be in the wild for a variety of reasons, such as having run away, gotten lost, or been abandoned. The most sustainable method for keeping birds and small animals safe from

these cats is to keep the cats indoors as much as possible. Feral cats, on the other hand, do not typically socialize with humans and can be scared or aggressive, so it's not usually safe to bring them into a household. The best method for protecting birds from feral cats is to trap and neuter the cats so the feral population does not grow.

Domestic cats, whether feral, stray, or free-ranging, also spread a disease called toxoplasmosis, caused by a parasite found in their feces. Though the parasite reproduces in cats' digestive tracts, it can spread to a variety of mammalian species, including humans and marine mammals. This is why it's recommended pregnant women do not change litter boxes. Storm water washes cat feces carrying the parasite into our water system and out into the bay, where manatees and dolphins have been known to get infected. The takeaway? Keep Mr. Mittens inside.

Conservation Connection

Miami-Dade County has a Trap Neuter Release (TNR) program to help curb the continued growth of feral cat populations. Trained professionals locate and trap cat colonies, take them to participating veterinarians for sterilization and ear clippings, and rerelease them back into the wild. A clipped ear on a feral cat indicates the individual has been sterilized and can live out its life without increasing the cat population. TNR does not immediately eliminate the threat of feral cats, but over time, it will hopefully reduce their numbers throughout neighborhoods and important South Florida ecosystems.

Florida Panther

Puma concolor coryi

`NATIVE` `ENDANGERED`

WHERE TO FIND THEM: Camino 305 Field Trips 14 and 20

Mountain lions, panthers, and cougars oh my! All are synonyms for the same animal, but in the scientific community, the term *puma* is preferred for these large cats. The Florida panther is a subspecies of puma. If you spot a giant feline that is uniformly tan in color, has lighter fur around its belly, and comes complete with a long tail, it's pretty safe to assume you're looking at a Florida panther. Florida's only other large feline species, the bobcat, is smaller than a Florida panther and has darker streaks on its coat and stubby tail.

Florida panthers were first described by Charles B. Cory in 1896 and they are Florida's official state animal. Historically, they ranged throughout the southeastern United States, but the dwindling population, now estimated at roughly 200 individuals, lives mostly in southwestern Florida. This dramatic decrease in numbers is due to their need for large territories, an average of 200 square miles, for roaming. As more humans move south,

Fun Fact

Pumas can't roar! They can purr or growl, but they lack the elastic ligament on their hyoid bone (a small neck bone) that allows big cats to belt their mighty roar.

developing and building land, rerouting water, and chopping down trees, Florida panthers have less and less space in which to live. Panther conservation strategies focus primarily on securing more land for preservation and closely monitoring the remaining population. The Florida panther has been protected under the Endangered Species Act since 1967. They are extremely rare, but if you're lucky enough to spot one in the wild you can report your sighting to the Florida Fish and Wildlife Conservation Commission (FWC), which manages and tracks Florida panther populations as part of its efforts to protect our state symbol.

If you ever get a good look at a Florida panther, you might notice a right-angled kink at the end of its tail. Scientists believe this is a result of inbreeding due to their small population. A kink in the tail isn't the only negative result of an undersized breeding population—infertility, heart defects, and increased mortality were all documented in the Florida panther population. In 1992, a team of geneticists and conservation biologists warned that

Conservation Connection

Sadly, almost 60 percent of Florida panther casualties today are caused by vehicle strikes. Roads built in South Florida to connect the west coast to the east coast drive right through the unique and important ecosystems the panthers rely on. You'll sometimes come across a PANTHER CROSSING sign, and on many of these roads, construction is underway on wildlife passages so the cats and other animals can safely make their way back and forth. With a combination of patience, understanding, and ingenuity, we can help ensure the Florida panther's continued survival.

the whole population could be eradicated in as little as twenty-five years. Alarmed by the possibility of losing one of Florida's apex predators, FWC, the National Park Service (NPS), and the US Fish and Wildlife Service (FWS) made a plan to introduce eight female pumas from Texas to the Florida population. These pumas historically lived throughout the southeast United States, and the Texas and Florida populations would have interacted in the days before human development separated them.

The experiment was deemed a success. Five of the introduced mama pumas were able to give birth to twenty cubs, and in today's Florida panther population, we see fewer kinks in tails, fewer inbred defects, and a higher survival rate in both adults and cubs.

Coyote

Canis latrans

NATURALIZED

WHERE TO FIND THEM: Camino 305 Field Trips 14, 20, 22, and 23

A relative to our trusty canine companions, coyotes are known for being vocal through barks, yips, and howls—so much so that their scientific name translates as "barking dog."

Fun Fact
It is possible, although rare, for dogs and coyotes to mate and produce hybrids called *coy-dogs*.

The coyote isn't considered an introduced or native species but a naturalized one, a designation which refers to non-native species that have established themselves within an area, found a "balance" with the new ecosystem, and do not require human intervention. Coyotes naturalized in southern Florida after expanding their range across most of North America, and they're now present in every US state except Hawaii. They thrive in urbanized and agricultural settings. With increased agricultural development across the United States and no competition from the gray wolf (*Canis lupus*) or the red wolf (*Canis rufus*), which were eradicated from most of their ranges in the 1900s, coyote populations have grown and expanded. These opportunistic omnivores will dine on almost anything, including plants, animals, and even decaying carcasses—yum! Coyotes can reach just under three feet in length and about thirty pounds in weight. They are usually a rusty brown or gray color with a bushy tail. Unlike wolves with their famous packs, coyotes usually travel alone unless raising offspring.

Eastern Gray Squirrel

Sciurus carolinensis

NATIVE

WHERE TO FIND THEM: Camino 305 Field Trips 1–24

Maybe one of the most familiar rodents, the eastern gray squirrel is known for its big, fluffy, silver tail and its habit of hoarding acorns. It is found throughout eastern North America and is the most common species of squirrel seen in South Florida. Often observed climbing

trees or telephone wires, these little mammals live in both residential and natural areas. If you see them chasing each other, it's usually not a game of tag but rather a sign that it's squirrel mating season. Although skittish, they will do anything for some grub, especially in heavily populated parks and campuses where they've grown accustomed to people, even going so far as to snatch a snack from a human hand.

Gray squirrels have a habit of not eating their meal immediately, instead burying it so they can be sure to have something to eat during seasons when food is scarce. However, their attempts at saving a meal for another day often result in forgetting the exact location of said meal. While this might lead to a slightly hungry and frustrated squirrel, these forgotten nuts and seeds later germinate, becoming the next generation of plants. In this way, squirrels help forests grow and expand their ranges.

Florida Black Bear

Ursus americanus floridanus

NATIVE

WHERE TO FIND THEM: Camino 305 Field Trips 19 and 20

The Florida black bear is a subspecies of the American black bear and the only species of bear found in Florida. Although American black bears can be found throughout the country in a variety of colors, the Florida subspecies is distinctively black with a blonde or white patch of hair on its chest.

These medium-sized bears average about 330 pounds, but there's no need to fear them—their size is supported by a diet that consists of about 80 percent fruits, nuts, and berries, 15 percent insects, and only 5 percent meat, usually from small mammals. Found in forested areas, Florida black bears are excellent climbers and usually hide out in trees if they feel threatened. Historically, they were found throughout Florida, but today they live in about 50 percent of their original habitat, with subpopulations around the state and into Alabama and Georgia. Florida's Fish and Wildlife Commission (FWC) manages their population with a goal of preserving the sustainability of the species and the habitats they rely on.

Gray Fox

Urocyon cinereoargenteus

NATIVE

WHERE TO FIND THEM: Camino 305 Field Trips 1–23

Like all foxes, our native gray fox belongs to the dog family. Their omnivorous diet allows them to snack on anything from small birds, mammals, or insects to fruit and various vegetation. Since they're nocturnal, you're most likely to encounter them late in the evening while they're on the prowl scavenging for food in forested areas.

Less frequently encountered in South Florida are red foxes, which are non-native and were introduced primarily for sport through hunting clubs. Their names give you a big clue to identifying whether you're looking at a native gray or a non-native red. The red fox is normally rusty in color, with hints of white

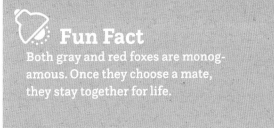

Fun Fact

Both gray and red foxes are monogamous. Once they choose a mate, they stay together for life.

on its belly, feet, and tip of its bushy tail. The back of its ears are typically black and it's often mistaken for a feral cat. Gray foxes usually have darker coloring, with black on their tail and snout.

Nine-Banded Armadillo

Dasypus novemcinctus

~~NATURALIZED~~

WHERE TO FIND THEM: Camino 305 Field Trips 20, 21, 22, and 23

Closely related to anteaters and sloths, the nine-banded armadillo has a narrow snout with a long, sticky tongue, which it uses to slurp up its preferred diet of ants and termites (flexible in its dietary habits, it has sometimes been observed eating small eggs and plants if needed). One of the more unusual-looking species on this list, the nine-banded armadillo can grow to about sixteen inches long and is protected by armored skin embedded with bone, which is separated by nine leathery moveable bands, allowing it to move about and dig quickly.

They have poor eyesight and dig burrows for shelter. Female armadillos produce one egg that splits four ways, meaning she always gives birth to identical quadruplets. Having expanded their range to Florida in the early 1900s, nine-banded armadillos are now considered naturalized. Historically, Florida did have a native armadillo, but it's been gone awhile. During the Pleistocene, an era which began 2.6 million years ago and ended roughly 11,500 years ago, the giant armadillo (*Holmesina septentrionalis*) roamed these parts, weighing more than 500 pounds.

Fun Fact

Think you saw a mini manatee? It could have been a nine-banded armadillo. They are surprisingly strong swimmers, with the ability to walk along the bottom of shallow waters, hold their breath for up to six minutes, and even swallow air to expand their stomachs, making themselves more buoyant.

Roof Rat

Rattus rattus

NON-NATIVE

WHERE TO FIND THEM: All Camino 305 Field Trips

Warning, this entry is not for those who suffer from musophobia (fear of mice and rats). The roof rat, or black rat, is one of the most abundant rodents in Florida. A non-native species from southwestern Asia, this destructive mammal was introduced to North America (and many other locations) in the 1800s as a stowaway on ships. Infamous for spreading the bubonic plague, the roof rat can wreak havoc wherever it goes through the destruction of food products, crops, and structures. They've been known to occupy any space in a home, damaging walls, pipes, plastic, and even electrical wires. When not acting as uninvited houseguests, they typically hang out in elevated areas, nesting and feeding in trees or telephone poles. Omnivorous and opportunistic, they will eat anything, even birdseed from backyard feeders.

They're typically black, gray, or brown, with a lighter-colored belly and a long, hairless tail. Sometimes, they're confused with the smaller, native marsh rice rat (*Oryzomys palustris*).

Skunks

Eastern Spotted Skunk

Spilogale putorius

NATIVE

Striped Skunk

Mephitis mephitis

NATIVE

WHERE TO FIND THEM: Camino 305 Field Trips 1–23

▲ Eastern spotted skunk

South Florida is home to two species of skunk, the eastern spotted and the striped, with both belonging to the family Mustelidae. Mustelids are unique because they are equipped with anal glands that produce a strong-smelling musk. Both the eastern spotted and striped skunks take this musk to another level with the ability to aim and squirt extremely fragrant (not in a good way) droplets more than twelve feet.

The striped skunk has two large white stripes down its back, which sometimes run onto its tail. They are excellent diggers. Eastern spotted skunks climb trees rather than digging and can be found thieving eggs from bird's nests. They are a bit smaller than striped skunks and have spots and stripes all over their head and back and at the tip of the tail. Despite their names, it can be difficult to differentiate between the two species without an extremely close inspection, and you'll have to decide for yourself if proper identification is worth a potential tomato juice bath (a good way to remove skunk musk).

▲ Striped skunk

Virginia Opossum

Didelphis virginiana

NATIVE

WHERE TO FIND THEM: All Camino 305 Field Trips

Play dead! Or not? It's honestly difficult to tell.

The thespians of the animal kingdom, Virginia opossums are a frequent visitor to local Miamian backyards and can often be seen climbing along fences or trees at night.

But when caught on the ground and unable to escape a perceived threat, these marsupials attempt to confuse their predator by mimicking a corpse. In an incredible and realistic portrayal of death, their tongue falls from

Fun Fact

Opossums are immune to pit viper venom.

their mouth, their body seemingly ceases to breathe, and they excrete a foul odor that smells like rotting flesh. Once the threat has disappeared, they make a miraculous recovery and walk off into the shadows to fight—or "die"—another day.

Although some may believe them to be a pesky rodent (especially considering they're not exactly the cutest mammal you've ever seen) these are actually the only marsupials found north of Mexico. That's right, they are related to kangaroos! Females have a fur-lined pouch where, after a quick thirteen-day gestation period, young opossums live with their mothers for another fifty days or so before moving about on their own. Although they may seem threatening with their rat-like hairless tail, long snout, and sharp teeth, their diet makes them useful critters to have in your yard. Loose in their dietary preferences, opossums will eat fruits, vegetables, and bugs, but also pests such as ticks, fleas, and even venomous snakes.

White-Tailed Deer

Odocoileus virginianus

NATIVE

WHERE TO FIND THEM: Camino 305 Field Trips 14, 19, and 20

Florida (and almost every other state in the United States) is home to white-tailed deer. These hooved mammals get their name from the coloring and usefulness of their stubby tails, which are usually brown on the top and bright white underneath. When frightened, the deer freeze their whole bodies except their tail, which they stick directly up in the air and wave slowly (like a surrender flag). This serves as a warning for others that danger is near. Known for grazing on a variety of vegetation, they can be pretty damaging to crops and gardens when they find a tasty treat. Often active at dawn and dusk, their greatest threat is being struck by an unexpected vehicle. Quite the opposite of an endangered species, white-tailed deer are considered overpopulated throughout the country and are subject to regulated hunting practices.

Fun Fact

In order to preserve healthy habitats in which deer and other game could thrive, hunters fought to protect land from development. Hunters are often credited with the start of the conservation movement.

Reptiles and Amphibians

Brown Anole

Anolis sagrei

`INVASIVE`

WHERE TO FIND THEM: All Camino 305 Field Trips

The highly invasive brown anole, which hails from Cuba and the Bahamas, was introduced in the 1970s through either the pet trade or as a hitchhiker on cargo ships. Ever since arriving in South Florida, it has expanded rapidly throughout the state, even becoming established in southern coastal Georgia. Scientists expect it to continue migrating north as climate change brings warmer winters that aren't cold enough to keep its population in check.

The brown anole is the mortal enemy of Florida's green anole. Not only will the former attack and provoke its native cousin, but its presence is altering the behavior and habitat of the green anole—causing them to move higher up into the canopies of trees. The two anoles are almost identical in shape and size, and to confuse matters even further, the green anole can change color from bright green to the same brown as its invasive counterpart.

Green Anole

Anolis carolinensis

`NATIVE`

WHERE TO FIND THEM: All Camino 305 Field Trips

Abundant and adorable, Florida's very own green anole (also known as the Carolina anole) can often be found staring at you from a tree trunk or fence post. Anoles are found throughout the Caribbean. In fact, 173 of the roughly 400 anole species throughout the world call the Caribbean and tropical Americas home. Florida, with a climate similar to much of the Caribbean, has just one native species. Found as far west as Texas, the green anole is an arboreal species that lives in trees—you'll often see them hanging upside down from tree branches. Their long, slender bodies are accessorized with a pink dewlap, a brightly colored flap of skin that extends from their neck. Males use their dewlaps to communicate territoriality and to court females. Green anoles can change color from bright green to brown depending on their surroundings or mood.

Recent research shows anoles are extremely adaptive to their surroundings—Caribbean anoles have developed larger footpads for additional support in areas where hurricanes are frequent. Unfortunately, the introduction of the Cuban anole, or brown anole, has displaced Florida's native greens, pushing them into more constrained habitats.

Knight Anole

Anolis equestris

NON-NATIVE

WHERE TO FIND THEM: All Camino 305 Field Trips

Similar to the native green anole, the knight anole is brilliant green in color, but this species, also called the Cuban anole, has yellow ridges on its head and is substantially larger than its cousins, sometimes measuring up to twenty inches long. An arboreal species, they aggressively defend their territory with displays that include a propped-up body and open jaw paired with an up and down head-bobbing motion. Introduced to South Florida from Cuba in the early 1950s via the pet trade, their population has expanded steadily, making them an established species. Though its range is restricted by cold weather, there is no indication this species will bow down to any native species in a warmer future.

Argentine Black and White Tegu

Salvator merianae

INVASIVE

WHERE TO FIND THEM: Camino 305 Field Trips 14, 19, and 20

Tegus are large terrestrial lizards with mottled black and white bands down their back and tail. Males can grow up to five feet long. Though they live on land, they are capable of swimming and can tolerate both marine and freshwater environments.

Native to southern Brazil and Argentina, tegus arrived in Miami through the pet trade. Omnivorous by nature, they consume the eggs of protected species such as the American alligator, American crocodile, and gopher tortoise. While not as common as green iguanas or knight anoles, they have been documented throughout Miami and as far north as Tampa Bay.

 ## Conservation Connection

Flushing an unwanted pet fish down the toilet or releasing a reptile in an open field is not only inhumane to the animal but can begin a new species invasion. In an attempt to prevent the spread of non-native and invasive species in Florida, the Florida Fish and Wildlife Conservation Commission (FWC) runs the Exotic Pet Amnesty Program at zoos, aquariums, and environmental events, which allows people currently in possession of exotic pets (legal or illegal) to yield ownership to FWC with zero penalty or questioning. At these events, responsible and permitted pet owners or facilities can adopt the surrendered animals. Usually open to the public, amnesty days can be fun and educational.

Brown Basilisk

Basiliscus vittatus

INVASIVE

WHERE TO FIND THEM: All Camino 305 Field Trips

Ever wanted to be able to walk on water? Look to the brown basilisk for pointers. Its lightweight, webbed feet and incredible velocity enable this reptile to travel where it pleases by temporarily running across the surface of water, earning it the nickname Jesus Christ Lizard. As if that isn't enough of a superpower, you can also add effective camouflage to its bag of tricks.

Growing up to two feet long, brown basilisks hail from Mexico and Central America and were most likely released via the pet trade as early as the 1970s. Males have a lobe-shaped crest on the back of their head, which can be used during courtship or to intimidate predators and competitors. Found in only a dozen or so counties in South Florida, they are most common in Miami-Dade and Broward counties.

Florida Box Turtle

Terrapene carolina bauri

NATIVE

WHERE TO FIND THEM: All Camino 305 Field Trips

One of four subspecies of box turtle found in the United States, the Florida box turtle is endemic to the Sunshine State. It can tolerate a wide variety of habitats and saltiness, and it is truly at home in the state, found as far south as the Florida Keys and as far north as Florida's Gulf Coast.

This turtle earned its name for its steep, dome-like carapace (shell), which it uses for protection and shelter. As for diet, it's an omnivore that eats gastropods (snails), leaves, and fruits and plays a role in spreading native plant seeds through its poop. Florida box turtles (and box turtles in general) are popular in the pet trade and are sometimes taken directly from the wild, but considering their important ecological role, it's almost always better to leave them be. Although it's not illegal to relocate them under certain circumstances (unlike the gopher tortoise), it can cause stress. Pick on someone your own speed.

Florida Scrub Lizard

Sceloporus woodi

NATIVE

WHERE TO FIND THEM: Not found at any Camino 305 Field Trips

A true representative of the Sunshine State, this lizard is entirely endemic to the state of Florida—meaning it is not only native but also only lives here and nowhere else. Resembling an anole, the Florida scrub lizard has a maximum length of about five inches, but the key to identifying it is the thick brown stripe that runs from behind its head to the base of its tail. Males have striking blue stripes along the sides of their bellies, which they display during courtship. Though they once lived all over Miami-Dade County, they are now only found in small patches of land, as far south as Palm Beach County. The scrub lizards' preferred habitat is upland, sandy, and sparsely vegetated, as in the County Line Scrub. This habitat can be found in Miami, but has shrunk over the years due to increased urbanization and climate change. This combined with an ever-growing number of feral cats has caused scrub lizard populations to suffer and pushed their range north.

In 2018, the Florida Fish and Wildlife Conservation Commission (FWC) organized a reintroduction of this species into promising habitats. Thankfully, these lizards don't require much habitat to sustain a long-term population. Though the reintroduction hasn't proven effective yet, time will tell if South Florida's environmental conditions will someday allow a population of scrub lizards to finally establish again.

Tokay Gecko

Gekko gecko

INVASIVE

WHERE TO FIND THEM: All Camino 305 Field Trips, except 19 and 20

The tokay gecko's stocky body is light blue, speckled with bright orange spots, and can grow to a whopping twelve inches long (quite long by gecko standards). As with most gecko species, it is nocturnal and relatively shy. Though it prefers to seek protection on the ground, you might also find one on a tree branch or even in your garage.

It is very vocal, with a call that often begins as a long cackle and eventually ends with a noise that sounds like "toe-kay"—hence the common name. The geckos use these loud calls primarily for courtship, and you're likely to hear them before you ever see them. Native to Southeast Asia, they escaped the pet trade, found Florida's warm weather and high humidity to their liking, established themselves quite quickly, and have been classified as a nuisance species ever since. Although they primarily hunt grasshoppers, moths, cockroaches, and spiders, you'd do well to steer clear of their large mouths, strong bite, and stubbornness to release their "prey" once they've locked their jaw onto something.

Tropical House Gecko

Hemidactylus mabouia

INVASIVE

WHERE TO FIND THEM: All Camino 305 Field Trips

On a warm summer night in Miami, point your eyes toward any light source on an external wall, and you've got a good chance of spotting one of these tropical house geckos. They have a habit of hanging out in close proximity to porch lights, waiting for a convenient moment to snatch an unsuspecting spider or flying insect.

Only four inches long, light grayish brown, and somewhat translucent, this tiny gecko hails from sub–Saharan Africa, but is now quite common in the warmer portions of the United States. Tropical house geckos are, like many geckos, quite vocal. On a quiet evening, you might hear their subtle yet distinctive squeaks and peeps. Though listed as an invasive species, tropical house geckos aren't as disruptive to the local ecosystem as some invaders. In fact, their biggest impact might be on an invasive cousin, the Mediterranean house gecko (*Hemidactylus turcicus*), whose population has shrunk since the tropical house gecko has become established.

Giant Ameiva

Ameiva ameiva

`INVASIVE`

WHERE TO FIND THEM: All Camino 305 Field Trips, except 19 and 20

The giant ameiva, or Amazon racerunner, looks like a cross between a monitor lizard and one of the various slender-headed snakes typically found in treetops. Originally hailing from the Amazonian areas of South America, specifically Brazil, the giant ameiva is a type of whiptail lizard that has invaded Florida as a result of the pet trade. This ground-dwelling giant maxes out at eighteen inches and prefers a diet of insects, spiders, and frogs. As a juvenile, it tends to be duller in color, exhibiting various shades of brown, but as it grows, it adopts brilliant shades of green and turquoise. It is an oviparous (egg-laying) reptile, and thrives in areas of open habitat, preferring to forage for food in locations where its speedy movements are an advantage in hunting and avoiding predators.

A second species of ameiva, the dusky giant ameiva (*Ameiva praesignis*), has been reported on Key Biscayne and Virginia Key. It is distinguished by its larger size and darker blue coloring.

Gopher Tortoise

Gopherus polyphemus

`NATIVE THREATENED`

WHERE TO FIND THEM: Camino 305 Field Trips 11 and 12

Taxonomists, make up your minds! Is it a gopher or a tortoise? With one glance, it's obvious this handsome reptile is absolutely a tortoise—its name comes from its ability to burrow holes up to forty feet long and ten feet deep.

Looking at a gopher tortoise, you might not assume they're effective diggers, but closer inspection reveals shovel-shaped front legs designed for scooping the sandy soil found in their preferred coastal dune, pineland, or hammock habitats. Found from Louisiana to

the Carolinas, this reptile is Florida's official state tortoise and the only native one found here. Cuteness and state pride aside, we can most appreciate the gopher tortoise as a keystone species, a term for an organism with a particularly important role in maintaining an ecosystem. Their deep burrows provide shelter for hundreds of other animals including frogs, small mammals, and the eastern indigo snake. Herbivorous, opportunistic grazers, they also spread the seeds of the native berries and other plants they eat.

Unfortunately, habitat destruction has been hard on the gopher tortoise. With a lifespan averaging fifty years in the wild (approximately ninety in human care) and a relatively slow reproductive rate, young tortoises face a harder time adapting to urbanization and development than shorter-lived species. The state currently lists them as threatened.

Fun Fact
The gopher tortoise is present in all sixty-seven Florida counties.

Black Spiny-Tailed Iguana

Ctenosaura similis

INVASIVE

WHERE TO FIND THEM: All Camino 305 Field Trips, except 19 and 20

A native of Central America, this voracious reptile is found almost everywhere in South Florida, basking in the sun on rocks in open grassy areas. Ranging in color from gray to brown, they

have spiny frills along the length of their backs and black vertical bars along the sides of their body and tails. Males can reach almost four feet in length and seem imposing, but you don't need to fear these omnivorous grazers. Other than a defensive whip from a tail or snap of the mouth when cornered, they aren't a danger to humans and will run away if you get too close—one of the fastest lizards in the world, they can sprint up to twenty miles per hour.

Spiny-tailed iguanas wreak havoc on landscaped gardens and native vegetation with their insatiable appetites. If they can't find their fill of vegetation, they will happily eat bird eggs, rodents, or fish, which makes them a threat to native species.

Green Iguana

Iguana iguana

INVASIVE

WHERE TO FIND THEM: All Camino 305 Field Trips, except 19 and 20

Florida is home to many reptiles, with a good portion having been introduced from else-where, including the green iguana. Though they are prevalent throughout South Florida and are often associated with Miami specifi-cally, they are just another tourist enjoying the fruits Miami has to offer (literally). Growing up to five feet long and resembling something more akin to a dinosaur than a modern-day lizard, these spiky-headed reptiles devour native vegetation and ornamental gardens and can dig deep nesting burrows that sometimes destroy pedestrian sidewalks and walls.

Introduced from Central and South America, iguanas are prolific breeders and compete with native reptiles. Other than culling (killing large numbers of them), our only hope for controlling their population in this agreeable environment, which suits them so well, is snaps of cold weather. A perfect representation of native versus non-native dynamics, the native reptiles in South Florida have adapted to survive our periodic winter temperature drops, while newcomers like the iguana, unaccustomed to the increasingly rare occasional low temperatures, grow stiff in the cold and can fall from trees. You'll never see a green anole slipping off a tree in January.

Oustalet's Chameleon

Furcifer oustaleti

INVASIVE

WHERE TO FIND THEM: Camino 305 Field Trips 13 and 14

South Florida's invaders come from far and wide—some as far as Madagascar. The Oust-alet's chameleon is one example. Discovered in a Miami-Dade County avocado grove in 2010, likely an escaped pet, it quickly established itself as a formidable predator—consuming everything from grasshoppers, ants, lizards, treefrogs, and weevils. It has even branched out to eat the berries of the prolific and invasive Brazilian pepper.

Large and bulky, Oustalet's chameleon can quickly grow to more than eleven inches and varies in color from green (female) to brown (male) with darker colored bands scattered across its body. So far, it hasn't shown the destructive characteristics common to most invasive species, but the full impact of its presence in Miami-Dade is still unknown. At this point, research and efforts to control the population are the best options.

Brahminy Blindsnake

Indotyphlops braminus

NON-NATIVE

WHERE TO FIND THEM: All Camino 305 Field Trips

While this snake is essentially blind (its eyes can only react to light intensity), it is the most wide-ranging terrestrial species of snake in the world, and like many globetrotters, it has found Florida to its liking. Though not native, the blindsnake's impact on Florida ecosystems has fortunately been minimal. Resembling more of a worm in size and appearance, this species first appeared in Miami in the 1970s, possibly hitching a ride from southern Asia within a shipment of potted plants, which earned it the nickname "flowerpot snake." Only about six inches long, slender, and nonvenomous, it poses no threats to humans. You're most likely to find it in leaf litter in pine rocklands and hammocks. Dig a hole almost anywhere in South Florida and there's a chance you'll encounter this snake.

Eastern Indigo Snake

Drymarchon couperi

NATIVE THREATENED

WHERE TO FIND THEM: Camino 305
Field Trip 20

The eastern indigo snake is a Florida native, and most of its population lives almost entirely within state boundaries. It holds the title of longest native snake in the United States, reaching lengths just under eight feet. Luckily for us, length doesn't equal danger, as it is nonvenomous and shy—unless you are a small bird, mammal, or reptile.

Bluish-black in color, the eastern indigo snake appears almost metallic in sunlight. It prefers to dwell in pinelands, swamps, and hammocks and shares an interesting, commensal relationship with Florida's state tortoise, the gopher tortoise. Roughly once per year, the snake relies on burrows created by the gopher tortoise as a safe location to deposit its eggs. Unfortunately, the once ubiquitous habitat favored by gopher tortoises and eastern indigo snakes is continuously being lost to urban development—so too are the chances of survival for this currently threatened species.

Rim Rock Crowned Snake

Tantilla oolitica

NATIVE THREATENED

WHERE TO FIND THEM: Camino 305 Field Trips 11 and 12

This nonvenomous snake's name is derived from Miami's famous rock ridge geological formation. While many species are endemic to Florida, this rare snake is only found in Miami-Dade and Monroe counties, making it a true representative of the 305. Generally small and only reaching twelve inches at its maximum length, it is somewhat nondescript, with shiny black scales, a black to light brown head, a yellowish belly, and black spots. Though it was recently added to the International Union for Conservation of Nature (IUCN) Red List as an endangered species, as a result of much of its pine rockland and hardwood hammock habitat having been lost to development, the rim rock crowned snake has defied expectations and continues to hang on.

Ringneck Snake

Diadophis punctatus

`NATIVE`

WHERE TO FIND THEM: All Camino 305 Field Trips

One of the smaller snakes found in Miami, the ringneck snake has had enormous success expanding its range through North America. With fourteen subspecies ranging throughout the United States, Mexico, and Canada, this fifteen-inch long snake is found in every Florida county. Shy and nocturnal, they often turn up under rocks in moist hardwood forests and at wetland edges.

Despite being classified as venomous, these snakes are essentially harmless to humans. The small amount of venom mixed with their saliva is ineffective against a person, but it's enough to subdue their preferred prey of smaller invertebrates and amphibians. If you're ever unsure of identification, focus on the yellow collar circling the neck at the back of the head. In nature, bright colors often indicate a poisonous individual, but some species sport bright colors as a way to trick predators into leaving them alone. When disturbed, a ringneck snake's initial defense is to twist its body upside down, revealing a bright red, orange, or yellow underside. Scientists believe this behavior is an attempt to say, "Don't eat me—I'm poisonous!" We suggest you don't try to call the bluff.

Cane Toad

Rhinella marina

`INVASIVE`

WHERE TO FIND THEM: Camino 305 Field Trips 1–24

Some of South Florida's current invasive species were introduced with good intentions,

namely controlling agricultural pests. The cane toad, or bufo, is an example of an intentional introduction gone awry. A native of Central America, this omnivore was brought to Florida in the 1930s and 40s as a means of controlling the rat and beetle populations wreaking havoc on sugar cane fields. It has been thriving in our subtropical climate ever since. Managing the species has proven difficult, as few predators are equipped to eat something so toxic. The cane toad's skin secrete bufotoxins, which can irritate human skin and cause lasting harm or even kill animals like dogs and cats. To top it off, even their eggs are toxic.

Though adult cane toads are larger than native southern toads, it can be difficult to distinguish the two. When in doubt, just keep yourself and your furry friends away.

Conservation Connection

Outside Florida, cane toads have proven to be one of the most widespread and destructive invasive species on the planet, destroying native fauna wherever they go (especially where sugarcane is cultivated). In Australia, the economic impact is measured annually in the millions of dollars. Since the first 102 cane toads were introduced to Queensland in 1935, their populations have exploded, threatening domesticated animals and native wildlife, particularly the northern quoll—a carnivorous marsupial endemic to Australia. In Florida, containing the problem of the cane toad is up to homeowners and their ability to tell cane toads from native cousins. Florida Fish and Wildlife Conservation Commission (FWC) has an identification guide on its website, which instructs users on how to humanely and safely remove cane toads.

Southern Toad

Anaxyrus terrestris

NATIVE

WHERE TO FIND THEM: Camino 305 Field Trips 14, 19, and 20

The southern toad has an enormous range, extending westward to Louisiana and as far north as Virginia, which really earns this amphibian its name. Though it closely resembles the highly invasive and toxic cane toad, you can distinguish the species by the two knobs on the southern toad's head, just above its eyes—cane toads lack any cranial ridges.

Nocturnal by nature, southern toads aren't a particularly large toad, with males reaching the size of an average adult human's hand. They are very common in Florida and you can probably spot them whenever a pond or other freshwater source is nearby. During the day, they hang out in burrows, emerging at dawn and dusk to hop around in leaf litter. March and October are their breeding seasons, and that's when you'll hear their screeching calls, which can last from two to eight seconds and tend to be an octave or so higher than American toad calls.

Cuban Treefrog

Osteopilus septentrionalis

INVASIVE

WHERE TO FIND THEM: All Camino 305 Field Trips

The largest tree frog in North America came from our southern neighbor across the Florida Straits, the isle of Cuba. While many reptile and amphibian species have made it to Florida across the ocean by way of storms, pet trade, or even hitchhiking on mats of vegetation, the Cuban tree frog ventured here as a passenger on cargo ships in the 1930s. Once introduced, nothing could stop it. This voracious predator wantonly gobbles up native frogs, lizards, and even baby snakes. Female Cuban tree frogs can lay thousands of eggs per clutch, giving them enormous reproductive advantages over

native species. They can also release a mucus from their skin which makes them repulsive to native predators. In specific Florida habitats where efforts have been organized to remove Cuban tree frogs, native frog species have been able to recover quickly, emphasizing the invaders' dramatic effect on local populations.

To find Cuban tree frogs, you need not travel far. They have a preference for moist areas often associated with outdoor showers and shaded areas. They can be spotty green, pale brown, or even cream white, and when at rest, they tend to sit with their legs tightly tucked against or underneath their bodies.

Green Treefrog

Hyla cinerea

NATIVE

WHERE TO FIND THEM: All Camino 305 Field Trips

Fun Fact

Both Georgia and Louisiana claim the green treefrog as their official state amphibian.

The male green treefrog is quite the vocalist, using its unique song and puffed-up chest to emit an attractive sound for the larger females. An arboreal species, it lives in trees throughout the southeast. Though it prefers warmer, wetter areas such as swamps and ponds, you might also spot one around your patio or porch, waiting for an opportunistic moment to snatch a light-distracted insect. These insectivores eat a tremendous number of irritating pests, including mosquitoes and various fly species—so keeping their populations healthy isn't just ecologically important but also useful for minimizing annoying mosquito bites. Fortunately, despite competition with the Cuban treefrog, the International Union for Conservation of Nature (IUCN) Red List lists their status as least concern.

Bright green with a pale-to-white underside, green treefrogs measure roughly an inch and a half long. Their long legs, combined with adhesive pads on their long fingers and toes, make them pretty easy to ID as treefrogs. On any given night, you can hear them going about their nocturnal habits in your backyard, and you can rest a little easier knowing their dinner is making your night a little more comfortable.

Birds

American Crow

Corvus brachyrhynchos

NATIVE

WHERE TO FIND THEM: Camino 305 Field Trips 19 and 20

Although the word *murder* is mostly associated with the act of killing, it is also the word given to a group of crows. Nobody is sure where the term originated, but this ominous descriptor has been used in folktales and historical references. In today's world, the American crow has proven to be a true survivor, acclimating well to urban environments and demonstrating high intelligence. Despite some attempts to exterminate them—some people have even gone so far as using dynamite to demolish their nesting areas—this opportunistic scavenger has continuously shown resilience.

Jet black, with large, broad beaks and a distinctive cackling song, crows are found throughout the United States and Canada. They will eat almost anything they happen upon and sometimes gather in communal roosts numbering in the tens of thousands—if you happen to be a small reptile, insect, or berry, perhaps calling these groups a murder feels appropriate.

American Kestrel

Falco sparverius

NATIVE

WHERE TO FIND THEM: All Camino 305 Field Trips

The smallest raptor (birds of prey) in North America, this species of falcon is also known as the sparrow hawk. With an average height measuring approximately ten inches, its smaller size may not strike fear in most land animals, but any grasshoppers, mice, lizards, or smaller birds on the menu should be wary of the American kestrel's hunting skill. Their

varied diet has proven advantageous, allowing them to occupy a perching-predator niche in many environments and expand their range to both Canada and South America. Males and females are very similar in size and appearance, possessing a small black beak, a gray crown, and vertical stripes along the side of the face. Their wings are gray, and their chest and back are a mottled orange and black. Because they are skilled at hunting and diving from extreme heights, you're most likely to spot an American kestrel searching for prey from the top of a tall tree or a similarly elevated spot.

Blue Jay

Cyanocitta cristata

NATIVE

WHERE TO FIND THEM: All Camino 305 Field Trips

Common throughout the eastern United States and Canada, the blue jay is arguably the most common bird you're likely to see within Florida's wooded areas, and it's definitely one of the easiest to identify. As its name suggests, it is light blue, specifically on the crest, wings, and tail feathers. Its primaries, secondaries, tail feathers, and upper tail coverts (the area above the tail) are particularly vibrant, hosting multiple shades of brilliant blue in a checkered pattern.

Blue jays eat a wide range of foods: berries, seeds, insects, snails, and lots of other small animals, so they have adapted well to a suburban lifestyle, even going as far as to rob other birds' nests for eggs. They also have a particular fondness for acorns. Just like squirrels who bury their nuts and don't always remember to come back and eat them, blue jays do their part to spread acorns, helpfully supporting native live oak regeneration.

Florida has its own subspecies of blue jay, *Cyanocitta cristata semplei*, which is slightly smaller than the more temperate species but still retains the signature intelligence and adaptability often associated with this opportunistic omnivore.

Carolina Parakeet

Conuropsis carolinensis

`NATIVE` `EXTINCT`

WHERE TO FIND THEM: Not found at any Camino 305 Field Trips

Although it's hardly surprising to learn parrots are native to the tropics, you might be surprised to learn there are nearly 400 different species of parrots living worldwide, most near the equator. Some parrot species do live in temperate locations, but the majority are found in Central America, South America, and the Caribbean.

The Carolina parakeet—now extinct—was the only parrot species native to the eastern United States. The last time it was spotted in the wild was in Okeechobee County, Florida, in 1904. Before its demise, it roamed dense forests, particularly near rivers, as far north as New York and Wisconsin. It was common in Florida, and the Seminole called it *puzzi la née* (head of yellow), due to its bright yellow neck sandwiched between a vibrant red crown and brilliant green wing feathers.

The parakeets' habit of gathering in large noisy flocks so angered farmers that they shot the birds en masse. This, combined with habitat loss from clearing forests for farming and a market for using their plumage to decorate hats, eventually exterminated the species.

Although extremely similar in appearance, Mitred parakeets (*Psittacara mitratus*) are from South America. Originally brought to the United States as pets, they have since escaped and established their own feral populations.

Cattle Egret

Bubulcus ibis

`NATURALIZED`

WHERE TO FIND THEM: All Camino 305 Field Trips

In the 1950s, Florida welcomed a new resident. The cattle egret flew across the Atlantic Ocean from its native range in Africa and Asia and became an established Floridian, a thriving naturalized species. There is evidence of them competing for nesting sites with native birds and even eating their chicks, but scientists

BIRDS

haven't yet documented any long-term negative impacts of their introduction.

Cattle egrets get their name from their habit of following around livestock or other large animals in order to eat bugs and parasites that feed on grazing herbivores, and they're often seen feeding in flocks. They are small, mostly white in color, with a long yellow bill and yellow legs. They can reach up to twenty-two inches tall and are usually found nesting in dense colonies in upland habitats.

Cave Swallow

Petrochelidon fulva

`NATIVE`

WHERE TO FIND THEM: Camino 305 Field Trips 11, 12, and 13

Cave swallows have distinctive orange coloring on the face and throat and a black cap on the crown of the head. Small birds, with a maximum height of around five inches, they are excellent fliers and strict insectivores who forage while in flight—meaning they catch every meal without ever touching the ground. Although most of the population is located in Yucatan, northern Mexico, Texas, and New Mexico, South Florida hosts a small colony. Originally limited by a reliance on natural caves, cave swallow numbers were on the decline in the 1960s, but their ability to adapt and start using artificial surfaces in urban environments has been a huge benefit to the species. Their nests can now be spotted beneath bridges and buildings. Formed from an accumulation of mud, plants, feathers, and guano, these nests can last for years if positioned well.

Common Peafowl

Pavo cristatus

`NON-NATIVE`

WHERE TO FIND THEM: Camino 305 Field Trips 11, 17, and 21

The common term *peacock* actually refers only to the males of this species. Similar to chickens, the females are known as hens, specifically peahens. At about three feet tall, adult males are the more colorful specimens, hosting white bands above and under the eyes, a delicate tufted blue crest above their blue heads, and, of course, that spectacular tail, which is called a train. A peacock's train comprises upward of 150 feathers with turquoise and iridescent blue color patterns that resemble eyes. Meanwhile, peahens have pearly green necks and brown feathers throughout their bodies. Peafowl, along with turkeys and chickens, are members of the pheasant family.

In Miami, peacocks have a noisy reputation—they loudly squawk about, provocatively flashing their trains in an attempt to attract a peahen mate. Introduced to Florida in the 1950s as ornamental birds, they are now ubiquitous in many neighborhoods; both Coconut Grove and El Portal have populations that draw visitors from far and wide. Originally from the Indian subcontinent, peafowl aren't terribly threatening to native birds or wildlife apart from occasionally eating native lizards and frogs. To the urban resident, however, they can be a nuisance. In addition to their noisy mating calls, they freely defecate (poop) in public areas, destroy gardens while foraging, and are incredibly slow moving in high-traffic areas. When encountering one, make sure to look for a fallen train feather to keep as a souvenir.

Fun Fact

Some people believe them to be flightless, but peafowls are actually proficient flyers; they just prefer to spend a majority of their time on the ground.

Eurasian Collared Dove

Streptopelia decaocto

INVASIVE

WHERE TO FIND THEM: All Camino 305 Field Trips, except 19 and 20

A non-native species that originated in the Middle East before making its way to Europe then the Bahamas, the Eurasian collared dove eventually migrated to Florida and now occupies most of the continental United States. Clearly, it's an adaptable bird species. Maybe too adaptable, as it outcompetes native birds for resources.

Small and stocky, it has a black bar on its nape that makes it easy to identify. You'll find it in urban neighborhoods, where it has acclimated well to different Miami lifestyles.

Its primary diet consists of berries and insects, but many live off the birdseed given to them in Latin American neighborhoods where doves are a symbol of good luck.

Mourning Dove

Zenaida macroura

NATIVE

WHERE TO FIND THEM: All Camino 305 Field Trips

The first thing you may notice about this bird is its name, particularly how it's spelled. It is named for its haunting and mournful cooing sound and not for the start of the day. Mourning doves are native to Florida, but most American states can also claim them. As one of the most commonly found birds in the country, they have proven their ability to adapt to almost any climate and habitat.

The black spots on the outside of the wings are a mourning dove's most easily identifiable feature. With a closer look, you might also notice a pinkish blush on the sides of its head beneath its eyes. As a result of the warm weather in South Florida, mourning doves can multiply quickly, raising roughly six broods of chicks per year, with generally two chicks in each brood.

 Fun Fact

Doves and pigeons are two names for the same birds. In the first few days of their lives, young doves live off a liquid called pigeon milk or crop milk. Adult pigeons have a special organ called a crop that projects from the bottom of their throat and both produces and stores the "milk." This liquid makes a nutritious meal for hatchlings until they're old enough to begin foraging for food.

Egyptian Goose

Alopochen aegyptiaca

INVASIVE

WHERE TO FIND THEM: Camino 305 Field Trips 1–4, 6–12, 15–18, and 21–24

If you are in a terrestrial area with a host of freshwater habitats such as streams, lakes, and ponds, there's a chance you'll see at least two of these unique-looking geese grazing on grass, aquatic vegetation, or insects. The dark, reddish-brown patches around their eyes and breasts make them easy to identify.

The exact timeline or cause of the Egyptian goose's introduction into South Florida isn't clear, but speculation has it associated with the pet trade. An early sighting occurred in Martin County in 1994 when two were spotted, seemingly unafraid of humans, on a Hutchinson Island golf course (a barrier island east of Stuart, Florida). Now, mated pairs are often seen wandering around many of Miami's natural areas, including Crandon Park. They usually mate for life and there are reports of geese going into mourning after losing a mate. While the lifespan of these birds in the wild isn't well documented, one lived at the Woodland Park Zoo in Seattle, Washington, for fourteen years.

European Starling

Sturnus vulgaris

`INVASIVE`

WHERE TO FIND THEM: Camino 305 Field Trips 1–18 and 21–24

Considered a pest by most ornithologists, this highly adaptive bird has become common throughout North America since its introduction in the 1890s. Their populations have skyrocketed due to their ability to nest almost anywhere, negatively impacting native bird species who are restricted to nesting in small holes in trees and the like. Their omnivorous diet allows them to survive on a wide range of foods. Ironically, the only locations in which they are unlikely to be pests are wild forests or shrubbed areas.

One of the European starling's most famous habits is of flocking together in immense numbers, sometimes reaching the thousands. Maneuvering in unison, these murmurations (flocks of starlings) can become quite dense and are captivating to watch. They aren't particularly tall birds, with a maximum height of seven inches. Combine that height with a long, yellow beak and blackish-green feathers that can look purple in the light, and you have the very social, very adaptable, very vocal, European starling.

Florida Burrowing Owl

Athene cunicularia floridana

`NATIVE` `THREATENED`

WHERE TO FIND THEM: All Camino 305 Field Trips, except 19, 20, and the barrier island extensions

We dare you to find us a cuter bird species. If you ever dreamed of a mini owl that can fit in the palm of your hand, look no further than the adorable Florida burrowing owl. At only nine inches tall, with a white chin strap and yellow eyes, it resembles a regular-sized owl that has shrunk down small enough to fit right into our hearts.

As ground-dwellers, burrowing owls have longer legs relative to their size than most owl species. They can be found in almost any open, sandy field and often nest in colonies. Though

they are capable of flying, their instincts keep them close to the ground. When threatened, they will scurry away into their burrows. Burrowing owls eat mostly insects and, unlike other owls, are mostly diurnal, which means they're awake during the day. You're most likely to see them hanging out in or near the entrance to their burrow. Losing habitat to suburban development is their greatest threat.

Fun Fact

Burrowing owls can create a sound similar to that of a rattlesnake, which they use to warn others of nearby predators.

Florida Grasshopper Sparrow

Ammodramus savannarum floridanus

NATIVE ENDANGERED

WHERE TO FIND THEM: Not found at any Camino 305 Field Trips

Sparrows are common throughout most of North America, and you're probably used to seeing them everywhere. But are you aware of the Florida grasshopper sparrow? Specifically, how it is the most endangered native bird species in the United States? No more than five inches tall, our native grasshopper sparrows have flat heads and relatively nondescript black and gray feathers, which help them camouflage within the low, shrubby, grassy areas they prefer. They get their name from their call, which sounds like the buzz of a flying grasshopper. Not coincidentally, their primary food is grasshoppers. One of four subspecies of grasshopper sparrow in the United States, the Florida species doesn't migrate, residing year-round in the remote prairies of southern and central Florida.

Currently, the Florida grasshopper sparrow is protected by the Migratory Bird Treaty Act of 1918, the Endangered Species Act, and by Florida's Endangered and Threatened Species List. This little bird's demise is tied to its exclusive dependence on one type of habitat, the Florida dry prairie. This land once supported a few hundred individuals but is in high demand from farmers, cattle ranchers, and urban developers, and as it dwindles only a handful of Florida grasshopper sparrows remain. Recently, there have been conservation efforts focused on raising the birds in captivity then releasing them into the wild. So far, a total of 250 birds have been released into the Three Lakes Wildlife Management Area in Central Florida. While it's difficult to tell if the population has increased to healthier levels as a result, scientists have documented successful breeding, suggesting a new generation of Florida grasshopper sparrows could be off to a flying start.

Conservation Connection

Multiple organizations, including Florida Fish and Wildlife Conservation Commission (FWC), US Fish and Wildlife Service (FWS), and the National Audubon Society, organized the Florida Grasshopper Sparrow Working Group to initiate the captive breeding programs, some based in the biologists own homes.

Florida Scrub Jay

Aphelocoma coerulescens

`NATIVE` `THREATENED`

WHERE TO FIND THEM: Not found at any Camino 305 Field Trips

The Florida scrub jay is Florida's only endemic bird species, residing exclusively within the Sunshine State. Unfortunately, that doesn't mean it is common here. Found only in very remote parts of central Florida and the northern Everglades, scrub jays have been affected dramatically by habitat loss. Conservationists estimate that fewer than 10,000 birds live

within the state—thankfully most are within areas protected by state or national park jurisdictions. Their preferred habitats are barren areas with few trees, just clumps of bushes able to withstand poor, sandy soils. Though it may seem odd in a state so watery, this particular habitat (and much of Florida for that matter), is highly dependent on regular fires for balance. Fire clears out vegetation that would otherwise crowd out the delicate scrub ecosystem. In the absence of fire, the scrub habitat begins to shrink. Happily, scientists are closely monitoring the species' status, and, for now, population estimates appear stable.

A medium-sized bird, roughly ten inches in height, the Florida scrub jay has a short, sharp, black beak, a gray chest, and a light-blue head, back, and wings. It is also a rare example of a species that practices cooperative breeding, in which young birds remain in the nest to help raise new chicks and keep the nest safe from predators. Once these fledglings reach two to three years old, they leave the nest in search of mates with whom to begin the cycle again.

 ## Conservation Connection

Inland urban development has fragmented Florida scrub jay populations into many smaller, isolated groups, which could lead to reduced genetic diversity. Scientists from the Florida Fish and Wildlife Conservation Commission (FWC) are working on a program called genetic rescue, which involves translocating birds from larger populations, such as Ocala in central Florida, to areas with smaller ones, such as Jonathan Dickinson State Park in coastal Martin County. The goal is to freshen up the gene pool to make the birds more resilient. In 2020, biologists saw evidence of the introduced birds interacting with resident birds.

House Sparrow

Passer domesticus

NON-NATIVE

WHERE TO FIND THEM: Camino 305 Field Trips 1–18 and 21–24

An adaptable survivor, this non-native resident may be the most widespread bird in the world thanks to its comfort level around human development and its ability to adjust to new environments and available diets. Some scientists have even observed that house

sparrows prefer nesting in man-made structures to natural landscapes. If you drop some food on the sidewalk, and a small, stubby bird with a brown head wanders over to snatch it up, chances are it's a house sparrow. A native of Eurasia and North Africa, the house sparrow was introduced to the United States in 1851 and has since spread throughout the entire western hemisphere.

Loggerhead Shrike

Lanius ludovicianus

NATIVE

WHERE TO FIND THEM: Camino 305 Field Trips 1–24

Despite its small, plump body and somewhat puffy appearance, this bird has quite the unnerving reputation as a ruthless killer. It's often referred to as the butcherbird—partly because it uses its hooked bill to kill prey, but mostly because of its habit of using thorns (or some convenient barbed wire) to impale its prey temporarily, until the shrike is ready to return and eat it.

Although similar in appearance to the northern mockingbird with its gray feathers, pale chest, and black slash across its eyes, this shrike maxes out at eight inches and less than two ounces. Its predatory skills are similar to that of a raptor; perching high on a vantage point while scanning below for prey, it will swoop down, just like a hawk, and pick off oblivious reptiles and rodents before they know what hit them. To increase predatory efficiency, the shrike focuses its attack on the neck or head area, making this tiny bird a fearsome hunter.

However feisty, loggerhead shrikes have unfortunately been declining rapidly in recent years throughout its North American range. Scientists are not entirely sure why. Generally, vehicle strikes, pesticide contamination, and habitat loss are known threats, but no specific reason has been attributed to their recent population decrease.

Muscovy Duck

Cairina moschata

`INVASIVE`

WHERE TO FIND THEM: Camino 305 Field Trips 1–18 and 21–25

While ducks are most commonly associated with ponds or lakes, muscovy ducks are often found hanging out and nesting in tall trees. From the moment they hatch, they have sharp claws, which help them with tree climbing. Their diet, like that of most ducks, consists of aquatic plants, seeds, insects, and other invertebrates. Males are on the large side, with glossy black-and-white feathers and reddish wart-like wattles around their beaks. Females are roughly half the size of the males and tend to have duller coloring.

While their name suggests an origin close to Moscow, Russia, they are in fact from Central and South America and were introduced to Florida in the 1960s. Found near suburban lakes and farms, muscovy ducks compete and interbreed with Florida's native ducks and can spread diseases in duck populations. Many homeowners and businesses consider them a nuisance because they aren't afraid of humans and can sometimes become aggressive.

Northern Mockingbird

Mimus polyglottos

`NATIVE`

WHERE TO FIND THEM: All Camino 305 Field Trips

"Hush little baby, don't say a word. Mama's gonna buy you a mockingbird." This well-known lullaby isn't just a random promise. Unfortunately, it represents a dark chapter for the northern mockingbird. For nearly 200 years, these birds were commonly collected for the pet trade, almost leading to their extinction in the wild. Fortunately, their population was able to rebound, once again becoming common in the southeastern United States.

 Fun Fact

Although the northern mockingbird is the state bird for five states (Arkansas, Florida, Mississippi, Tennessee, and Texas), Florida and Texas were the first states to make it official. Though Texas adopted it in January of 1927 and Florida in April, we're pretty sure they stole the idea from us and just beat us on the paperwork.

The only mockingbird native to North America, this slender, long-legged bird is mostly gray with black feathers on both its wings and tail. It typically eats insects, worms, and berries on the ground. During nesting season, which occurs in late spring and summer, its loud trademark call is audible almost everywhere. True to its name, it has the ability to imitate the sounds of birds, cats, dogs, crickets, and even car alarms.

Painted Bunting

Passerina ciris

NATIVE

WHERE TO FIND THEM: All Camino 305 Field Trips

Few birds in the United States are as stunningly colorful as the male painted bunting. Its blue, red, yellow, and green plumage suggests it comes from a rainforest, but its body resembles that of a typical North American songbird. Its preferred habitat is bushy vegetation, but as a ground forager, it has been known to venture into suburban backyards in search of food.

These birds migrate to Florida every spring from eastern US woodlands; however, their numbers have declined rapidly in recent years. While some scientists believe the decline is related to the birds being captured for the exotic pet trade, others believe it has fallen victim to the brown-headed cowbird (*Molothrus ater*), which also winters in Florida. Rather than building their own nests, cowbirds remove eggs from the nests of other birds and replace them with their own eggs, leaving the task of raising the chicks to an unknowing new mother.

 Fun Fact

The French word for the painted bunting is *nonpareil*, which, in reference to their brilliantly colored plumage, translates to "without equal."

Palm Warbler

Setophaga palmarum

NATIVE

WHERE TO FIND THEM: All Camino 305 Field Trips

In Florida, we all know a snowbird or two—a person who moves from the cold northern parts of North America to our warm sunny climate during winter. The palm warbler is an avian equivalent. It migrates so it can enjoy warm weather all year around. After summering

in the northern United States and Canada, it flies thousands of miles south toward Florida in winter. Once here, it primarily feeds on a range of insects, including grasshoppers, ants, and bees, but it will also eat berries and seeds as needed.

Despite the long, cross-country flights, this is not a species known for flying high—you're more likely to spot one near the ground. Palm groves are a good place to look for them. Short and somewhat plump, they have a yellow chest and a tuft of crimson on the crown of their head. While foraging for food in open areas with low-growing vegetation, their elongated tail is seemingly always wagging, which can be a helpful detail when trying to ID them.

Red-Bellied Woodpecker

Melanerpes carolinus

NATIVE

WHERE TO FIND THEM: All Camino 305 Field Trips

This bird's name is a little misleading. Though it does have a small patch of feathers tinted slightly red on the lower half of its belly, its crown is where the red is most pronounced, extending from the beak over the head to

 ## Conservation Connection

One hundred years ago, due to habitat loss and pesticide use, this bird was quite rare. But thanks to its omnivorous diet and ability to adapt to suburban areas, it has since expanded its range and population.

Two of the best ways to protect woodpeckers and other birds are to neuter stray cats and to make your own outdoor cat wear a colored collar with a bell that can alert birds of impending attack.

the nape and contrasting brightly with its light-gray body feathers and black-and-white mottled wings.

The red-bellied woodpecker is native to the eastern United States, including Florida, where it's quite common. It is most famous for pecking trees while foraging for insects, but it also eats fruits, the occasional smaller reptile or bird, and acorns, which it might hide in a tree for later, just like a squirrel. The sound of its pecking can be quite loud but doesn't always mean the woodpecker is on the hunt—males can also use loud tree-pecking as a mating display to attract females.

Red-Shouldered Hawk

Buteo lineatus extimus

NATIVE

WHERE TO FIND THEM: All Camino 305 Field Trips

It's always convenient when a name perfectly captures a key identifying feature. If you see a hawk in Miami that has red shoulders, and you happen to be in a woodland area near a body of water (easy to do in South Florida), then there's a good chance it's the red-shouldered hawk. They prefer tall trees, typically pine woods, but have also been observed in mangroves. There are five subspecies of the red-shouldered hawk, but the one in southern Florida, *extimus*, is the smallest and palest of the bunch, with a head that is grayish, almost white.

These hawks dine from an extensive menu—they'll eat any prey they can scoop up via swoop—from small mammals and reptiles, to birds and amphibians, even insects and fish on occasion. In South Florida, the red-shouldered hawk population is stable, and they can often be found in urban habitats. So, keep your eyes open and try to look bigger than a rabbit.

Ruby-Throated Hummingbird

Archilochus colubris

NATIVE

WHERE TO FIND THEM: All Camino 305 Field Trips, except 19 and 20

If you see a hummingbird in Florida (or anywhere on the east coast of the United States), it's probably this one. Another species, the black-chinned hummingbird (*Archilochus alexandri*) occasionally appears in Florida during winter, but the ruby-throated hummingbird is the most common. Despite its small stature, it migrates up and down the eastern seaboard, as far south as Costa Rica to as far north as Canada.

Ruby-throated hummingbirds are easy to identify, thanks to their green head and wings adorned with a bright-red throat. You're most likely to spot them at the edge of a forest or in a backyard garden. While hovering in front of a flower to sip nectar, a hummingbird can beat its wings more than fifty times per second while it extends its surprisingly long tongue deep into the center of the flower to drink nectar. An insectivore, this bird likes to eat bugs too. It will also prey on spiders, and will sometimes even steal the insects trapped in the spider's web.

Turkey Vulture

Cathartes aura

`NATIVE`

WHERE TO FIND THEM: All Camino 305 Field Trips

With a wingspan of up to six feet, combined with strong eyesight and an excellent sense of smell, turkey vultures are adapted to soar with minimal effort while searching for food from great heights. They hold their wings in a V pattern as they hover and often gather in groups around dying or decaying animals. These black-feathered scavengers also possess a handful of adaptations that make them good carrion (dead meat) eaters. The lack of feathers on their face, which shows off their red, wrinkly skin, might not be too appealing to look at, but it reduces their chances of picking up an infection as they dig through a rotting carcass. Their hooked beaks are perfect for picking their food apart. Although you may find their eating habits disgusting, they are federally and state protected, so let them eat their roadkill in peace.

Wild Turkey

Meleagris gallopavo

NATIVE

WHERE TO FIND THEM: Camino 305 Field Trip 14, 17, and 20

Perhaps one of the most famous large birds found in Florida, wild turkeys are ground-dwelling birds in the order Galliformes and are often hunted for sport with other

members of this order—pheasants and quails. They were almost hunted to extinction in the early 1900s, but thanks to reintroduction programs, today they are common throughout all of North America. Wild turkeys are found in forested areas and, in Florida, are vital from an ecological, recreational, and economical perspective. They are important prey for apex predators such as Florida panthers, and contribute 1.9 billion dollars to the hunting industry and 4.9 billion to the wildlife viewing industry in Florida.

Though you might be able to identify a turkey thanks to your hand paintings in elementary school, a refresher never hurts. Males have a round shape, with long legs, a small featherless head, and a slim neck with a pinkish red wattle (a flap of skin that regulates body temperature) that hangs from their throat. They are typically dark brown or bronze colored. Females are usually slimmer, duller in color, and don't have a wattle.

Conservation Connection

The Florida subspecies of wild turkey (*Meleagris gallopavo osceola*) used to be abundant in southern Florida. They inhabited upland areas such as pinelands, cypress swamps, prairies, and hardwood hammocks, but excessive logging dramatically reduced their habitat and overhunting reduced their numbers. Efforts to reestablish a population of wild turkeys in Everglades National Park began in the early 2000s. So far, two separate attempts have been made to establish a successful wild breeding population, but they've been challenged by predators and reproduction difficulties, and long-term success isn't a sure thing yet.

Insects and Arachnids

Florida Carpenter Ant

Camponotus floridanus

`NATIVE`

WHERE TO FIND THEM: All Camino 305 Field Trips

South Florida's winters tend to be relatively warm, with only a handful of days reaching temperatures low enough to be categorized as cold. But on chillier evenings, nothing beats setting a wood fire in the yard to make a few s'mores and spend time with family. If you keep a woodpile, you might be surprised at some point when you pick up a log and are met with hundreds of large red and black ants streaming from the wood. These are likely Florida carpenter ants; our most intimidatingly bulky native ant species. Be careful if you do disturb them, as they will bite while defending their nest.

Like termites, these carpenter ants make their burrows in wood. Unlike termites, they

don't eat it, preferring to make their homes in wood that is already partially decomposed and relatively soft (such as rotting logs), which means they don't pose much of a threat to people's homes.

Red Imported Fire Ant

Solenopsis invicta

`INVASIVE`

WHERE TO FIND THEM: All Camino 305 Field Trips

You can't call yourself a true Floridian if you've never accidentally stepped on a fire ant nest. Ok, maybe you still can, but many of us aren't so lucky. Red imported fire ants (RIFA) are small and colored dark red and black. The first record of the dastardly RIFA in the United States was in Alabama in the 1940s, likely introduced with goods imported from South America, where RIFA is native. Fast forward several decades, and they have successfully conquered most of the southeastern part of the country, including the entirety of Florida. Though the insect is small, its sting packs a painful punch. Multiply this by several dozen for the unfortunate person who steps on one of their anthills, and you're looking at a nasty rash lasting several days. Fire ants are very territorial, often warring with other colonies to take over an area of land, and with their superior firepower, they're able to displace other ant species, including native ones.

Fun Fact

Fire ants are essentially flood-proof. If their burrows begin to flood, the ants clasp onto each other. One by one, they form a waterproof raft out of their linked bodies and allow the water to take them where it may. When the flood recedes, they release their grasp and start digging a new burrow. Anything for the queen!

European Honeybee

Apis mellifera

NON-NATIVE

WHERE TO FIND THEM: All Camino 305 Field Trips

The European honeybee is the poster child for global bee conservation. These inch-long insects are very recognizable by their fuzzy, brownish-yellow bodies with bold black stripes on their abdomens and their habit of clustering together. They have had an important relationship with humanity for tens of thousands of years as a crop pollinator and honey provider. Though they are able to sting us, they rarely do. In their native environment they coevolved with plants for millions of years, establishing themselves as an important component of the ecosystem. Their importance in agriculture is hard to overstate, as they are responsible for 35 percent of the world's agricultural product. Although they are an important species, they are not the only bees we rely on; there are a plethora of native bee species in the United States and throughout the world that also need help.

In South Florida, as in most of the world, the honeybee was introduced. It is now a common visitor to blooms in and around the city. As it has been in the United States for so long, and plays such a commercially important role, it seems hard to justify removing this species even if it is non-native.

Green Orchid Bee

Euglossa dilemma

NON-NATIVE

WHERE TO FIND THEM: All Camino 305 Field Trips

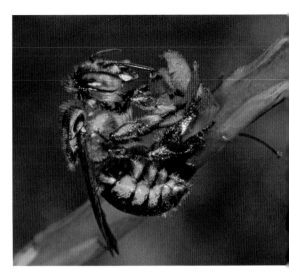

This beautiful bee, with its shiny metallic green body and hummingbird-like flight habit, is an introduced species in South Florida. About an inch long, it comes from Mexico and Central America. Nobody quite knows how it got here, but the first documented sighting in Miami was in 2003.

Research is currently underway to understand what impacts green orchid bees are having on Miami's local ecosystems. They seem to be established and spreading throughout the state. So far, they have proven to be effective pollinators of native Florida plants, and any negative impact from their presence has yet to be determined.

Poey's Furrow Bee

Halictus poeyi

NATIVE

WHERE TO FIND THEM: All Camino 305 Field Trips

Poey's bee is Miami's most common native bee. Their native range is east of the Mississippi River from New Jersey to Florida, but people have found them as far south as Cuba and Jamaica. The Poey bee was named after Felipe Poey y Aloy, the Cuban father of biodiversity who, in the nineteenth century, named and catalogued thousands of species native to the Western Hemisphere.

You need to look closely at a blooming flower to notice these little pollinators, as they are significantly smaller than honeybees. They belong to the sweat bee family, a name they earned because they are attracted to the salt in our perspiration. Though Poey's are a social species, they lack the complex labor division exhibited by honeybees.

Atala Butterfly

Eumaeus atala

NATIVE

WHERE TO FIND THEM: Camino 305 Field Trips 3, 9, 11, 12, 15, 17, 18, 21, and 23

The atala butterfly and the coontie plant are inseparable. This butterfly, which lives throughout the Caribbean but only in the extreme southeast corner of Florida, eats what no one else can (or dares). The waxy sap of the coontie leaf is poisonous to every animal except for atala caterpillars, which not only devour it but also gain power from its toxins by incorporating them into their tissues. Any bird or insect who sees the telltale yellow spots and bright red coloring of the atala caterpillar knows not to eat it. Adult butterflies retain the toxins and let predators know it—their strikingly beautiful jet-black wings are speckled with an iridescent blue and their abdomens are a deep red.

Though hungry predators and grazers don't pose much of a threat, the atala and the coontie almost went extinct together. Early South Florida colonists learned from the native Seminole how to turn the starchy roots of the coontie into flour for bread, eventually overharvesting the plants to fuel a large flour industry. As the coontie population was devastated, so too was the butterfly that depended on it for survival. However, with the return of the coontie and its popularity as a native landscaping plant, atalas are becoming much more bountiful. Their return is a gift to those who appreciate beauty in nature.

 ## Conservation Connection

There's just something about butterflies that people love. Like colorful fairies, they add a magical touch wherever they flutter. Bound by Beauty is a local organization that uses butterflies as a gateway organism to inspire people to love (and subsequently protect) the natural world around them. They help butterflies thrive through education and outreach, garden installations that focus on native nectar and host plants, and a seed kit program called Seeds2Share. Many an atala butterfly owes its existence to their Atala Foster Garden Program, which rescues and redistributes atala caterpillars. The group's passionate efforts teach that when time and care is put into creating a habitat, the results are bound to be beautiful.

Cloudless Sulphur Butterfly

Phoebis sennae

NATIVE

WHERE TO FIND THEM: Camino 305 Field
Trips 1–24

This species has a large range throughout
North America, particularly on the east coast.
Highly migratory, they move south in fall as
temperatures decrease—people have spotted
them as far south as Argentina! They get their
species name, *sennae*, from their preferred
host plants, which are in the genus *Senna*.
Miami's native sennas are medium to large
shrubs, but several tree species of senna have
been introduced to South Florida as well.
The color of a cloudless sulphur caterpillar
will depend on which part of the senna plant
it eats. If it munches mainly on the leaves, it
will adopt a greenish color, while a diet of the
yellow flowers will turn it yellow instead. The
caterpillar's coloring doesn't seem to affect
the color of the adult butterfly—it's wings are
always a cheerful yellow. Adult cloudless sulphurs have a wingspan of up to three inches.
Females have a thin, dark border around the
edge of their wings while the males do not.

Heliconian butterflies

Zebra Longwing Butterfly

Heliconius charithonia

NATIVE

Gulf Fritillary Butterfly

Agraulis vanillae

NATIVE

Orange Julia Butterfly

Dryas iulia

NATIVE

WHERE TO FIND THEM: All Camino 305
Field Trips

You may be unaware that, along with an official
state tree and flower, we also have an official
butterfly (only about half of US states have
one), but if you've spent any time exploring
Miami's green spaces, chances are you're
already familiar with Florida's erratically flying
lepidopteran representative. The zebra longwing butterfly, named for its distinctive black
and yellowish-white stripes that run parallel
to its unusually long wings, is a common sight
year-round.

The zebra longwing, Gulf fritillary, and
orange Julia form a trio. Despite belonging to
separate genera, they are all in the subfam-
ily Heliconiinae, making them heliconian
butterflies, and they all share the same
larval host plant—Florida's native corkystem
passionflower. This unassuming vine grows
vigorously in a wide variety of habitats, from
coastal strands to pine rocklands and upland

▲ Zebra longwing

hammocks. With its dull-hued, dime-sized flowers, it might not be your first pick for the garden, but to these butterflies, the fresh and tender tendrils of this plant and closely related species in the genus *Passiflora* are the only suitable places to lay eggs, making passionflower a must-have for any native Miami garden.

Once hatched, the caterpillars exhibit a prodigious appetite, eating passionflower leaves throughout the daylight hours and incorporating toxins from the plants into their bodies. If you look closely at a passionflower vine, you may be lucky enough to see all three kinds of caterpillar. Their shapes and the stingless, soft spikes on their bodies are similar, but they are different colors. The zebra longwing caterpillar is white with black spots, the Gulf fritillary is a solid orange, and the orange Julia is black with white spots.

Firebush and butterfly sage (*Varronia globosa*) are magnets for the adult butterflies and have the added garden benefit of attracting birds who like to eat the fruits. Don't worry about the birds eating the butterflies—the adult insects retain passionflower toxins in their bodies as adults, making them unpalatable to predators. Most adult butterflies feed exclusively on nectar, a sugary fluid that flowers produce in their attempt to attract pollinators. But zebra longwings have the unique ability to consume and digest protein-rich pollen, the same highly nutritious substance honeybees feed to their queen and her larvae. Their more robust nutrition gives them a

▲ Gulf fritillary

▲ Orange Julia

considerably longer lifespan compared to other butterflies. Whereas most species may live for about a month, the zebra longwing can survive for up to six. That's the equivalent of a human living to the age of 450!

Miami Blue Butterfly

Cyclargus thomasi bethunebakeri

`NATIVE` `ENDANGERED`

WHERE TO FIND THEM: Not found at any Camino 305 Field Trips

Miami who? Miami blue! This light-blue butterfly is a native Floridian and the only member of the Cyclargus genus. Once found as far north as Daytona Beach and as far west as Tampa, the Miami blue saw its fortunes fade with the loss of its hardwood hammock and pine rockland habitat as Florida's aggressive urban development progressed. In the 1990s, scientists thought the species had become extinct, but in 1999 some were spotted in the Florida Key's Bahia Honda State Park. The sighting triggered a coordinated campaign between the state and the University of Florida to begin raising and releasing Miami blues in protected areas. While some efforts have failed, others have shown potential.

Continued conservation efforts are an absolute must if we ever want to see these baby blues fluttering throughout the city again.

Conservation Connection

The Miami Blue chapter of the North American Butterfly Association (NABA) champions butterfly conservation wherever it's happening (and for all species of butterflies throughout the state), collaborating with various organizations who share their common goals. This includes educational programming, summits that try to spark conversation between experts in the field, habitat restoration work, and more. They host quarterly public meetings that provide an opportunity for anybody to learn about the latest work and research. Their website also has a plethora of resources to help you learn how to attract native butterflies to your home.

Monarch Butterfly

Danaus plexippus

`NATIVE`

WHERE TO FIND THEM: All Camino 305 Field Trips

As one of the most recognized and beloved butterflies not just in Miami but throughout its enormous range in North and Central America, the monarch is a mainstay for butterfly gardens. You can recognize them by their deep orange wings marked by a lattice of bold, dark black stripes. A related species, the viceroy butterfly (*Limenitis archippus*), has

Fun Fact:

People's love for monarchs have spurred many to plant milkweed to support their caterpillars. Unfortunately, the most readily available species of milkweed, the tropical milkweed, is non-native, and it has begun to exhibit invasive potential. If you want to support the monarchs, make sure to only plant native milkweeds such as butterfly weed (*Asclepias tuberosa*) and swamp milkweed (*Asclepias incarnata*).

similar coloring but with an additional black, horizontal stripe along its back wings. To get close enough to truly differentiate between the two, you might need to practice your tiptoeing skills.

Monarch caterpillars feed exclusively on milkweeds, which are extremely poisonous to most animals, containing a class of chemical compounds called cardiac glycosides. Similar to the atala, monarch caterpillars incorporate the toxins into their tissues and retain them through adulthood. It's a rare thing to catch a bird or other predator trying to make a meal out of these foul-tasting caterpillars and butterflies.

Giant Swallowtail

Papilio cresphontes

NATIVE

WHERE TO FIND THEM: All Camino 305 Field Trips

The giant swallowtail is found throughout North America from southern Canada to Mexico. It can even be found in Cuba and Jamaica. North America's largest butterfly, they are the jumbo jets of Miami's butterfly species— seeing one never fails to inspire awe. Though they are magnificent, it takes an adventurous gardener to plant their preferred native host plant, the prickly wild lime. The thorns on this tree make it less than ideal for a yard's central feature, but you might tuck one away behind a line of other, safer plants. If you're working with limited space, a citrus tree is a great alternative, as giant swallowtail caterpillars enjoy them too.

To observe the caterpillars, you'll need to look closely and carefully because they have evolved unusual methods of camouflage and defense: during their first development stage (called an instar), they look just like bird poop, and if that doesn't convince predators to pass them by, then the foul, rotting-citrus smell they release when disturbed will surely do the trick.

189

Schaus' Swallowtail

Papilio aristodemus ponceanus

NATIVE ENDANGERED

WHERE TO FIND THEM: Camino 305 Field Trips 24 and 25

Sometimes, bullets are dodged in conservation. Continually threatened by habitat loss and broadscale mosquito spraying, the Schaus' swallowtail butterfly was added to the federal endangered species list in 1984. The listing didn't seem to solve much, as the Schaus' population continued to decline to a point where an annual monitoring event in 2012 spotted only four individuals. Though there are other Schaus' populations in the Caribbean, the Florida subspecies is unique, and it was facing extinction. Luckily, enough individuals were found to start a captive breeding program, in which many of these beautiful black-and-yellow butterflies were reared in captivity then released to suitable habitats. Though it was a remarkable success, and there are now hundreds of Schaus' swallowtails inhabiting Biscayne National Park and the Florida Keys, the species is still listed as endangered. If a species is to be saved from extinction, proactivity is much more successful than passivity.

Carolina Mantis

Stagmomantis carolina

NATIVE

WHERE TO FIND THEM: All Camino 305 Field Trips

If you know where to look, a cunning eye can spot these large insects camouflaged in the greens and browns of tall grasses, shrubs, and trees. Mantises are known for their large and spiny front legs, which they keep close to their body while at rest, in a position that looks like a person praying. This hunter is a sit-and-wait predator, using its bulbous eyes on its triangular face to gaze about for potential prey. Camouflaged well, it sits very still and waits for a meal to come within striking distance before lashing out with its long "praying" legs to capture dinner.

In tall grassy areas, you may find what looks like a ridged cocoon attached to a grass blade. This may be a mantis' egg case. Before she can deposit these eggs, a female mantis will mate with a male. If she is very hungry (making egg cases takes a lot of energy!), she might decapitate the male and eat him. The Carolina mantis is the most common species of praying mantis in Miami. It can be green, brown, or gray, with a small black spot on the upper part of its abdomen.

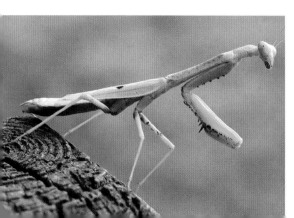

American Cockroach

Periplaneta americana

NON-NATIVE

WHERE TO FIND THEM: All Camino 305 Field Trips

Few insects evoke as much revulsion as cockroaches. In Miami specifically, it sometimes seems as though the city is only afraid of two things: slightly colder temperatures and cockroaches. In proportion to its body, the American cockroach is the fastest of all roaches, scuttling its way up walls, kitchen appliances, and even food. They have brown, shiny, two-inch long bodies, long back legs with small tactile spines (sensory organs that provide sense of touch) running along them, and a pair of large wings. Additionally, as if we weren't already spooked enough, those wings were made for flying—which, the moment those six legs leave the ground, often sends people straight into panic mode.

The name "American cockroach" is a misnomer. They aren't from the Americas at all, but are instead native to Africa and the Middle East.

Florida Woods Cockroach

Eurycotis floridana

NATIVE

WHERE TO FIND THEM: All Camino 305 Field Trips

Also known as a palmetto bug, this native cockroach is somehow much less intimidating than its "American" counterpart, probably because it would rather stay out in its natural habitats and rarely comes inside homes or buildings. Native to South Florida's damp hammock forests but found as far north as the Carolinas, you can often spot it under leaf litter or rotting logs.

Though it is slower than the American cockroach and cannot fly, don't count this species out just yet. What it may lack in speed and flight capability, it more than compensates for in chemical defenses. When disturbed by a hungry predator or, say, someone casually opening their outside shed door, the Florida

woods cockroach can spray a foul-smelling deterrent. This skill has earned it the nickname skunk roach.

Common Oblique Syrphid Fly

Allograpta obliqua

NATIVE

WHERE TO FIND THEM: All Camino 305
Field Trips

Thanks to its yellow and black stripes, at first glance, you might identify this buzzy native as a bee, but upon closer inspection, you'd realize it is actually a fly. Don't feel silly for this confusion. In fact, the fly is counting on it. It evolved the color pattern as a way to trick and deter any would-be predators.

A type of hover fly (can you guess how they got this name?), the common oblique syrphid fly is best known in gardening circles for its appetite for aphids, a common insect pest that can destroy plants by sucking out their water and nutrients. The most ecologically sound way of controlling aphids is to attract predatory insects such as these to an area where you want plants protected. Spraying pesticides can work temporarily but, among other harmful environmental impacts with long-lasting consequences, they also kill helpful insects like the syrphid fly, leaving plants vulnerable to the next aphid attack.

Eastern Lubber Grasshopper

Romalea guttata

NATIVE

WHERE TO FIND THEM: All Camino 305 Field Trips

Eastern lubbers are large grasshoppers native to the eastern US coast. Varying between yellow and red in color, they can reach lengths over three inches, with the females being larger than the males. They are also at the center of a fair bit of controversy among nature enthusiasts in Miami. Some love them for their docility, bright coloring, and impressive size, while others find them bothersome due to their destructive appetites. Because they are a generalist species in terms of diet, they don't really discriminate between wild native plants, backyard vegetables, and ornamental gardens, so they can be quite destructive. And because they are fairly poisonous to eat, they don't have many predators.

If you encounter one, you'll notice their passiveness quite quickly. You could easily pick one up, hold it in your hand or even place it on your shoulder—but it's probably best to just watch it hop along toward its next plant-based meal.

Florida Blue Centipede

Scolopendra viridis

NATIVE

WHERE TO FIND THEM: Camino 305 Field Trip 16

The Florida blue centipede reaches a maximum length of three inches and is able to zoom across the ground on many pairs of legs. It has a bluish-gray topside and reddish sides, with two fang-like pincers on the side of its head that can deliver an uncomfortable sting. Though they look scary, they rarely bite humans (if you were to get bitten, it would hurt about as much as a mild bee sting). Centipedes are predatory arthropods that eat insects, spiders, and worms. You may come across a Florida blue centipede while moving things around in your yard. If that happens, remember that it means you no harm and your best course of action is to just step back until it scurries away. Understandably, they don't like their hiding spots disturbed and will quickly move elsewhere.

Headlight Elater

Pyrophorus noctilucus

NATIVE

WHERE TO FIND THEM: All Camino 305 Field Trips

The headlight beetle is a kind of click beetle. When flipped onto their backs, they quickly thrust their bodies to flip themselves upright; the movement makes a loud clicking sound, which gives them their name, and often launches them into the air. What sets the headlight elater apart from other click beetles is their bioluminescence. By creating chemical reactions in specialized glands, they can emit a glow from two spots located on the sides of their thorax. This makes them similar to fireflies (family Lampyridae), except where fireflies emit pulses of light, headlight elaters are constantly flashing at different intensities.

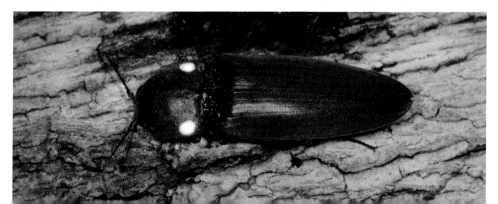

Housefly

Musca domestica

NATIVE

WHERE TO FIND THEM: All Camino 305 Field Trips

Few things are more annoying than laying down in bed, enjoying the silence of the night, and drifting off to sleep only to be awakened by the buzz of something flying close to your ear. Having a housefly buzzing around in your room is as disturbing as it gets (second maybe to a mosquito). One of the most widely distributed species in the world, the housefly has successfully taken full advantage of human settlements, where it finds many sources of food. When food is abundant, housefly populations can explode, a serious issue considering they are effective transmitters of disease. It's important to control them; increased sanitation is the best route because it is preventative.

> **Fun fact**
> Over 110,000 species of flies are known to science. Many of them are actually important pollinators in their ecosystems.

Io Moth

Automeris io

NATIVE

WHERE TO FIND THEM: All Camino 305 Field Trips

Named after the mythological Greek priestess Io (pronounced "eye-oh"), for which one of Saturn's moons is also named, the Io moth is one of the most easily recognizable of Miami's native moths. Its first distinguishing characteristic is its size. With a wingspan of up to three inches, it's larger than most moth species found here. When perched, it often has its forewings tucked over its hindwings, but if disturbed, it raises the forewings to reveal two yellow-and-black spots that look like a pair of owl eyes. This mimicry is a defense mechanism intended to spook any would-be predators into thinking twice before attacking. Io moth caterpillars have a variety of host plants, but if you want to attract this species to your home, your best bet is planting cocoplum. An easy-to-grow shrub that likes full or partial sun, it'll do well pretty much anywhere in your yard. Remember to be careful around the green Io caterpillars—they're covered with small spines that will give you a mildly painful sting that lasts for a good ten minutes. A small price to pay for having such a beautiful moth around.

June Beetle

Phyllophaga species

NATIVE

WHERE TO FIND THEM: All Camino 305 Field Trips

In May and June, large brown or black beetles begin to emerge from the soil. In the months prior, the larvae of these beetles were steadily growing underground, forming a pupa before emerging in the rainy season. Most June beetles are brown, but the green June beetle (*Cotinis nitida*) is distinguished by its green and gold coloring. Some consider the larvae of these species, commonly referred to as white grubs, to be undesirable in their soil. Many store-bought insecticides are formulated to target them, but the best defense is to grow a diversity of native plants at home. This creates a habitat that attracts various insect predators that will eat the grubs for you. Ecologically based solutions are almost always the best.

Ladybird Beetles

Trident Ladybeetle

Hyperaspis trifurcata

NATIVE

Asian Ladybeetle

Harmonia axyridis

NON-NATIVE

WHERE TO FIND THEM: All Camino 305 Field Trips

▲ Trident ladybeetle

▲ Asian ladybeetle

Ladybird, Ladybird, fly away home. Wait, we didn't mean that—please stay! Ladybird beetles, also known as ladybugs or ladybeetles, are an incredibly beneficial bug to have around. Many people who tend gardens swear by the recruitment of ladybeetles to keep other pest insects at bay. They mainly target aphids, sap-sucking insects that gather in multitudes and can weaken or kill plants. For ladybeetles and their larvae, aphids are easy targets. Florida has roughly 100 species of ladybirds in the Coccinellidae family, with some native and some not. Look closely at each ladybug you spot, each one is likely to look quite different from the one before.

195

As the name implies, the Asian ladybeetle is not from Florida. It came from East Asia and was introduced to the Americas in an effort to control pest insects. Biocontrol measures like this can have unintended consequences when the introduced species targets beneficial insects or native plants. It's important for scientists to consider all the nuances. If you're aiming to keep pesky aphids at bay in your garden, it's probably best to use native species such as the trident ladybeetle.

While the native species is typically black with lighter spots and patterns, the Asian ladybeetle comes in a wide variety of color patterns, all variations of red, black, and yellow. For the Asian ladybeetle, identification is relatively straightforward if you look for the black W imprinted on their white heads.

Lovebug

Plecia nearctica

`NATIVE`

WHERE TO FIND THEM: All Camino 305 Field Trips

A kind of march fly, lovebug males and females are often found paired up, abdomen to abdomen. This prolonged courtship has also earned the bug the name two-headed fly. If you ever drive on South Florida highways in spring and summer, you're familiar with love bugs. This is when they reach their peak flight, with many thousands of them buzzing around all over the place. The more you drive through these swarms, the more insect splatters you'll notice on your windshield and front bumper. A live specimen looks much less goopy, with oval-shaped black wings and a reddish thorax.

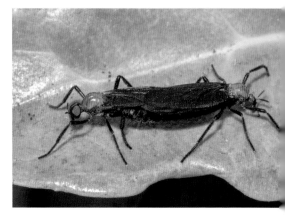

Milkweed Assassin Bug

Zelus longipes

`NATIVE`

WHERE TO FIND THEM: All Camino 305 Field Trips

Identifiable by its reddish-orange and black coloring and long proboscis (called a beak), the milkweed assassin bug is not out to kill the fan-favorite milkweed plant. As a generalist hunter, it preys on a variety of other bugs often found on milkweed. These include pest insects like flies, stink bugs, and caterpillars, which sometimes can cause damage to the plants they eat if their populations are unchecked. They also consume aphids, often found in large numbers sucking fluid out of milkweed plants. The milkweed assassin bug uses venom to incapacitate its prey, and it can potentially bite people; if you ever need to pick one up, do so gently and not for too long. The milkweed assassin bug indirectly assists monarch butterflies, which require ample amounts of milkweed to complete their larval stage.

Parasitic Wasps and the Caribbean Fruit Fly

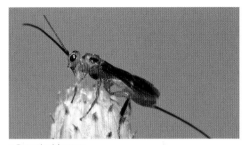

▲ Parasitoid wasp

Parasitoid Wasp

Doryctobracon areolatus

NON-NATIVE

Caribbean Fruit Fly

Anastrepha suspensa

NON-NATIVE

WHERE TO FIND THEM: All Camino 305 Field Trips, except 19 and 20

▲ Caribbean fruit fly

Parasitic wasps are generally beneficial to humans; they keep populations of nuisance insects, including agricultural pests, in check. However, the situation gets a little more gray when the parasitic wasp in question is an introduced species like *Doryctobracon areolatu*, a relatively miniscule brown wasp that was brought in from the Dominican Republic to control fruit flies.

Some fruit flies have the potential to destroy entire harvests. One of the species that spurred the introduction of the parasitoid wasp is the Caribbean fruit fly, also called the caribfly. This non-native fly is identifiable by its small size, brown body, and wings patterned with bold, black stripes. It invades over eighty species of fruit trees, including citrus and mango, causing enough damage to these commercial crops to justify human intervention. In this case, the wasp parasitoid seems to have been a success. After initial releases in the 1970s, the fly's population quickly declined by 40 percent.

Some people make the argument that introducing biological control organisms in response to invasive pests is okay if scientists are certain it won't impact native species. Today, it takes many years of strenuous research before approval is given for the release of biological controls.

197

Rainbow Scarab

Phanaeus vindex

NATIVE

WHERE TO FIND THEM: All Camino 305 Field Trips, except 19, 20, and 25

Picture the scene: you're enjoying a peaceful morning in your yard when suddenly you hear a fast tap on a wall, then your fence, and then again on your shed. Unsure of the origins, you also hear a distinct buzzing, which you eventually follow to the culprit. Seeing this large colorful beetle may initially cause you to jump back, but its awkward clumsiness during flight and disinterest in your presence quickly calm your nerves. It's a humble rainbow scarab, and it's searching your yard for a very particular something—poop. Rainbow scarabs are a kind of dung beetle; they feed animal dung to their larvae. After locating some droppings, often from a cat or dog, the rainbow scarab in your yard will proceed to dig a deep hole in the ground beneath, roll some of the droppings into balls, and store the balls in the ground with its eggs.

Though many humans find its habits disturbing, few can argue with the beetle's gorgeous appearance. It gleams in the sunlight with iridescent green, red, and gold. The males take the show even further, with a singular long horn on their heads, which lends them a rhinoceros-like appearance and is used to impress females.

Scorpions

Order Scorpiones

NATIVE

WHERE TO FIND THEM: All Camino 305 Field Trips

This is one of the more uncommon critters in South Florida. Many Miamians will go their whole lives without seeing a wild scorpion,

 **Fun fact**

The main physical difference between arachnids and insects is that insects have six legs and up to four wings while arachnids have eight legs and no wings. Did you know horseshoe crabs are also arachnids?

especially considering how far we are from the desert. Even for outdoor explorers, scorpions of any kind will take some luck to find, but if you do manage to spot one, it's most likely one of three species: the Florida bark scorpion (*Centruroides gracilis*), striped bark or Hentz striped scorpion (*Centruroides hentzi*), or Guiana striped scorpion (*Centruroides guanensis*). One of the most recognizable arthropods in the world thanks to the recurved stinger at the end of their long tails, scorpions are not insects but arachnids, more closely related to spiders and ticks than they are to ants, butterflies, and beetles.

Southern Flannel Moth

Megalopyge opercularis

NATIVE

WHERE TO FIND THEM: All Camino 305 Field Trips

Common in Florida and found as far west as Texas and north as New Jersey, the southern flannel moth is small and yellowish, with a thick fur-like coat of bristles that earns the species a number of common names, including *perrito*, which is Spanish for puppy—in Florida their caterpillars called are puss caterpillars (as in pussycat).

Classified as the most venomous caterpillar in the United States, the puss caterpillar is teardrop-shaped and looks just as fuzzy as the full-grown version. A mature larva is similar in length to its adult form, roughly one and a half inches including the tail, and, like Cousin Itt from the Addams Family, all its features are completely hidden under a thick layer of hair (not actually hair but a structure known as setae). Among those hidden features are rows of hollow spines with venom glands at the base (this serious defense system isn't carried on to adulthood as moths). As if that wasn't enough, they can propel feces away from themselves as a distraction that lures would-be predators in another direction. This is one species of fuzzball that is far from cuddly.

Author Story: Thomas Morrell

In November of 2020, the fluffy yet ferocious southern flannel moth caterpillar provided me with a firsthand experience I'm not likely to ever forget. What started as a kind gesture, assisting a friend with some yard maintenance, soon unraveled into a blend of confusion and pain. While relocating some recently trimmed branches with ungloved hands, I felt a noticeable (but tolerable) pinch in my right palm. Regretting my bare-handed mistake, I assessed the damage but saw no evidence of a wound or a bite. Surely any dangerous interaction would have at least left a mark? Unfortunately, I couldn't have been more wrong. As the pain slowly intensified over the next couple hours, spreading through my hand, into my wrist, and up to my shoulder, panic ensued.

I thought I'd been attacked by some classic nightmare figure. An enormous spider? A venomous snake? Maybe an incredibly dangerous scorpion? After a virtual consultation with a medical professional and a confirmation from a friend who had recently endured a similar ordeal, the identity of my tormentor was confirmed—the fluffy little flannel moth caterpillar. All in all, the pain lasted twelve hours. Twelve hours of the most acute, cut-my-hand-off type pain. Then, as if someone had flipped a switch, the pain decreased to nothing, leaving only a temporary, caterpillar-shaped mark on my hand and some lingering ailments throughout my body. Puss caterpillars increase in size several times before they transform into moths, and while all sizes have the capacity to sting, the toxicity of the venom increases with the size of the caterpillar in question. I consoled myself by assuming that the caterpillar I encountered must have been somewhere around forty-four feet tall.

Gray Wall Jumper

Menemerus bivittatus

WHERE TO FIND THEM: All Camino 305 Field Trips

Jumping spiders are at the center of a deeply polarized controversy—are they insanely cute or downright terrifying? It depends on which of their features you consider. Their eyes are large and round and downright puppyish, but they also scurry around in a way that some people find alarming. Their movements can be so swift it sometimes seems like they're not moving at all, but rather just appearing in a new location.

What to do if you get stung

Hindsight is twenty-twenty. If you are ever stung, or think you *might* have been stung, the most effective remedy is to remove the spines from your skin as quickly as possible. Repeatedly sticking and removing tape (preferably duct tape) on the affected area should pull out the stinging cells and reduce your pain dramatically. If you can't find any tape, ice or a baking soda paste (water and baking soda mixed together) will work wonders to neutralize the pain. Some people suggest hydrocortisone cream or oral antihistamines, but in my case, they gave me no relief. If none of these treatments are available, restrict your movements so your blood moves more slowly and doesn't carry the toxin through your body. The sting is said to affect everyone differently, especially depending on where on your body you've been stung, but the usual symptoms seem to be intense burning pain, erythematous (blood-colored) spots at the sting site, general swelling, and swollen lymph nodes. You may also experience muscle spasms, fever, vomiting, stomach pain, convulsions, nausea, headache, and seizures.

What's the Takeaway?

I intruded into the caterpillar habitat. Although I would have definitely preferred to not be stung, I completely understand the actions of the caterpillar and am ultimately the one at fault. I altered their habitat by trimming the trees (they have a preference for oaks and elms, but my interaction occurred around a non-native ficus tree) and failing to wear proper safety equipment. Although the sting was unfortunate for me, it's hard to blame the caterpillar. Wouldn't you fight back if someone suddenly started cutting down your home? I'm truly sorry to the puss caterpillar and have learned from my mistake. As for future interactions, I politely request we never meet again.

Able to jump many times their body length, they also earn adoration as super athletes. In the end, it's all down to personal preference. Some people keep jumping spiders as pets, while others wonder what the heck is wrong with those people. South Florida homeowners are most likely to encounter the gray wall jumper, which has a pale brown body with two bold, black stripes along the sides. At a little less than a centimeter long, it is a particularly small species, and, as the name suggests, they're usually seen crawling on walls. Accidentally introduced from Africa, the gray wall jumper is now found throughout the tropics.

 Fun Fact

Even if you are scared of these speedy wall-crawlers, take comfort in knowing that jumping spiders rarely bite humans. Even if one did bite you, the worst you can expect is some itchiness for a day or two.

Golden Orb Weaver

Trichonephila clavipes

NATIVE

WHERE TO FIND THEM: All Camino 305 Field Trips

Throughout Miami you will hear the general public refer to these conspicuous arachnids as banana spiders. This is due to their large, bulbous abdomens, which are red and yellow in color. Because they often build their webs across forest trails, there's a chance you might have walked right through one of their sticky traps. This is precisely the intention of the golden orb weaver, except they're trying to catch smaller flying insects, not giant humans. By weaving a large circular web across tree branches, they are able to trap all manner of prey. Then they inject their dinner with venom, wrap it in silk, and take it back to the center of the web where they can eat at their convenience. If you spot the web before you walk through it face first, take the opportunity to examine it up close; you will see all manner of victims strung up on strands of shiny, golden silk. Between the sexes, females are much larger than males, reaching lengths of almost four inches.

Orchard Orb Weaver

Leucauge argyrobapta

NATIVE

WHERE TO FIND THEM: All Camino 305 Field Trips

Another common spider in Miami, the orchard orb weaver has distinctive green-and-black legs and a pretty yellow, red, green, and silver abdomen. It enjoys the shady areas along the edges of hammock forests but also lives in fruit groves. Orchard orb weavers are a common sight in the extensive orange groves of central Florida.

These orb weavers employ an economical (or perhaps downright stingy) method of web building, often seeking out the webs of golden orb weavers and using part of the other spider's web to support its own. This is clever because the less silk it has to use, the less energy it has to expend in weaving a web.

Just don't expect the other spiders to invite orchard orb weavers to the annual spider shindig. They know who'll show up with a half-eaten batch of bugchips.

Spiny Orb Weaver

Gasteracantha cancriformis

`NATIVE`

WHERE TO FIND THEM: All Camino 305 Field Trips

This species of spider is ubiquitous throughout Florida, and you're likely to encounter them in Miami. Also called crab spiders because their abdomens resemble a crab's carapace, spiny

orb-weavers are named for the ring of spikes around their abdomen and for their circular webs that hang in the air attached at several points to items like branches, poles, and fences. Sometimes, you can find several grouped together in the same general space. The webs are dotted with small clusters of white silk, which the spiders create to help birds avoid accidentally crashing into their otherwise invisible traps. Though this may seem like surprisingly considerate behavior, it's more selfish than neighborly. It takes several hours and a decent amount of precious energy to create a new web, and if a bird tears the web down, the spider may not be able to not catch enough food.

Wolf Spider

Family Lycosidae

`NATIVE`

WHERE TO FIND THEM: All Camino 305 Field Trips

On large stretches of grassy lawn, particularly those adjacent to natural areas, someone shining a light toward the ground at night may be met with hundreds of shining blue and

red specks. Is it dew on the grass refracting the light? If you have arachnophobia don't inspect any closer. What you're seeing are the eyes of hundreds of wolf spiders, each about an inch long. But fret not; despite their ferocious-sounding name, wolf spiders are exceedingly docile. If you pick one up off the ground, it will quickly hop off your hand and make its way back to the grass (and its little hop is actually quite adorable!). Their name comes from the way they catch prey. Rather than weave a web and wait patiently for prey to become entangled, wolf spiders take a more active approach, hunting through low vegetation for small insects, then pouncing on their dinner.

Thorn Bug

Umbonia crassicornis

NATIVE

WHERE TO FIND THEM: All Camino 305 Field Trips

By closely observing certain trees, you may notice what looks like an armament of thorns on the tree's branches. The thorns are a multicolored green, red, and blue, which may spur your curiosity further. Are those part of the tree? Taking a closer look, you realize these thorns have eyes! They are thorn bugs, a relative of the cicada. They love plants in the pea family, Fabaceae, which includes several native Floridian trees such as the common false tamarind.

Thorn bugs look cool, but they can be quite the pest on trees. They suck sap from and lay eggs in their twigs and branches, compromising the tree's ability to grow. Infestations can become so advanced, with hundreds of feasting thorn bugs, that the tree succumbs to their voracious appetites.

Tobacco Hornworm

Manduca sexta

NATIVE

WHERE TO FIND THEM: All Camino 305 Field Trips

Vine-ripened tomatoes are arguably unmatched for their red color and sweet taste. Many Miami residents plant tomatoes, excitedly waiting for the fruits to appear, only to wake up one morning and see that half the tomato plant is destroyed—where once there were leaves, there is only a bare stem. Upon

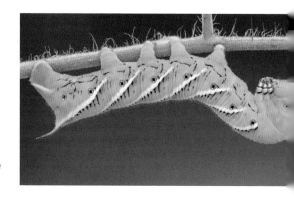

closer inspection, the camouflaged culprit is revealed: the tobacco hornworm. Just one of these green thumb-sized caterpillars can defoliate an entire plant in just a few days. They are voracious eaters of plants in the Solanaceae family, which includes tobacco, tomatoes, and peppers. Despite the damage they can do, the caterpillars are an important part of our ecosystems, providing a nutrient-rich food source for birds and bats. One of its predators, the parasitic hornworm wasp (*Cotesia congregata*), lays its eggs on the top of the caterpillar's torso. Once they hatch, these larvae will then devour the hornworms alive. If a tobacco hornworm is able to successfully dodge parasites and agitated gardeners, they will pupate and have a chance to morph into large Carolina sphinx moths.

Twostriped Walking Stick

Anisomorpha buprestoides

NATIVE

WHERE TO FIND THEM: All Camino 305 Field Trips

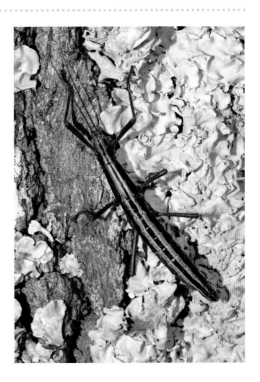

Look underneath that palm frond and you might find one of our more unusually shaped native insects. The twostriped walking stick is named for its slender, elongated shape and the two pale stripes running along the length of its dark black-and-brown body. They are sometimes found in small colonies, and the males are much smaller than the females. You might see a male piggybacking on a female during mating. Fortunately for him, the female twostriped walking stick doesn't have the same habit of eating her mate as the similar-looking praying mantis.

If you find a twostriped walking stick, don't try to pick it up. At the sign of a threat, they spray a musky chemical called anisomorphal that, in addition to smelling horrible, can cause severe irritation if it comes into contact with your eyes.

Woolly Oak Aphid

Stegophylla brevirostris

NATIVE

WHERE TO FIND THEM: All Camino 305 Field Trips

Live oaks are an exceedingly common tree throughout Florida's urban landscapes. You might sometimes notice fluffy tufts of white beneath their leaves and wonder if it is some

kind of unusual spider web. These tufts are most likely from woolly oak aphids, which excrete hairlike strands of wax as a means of protection. You're unlikely to see the aphids themselves since they are only about 0.04 inches long, possess no distinguishing features, and are completely covered in fluffy wool. Though they can become an issue in large numbers and some people may find them unsightly, they don't usually harm their host tree.

Yellow-Banded Millipede

Anadenobolus monilicornis

NON-NATIVE

WHERE TO FIND THEM: All Camino 305 Field Trips

Found under logs, in leaf litter, or just beneath the soil surface, this is one of Miami's most common millipedes, the other being the similarly shaped and sized rusty red millipede (*Trigoniulus corallinus*). These arthropods, distinguishable by the yellow and black stripes running down their bodies, are not native to Florida but rather the Caribbean. First sighted in Monroe County in 2001, their range is constantly expanding northward. Though they're not a threat to people, the increasing numbers of these detritivores (consumers of dead plant material in soil) can result in thick layers of millipede droppings in certain areas, which could be altering the dynamics of soil nutrients and soil ecology. The silver lining for gardeners is that they can be recruited in compost piles, where they break down food scraps and yard trimmings into a useful food source for plants.

 Fun fact

The word *millipede* means thousand foot. In reality, the average species only has about 300. Even the record setter, the siphonorhinid millipede (*Illacme plenipes*), only has 750.

Plants

American Beautyberry

Callicarpa americana

NATIVE

WHERE TO FIND THEM: Camino 305 Field Trips 3, 9, 11, 12, 13, 15, 17, 18, 20, 21, 22, and 23

American beautyberry gets its name from its gorgeous purple or white berries, which appear in dense, globular clusters along the shrub's branches during spring and summer. A favorite among native plant enthusiasts seeking color for their gardens, it's also preferred by birds seeking a tasty meal. Homeowners who plant American beautyberry can expect to find mockingbirds and small songbirds happily picking off the fruits. Though edible for humans too, they aren't very sweet and are better used as an ingredient in other foods; American beautyberry jam is perhaps the most popular recipe.

Author Story: Brian Diaz

American beautyberry has a special place in my plant-loving heart and played a part in developing my passion for botany. Though I was born and raised in Miami, my college career was in Baltimore, Maryland. In my final year and a half of college, I began exploring the city's forested parks and volunteering in urban reforestation events. I became enamored with plants, and those small pockets of forest acted as both my playground and sanctuary. Maryland is the northern bookend of American beautyberry's native range, and I often came across it while exploring. Upon graduation and returning to Miami, I began to learn about the diverse local flora that had existed around me throughout my childhood, but with which I'd been unfamiliar. During my studies, I was pleasantly surprised to learn that not only was beautyberry native to Miami but that South Florida was the *southern* bookend of its native range. Despite the vast differences in climate, topography, and soil composition between Miami and Baltimore, American beautyberry is nonetheless present. Part of my heart still dwells in those Maryland forests, and the vibrant beautyberry I have growing in my Hialeah home keeps me connected to the place where I began setting my botany roots.

Burma Reed

Neyraudia reynaudiana

INVASIVE

WHERE TO FIND THEM: All Camino 305 Field Trips

Originally brought to Florida as an ornamental, Burma reed has since escaped into Miami's natural areas. The pine rocklands have been particularly affected, for two main reasons: first, Burma reed grows densely and extensively, easily crowding out the pineland's characteristic low shrub and herbaceous understory. The second reason has to do with Burma reed's ability to drastically alter the fire regime of this fire-dependent ecosystem. Pine rocklands are naturally supposed to burn every three to seven years. Because not much fuel (for example, dead leaves and branches) can accumulate in that time, those fires typically aren't very intense or tall. But Burma reed can grow to heights exceeding ten feet. When they are set on fire, the flames become much taller and hotter than a pine rockland would naturally experience, to the degree that they can kill the usually fire-tolerant native flora (including veteran slash pines). Among other things, the long-term health of our pine rocklands will significantly depend on the eradication of this species from South Florida.

Cherokee Bean

Erythrina herbacea

NATIVE

WHERE TO FIND THEM: All Camino 305 Field Trips, Except 4 and 10

Cherokee bean is found in a variety of ecosystems including coastal uplands, hammocks, and pinelands. Growing as a tall shrub or small tree, it develops upright flower spikes in spring that contain many tubular, red flowers, which catch the eye of energetic hummingbirds whose long, pointed beaks fit into the flower like a key in a lock. After a hummingbird pollinates the plant, a seed pod forms containing several coral-red beans. These earn the plant its second common name, coral bean. Although their color is very attractive, they are extremely poisonous if ingested. Feast your eyes, but not your mouth.

Chinese Crown Orchid

Eulophia graminea

`INVASIVE`

WHERE TO FIND THEM: All Camino 305 Field Trips

Miami's native orchids are relatively rare. You just don't see them all that often, which is unfortunate because that makes most people's first encounter with a wild-growing orchid the Chinese crown orchid, a non-native species from Southeast Asia that was first observed in Florida in 2007 (as soon as it got through the door, it started establishing all over the place and is now classified as an invasive species).

Unlike most orchids, which live as epiphytes (plants that grow on other plants), the Chinese crown is a ground orchid, with large bulbs buried beneath the soil. If you were to dig one up, you might be surprised at how much these bulbs resemble onions (you would also be doing the ecosystem a favor). As far as orchids go, the Chinese crown orchid's appearance is relatively modest, with grass-like foliage and dainty mustard, pink, and white flowers. This invasive should not be confused with its native counterpart, wild coco (*Eulophia alta*), which can be found in freshwater wetlands.

Common Lantana

Lantana camara

`INVASIVE`

WHERE TO FIND THEM: All Camino 305 Field Trips

Invasive plants usually hurt native ecosystems by forming monocultures in natural areas, monopolizing resources (sunlight, water, space), and leaving little for other species. Common lantana goes a step further and has native species participate in making themselves extinct. In South Florida, the main grievance with common lantana is its genetic compatibility with our native lantanas. When they interbreed, the two species create hybrid offspring, crosses that begin to replace the native population. Specialist wildlife that depends on the native variant may not be able to use hybrids as effectively. Of particular conservation concern is pineland lantana (*Lantana depressa* var. *depressa)*, a short pine rockland species endemic to Miami-Dade. Its run-ins with common lantana have thrust it toward state-endangered status with a high risk of extinction. Hybridization has affected most of pineland lantana's populations, but thankfully some remain. The main characteristic to look for in the native is bright yellow flowers. Plants with flowers tinged with orange and red are most likely hybridized. Lantanas are a very popular garden plant, and you can help by not purchasing non-native lantanas of any kind and seeking native species only from reputable native nurseries.

Coontie

Zamia integrifolia

`NATIVE`

WHERE TO FIND THEM: Camino 305 Field Trips 2, 3, 9, 11, 12, 15, and 20–23

Coonties are Florida's only native cycad, an ancient plant family that originated over 280 million years ago; they are well represented in the fossil record and about 300 species exist today. At first glance, their foliage may trick you into believing they are a type of fern (whose lineage is even more ancient), but cycads are an entirely different group. In South Florida, coonties are most often associated with the pine rockland ecosystem, where their tuberous taproots lay anchored deep within pockets of soil between the exposed limestone rocks, but they also occasionally grow along the edges of tropical hardwood hammocks.

The coontie plant is incredibly poisonous thanks to a chemical compound called cycasin. The bright orange color of its fruits make them look like a tasty treat, but we cannot stress enough that absolutely no part of the coontie plant should ever be ingested. Its roots, when processed correctly, are the only exception—Indigenous Americans discovered that by grinding the roots, washing the mash several times to extract the soluble toxins, and then fermenting it, they could produce a nutritious flour we now call Florida arrowroot flour (please don't try this at home). Although it's highly encouraged to plant coontie at home for their wildlife value, please wear gloves when handling them and wash your hands afterward.

Corkystem Passionflower

Passiflora suberosa

`NATIVE`

WHERE TO FIND THEM: All Camino 305 Field Trips

Hiding beneath the shade of trees and shrubs, the seemingly inconsequential corkystem passionflower vine is actually a champion wildlife attractor. All *Passiflora* species have similar-looking flowers, and the more you look

Fun fact

Schnebly Redland's Winery in Homestead is one of Miami's most popular, specializing in unique wines that substitute grapes with tropical fruits. At this must-visit destination for those twenty-one or older, you can try locally made guava, carambola and—you guessed it—passionfruit wines.

at them, the more baffled you may become. Several dozen thin, wavy tendrils encircle an array of pale petals in a pattern that resembles a human iris. Protruding from the pupil are an array of anthers and stigmas that look like an extraterrestrial's eyestalks. How could a bloom that looks so alien be from planet Earth?

Corkystem passionflowers retain the shape found in other species, but are much smaller (about the size of a dime) and dully colored. Named for the cork-like outer layer of its stems, corkystem passionflower is the most common of Miami's five native passionflower species and is the most reliable food source for the caterpillars of Miami's three heliconian butterflies. Don't be surprised if you find the larvae of Gulf fritillaries, orange Julias, and zebra longwings all on the same plant. With three for the price of one, a South Florida butterfly garden would be incomplete without corkystem passionflower.

False Tamarind

Lysiloma latisiliquum

`NATIVE`

WHERE TO FIND THEM: Camino 305 Field Trips 3, 5–9, 11, 13, and 19–25

Don't try eating the fruits of this common tree. We promise you they taste nothing like the sour tamarinds you find at the grocery store—*false* was inserted into its name for a reason. False tamarind is in the bean family. It has papery seed pods that contain several tiny seeds and can grow to about eighty feet tall, making it a good candidate for the fabled beanstalk that Jack climbed in the fairytale. It's one the most prevalent species in rockland hammocks and forms a significant portion of the forest canopy. Just as well, as its seeds are a favorite food for many species of birds and a kind of lysiloma-specialized beetle called *Merobruchus lysilomae*. The relatively rare Florida tree snail is also found on the trunks and branches of false tamarind trees.

A common street tree, false tamarind now has competition in the form of its non-native counterpart, the sabicu (*Lysiloma sabicu*). Sabicu is distinguishable by its larger leaflets, reddish new growth, and scraggly bark. Though it's not invasive, why must we reinvent the landscape wheel when we have a perfectly good native version available?

Firebush

Hamelia patens

NATIVE

WHERE TO FIND THEM: All Camino 305 Field Trips

Firebush is one of the most commonly used plants in urban native landscapes, with some arguing that it is a must-have in any garden whose goal is to attract wildlife. Named for its clusters of reddish orange tubular flowers that look like miniature flames against the green leaves, firebush is a magnet for many species of butterflies including fritillaries, zebra longwings, and giant swallowtails. Hummingbirds are also fans, and, amusingly, so are bees—watching them try to get in the action by pushing their pudgy bodies into the narrow flower opening always elicits a chuckle. Songbirds, and particularly mockingbirds, flock to the fruits and sphinx moth caterpillars feed on the leaves.

If you grow just one native plant at home, firebush is likely to give you the most enjoyment. But use a discerning eye when shopping for it. A Central American firebush variety, *Hamelia patens* var. *glabra*, has been introduced to South Florida and is sold as "dwarf firebush." Native insects prefer not to eat the leaves of this variety. In addition to not offering the same ecological benefits, this plant unfortunately also hybridizes with our native variety, lessening the value to the next generation of wildlife. Indigenous firebush is distinguished by having bright red flowers and triplet leaves with short hairs on their surfaces—the non-native has light orange and yellow flowers and quadruplets of hairless leaves. Hybrids will exhibit features from both.

Gumbo Limbo

Bursera simaruba

NATIVE

WHERE TO FIND THEM: All Camino 305 Field Trips

In addition to being one of the most widespread and recognizable trees in South Florida, gumbo limbo has a name that's fun to say. Gumbo limbo! A common element of Florida's many upland ecosystems, they are also a popular native tree in Miami's urban landscape, often adorning streets and casting shade on the sidewalk. Gumbo limbo is easily recognized by the characteristic texture and color of its bark, which is particularly smooth and colored by a combination of coppery red, dark green, and white, and often has paperlike flakes peeling from the trunk. The tree's reddish color and peeling bark earns it another common name—tourist tree—as it resembles the flaking skin of an unwary tourist who stayed in the Miami sun for a bit too long.

The green color in the tree's bark comes from chlorophyll, the pigment that makes plants green and which is central to the process of photosynthesis. Usually, trees only have chlorophyll in their leaves and softer stems. By storing chlorophyll in its bark, gumbo limbo is able to extract additional energy from sunlight, an adaptation that probably helps it grow quickly.

In hammocks, gumbo limbo usually grows in proximity to poisonwood. Indigenous communities use gumbo limbo sap as a remedy for the stinging effects of poisonwood. But in a bit of irony, the leaves of the poisonwood and the curative gumbo limbo look fairly similar. Be sure not to mix them up!

Fun Fact

Gumbo limbo is easy to propagate (make more of) with seeds or from cuttings. So resilient is this tree, you could cut a piece of a branch, place it in soil, and expect roots to grow.

Hairy Awn Muhly Grass

Muhlenbergia capillaris

`NATIVE`

WHERE TO FIND THEM: All Camino 305
Field Trips

Grasses in general are wholly underappreciated, even among plant folks. You often hear botanists exclaim "oh no, I don't do graminoids" (the botanical term for grasses and grass-like plants). This is partly because it is difficult to identify many grasses and sedges in the field, especially if they aren't seeding. Oftentimes, it's the minutest details that let you tell one species from another. This aversion to grasses seems to have seeped into native landscaping, where they are often left aside in favor of more colorful wildflowers. But grasses have a range of benefits not provided by wildflowers. Native grasses act as habitat for critters that may not otherwise find their way to your yard, provide nest-building material for birds, aid in groundwater percolation thanks to their deep and complex root systems, and also just tie the garden together aesthetically. Hairy awn muhly grass is a beautiful and widely available species you can use to start your collection.

With dark green, wire-like leaves and fluffy purple flower panicles, muhly grass may be South Florida's prettiest native grass. You can find vast fields of it in the marl prairies of Everglades National Park and Big Cypress National Preserve, as well as in a variety of ecosystems throughout the state. Seeing the fantastical oceans of purple and green they create during their peak flowering period in fall should be on every Floridian's bucket list.

Holywood Lignum Vitae

Guaiacum sanctum

`NATIVE ENDANGERED`

WHERE TO FIND THEM: Camino 305 Field Trips 15, 21, and 25

For its fascinating history, unique biology, and natural rarity, lignum vitae is one of our personal favorite native trees. The native plant community shares our affinity, and the tree is a popular addition to home and public landscapes. The Latin words *lignum vitae* translate to "wood of life" and alludes to the wood's many uses in traditional medicine.

The genus *Guaiacum* contains only five species, with two naturally found in the

Caribbean. Of those, the holywood lignum vitae is the only one native to South Florida. These species are the world's only sources of the nearly mythical lignum vitae wood. It is believed Christopher Columbus introduced Europeans to this fantastic material. Since then, it has been highly sought after for its incredible density and oiliness. Lignum vitae is nearly unmatched in its hardness; it is so heavy that it immediately sinks in water. In

the centuries since its discovery, it has been harvested and used for making bowling balls, police batons, propeller shafts, and gears for machinery (its oiliness made it especially good for this last use, as turning gears are automatically lubricated).

In addition to its material utility, lignum vitae has a robust history of use as a medicinal tree. Among the ailments it has been used to treat are coughs, asthma, arthritis, syphilis, and gout, and its sap contributes to a resinous medicine called gum guaiacum. For these life-preserving properties, lignum vitae has been named the national tree of the Bahamas and national flower of Jamaica.

Lignum vitae has been intensely overharvested and all species are listed as potentially endangered by the Convention on International Trade in Endangered Species of Wild Fauna and Flora (CITES), which recommends better management of its commercial uses in order to secure the species' future. The hope is to spur people to be proactive in protecting these special trees. Though rarer in natural areas than in years past, lignum vitae is gaining popularity in landscaping. Its relatively low stature, dense foliage, and attractive blue flowers are ideal for small spaces that receive full sunlight. Because of the density of its wood, the tree is also incredibly slow growing, a feature many homeowners appreciate. Increased use in urban areas may prove to be a strong conservation boost, ensuring lignum vitae's legacy remains *near* mythical, but still part of our world.

Krug's Holly

Ilex krugiana

NATIVE THREATENED

WHERE TO FIND THEM: All Camino 305 Field Trips

The scorching South Florida summer sun can cause many to daydream about the cooler months of the end-of-the-year holidays. These folks may try getting an early start on the season, humming "deck the halls with boughs of holly" in June. With the complementary colors of their dark green leaves and vibrant red fruits, hollies are usually associated with colder northern climates. But Florida boasts twelve native species of holly, a diverse representation of the *Ilex* genus. One of these species is the Krug's holly, which typically grows as a small understory tree in rockland hammocks. Its leaves and fruits look no less festive than those of other species. When not in fruit, Krug's holly can be tricky to identify. One identifying characteristic to look for are the plant's dying leaves, which turn jet black before falling off.

Leavenworth's Tickseed

Coreopsis leavenworthii

NATIVE

WHERE TO FIND THEM: Camino 305 Field Trips 14, 19, and 20

Rather than have a single species of state wildflower, Florida chose to adopt an entire genus, *Coreopsis*, as its representative. These sunflower-like wildflowers received the honor in 1991 after many years of being extensively planted along the state's road-ways as part of a beautification initiative. Also known as tickseeds, for their seeds' passing resemblance to ticks, the State of Florida as a whole has twelve native coreopsis spe-cies, with only two of them native to Miami. Of those two, Leavenworth's tickseed is the most common, naturally occurring in moist prairies and used increasingly in urban and home landscaping. As an annual species, it completes its life cycle from germination to the production of new seeds within one growing season. If you plant some at home in an area that has moist soil and receives full sunlight, you can expect new plants to appear reliably in spring from seeds produced by the previous generation.

Fun Fact

The species is named after Ameri-can army surgeon and botanist Dr. Melines Conklin Leavenworth, who collected many plant specimens in the state in the mid 1800s.

Madagascar Periwinkle

Catharanthus roseus

NON-NATIVE

WHERE TO FIND THEM: All Camino 305 Field Trips

Madagascar periwinkle is a non-native flower-ing herb with an interesting history. Identified by its five-petaled, pinwheel-shaped flowers that are either magenta or white in color, it is naturally endemic to Madagascar, where heavy habitat loss has pushed it toward endangered status. Here in South Florida however, it gained popularity as an ornamental landscape plant and, after escaping cultivation, has since become a common sight in natural areas and roadsides, sometimes in dense patches. Though pretty, it's not recommended for urban landscaping because of its peskiness in our local natural areas. Still available throughout the nursery trade, especially in big box stores, it's not yet officially classified as a Florida invasive, but it may be on its way.

Hopefully the species will be better managed in Florida but conserved within its native habitat, as the world owes Madagascar periwinkle a debt of gratitude. It is tremendously important in the medical field, because it is the original source of the chemical compounds vincristine and vinblastine, potent chemotherapy drugs that have saved a lot of lives.

Mango

Mangifera indica

NON-NATIVE

WHERE TO FIND THEM: Camino 305 Field Trips 15, 21, and 23

¡Muévete al lado, naranjas, a comer mango se ha dicho!

Move over oranges, we will eat mangos, I say!

Mangos have replaced citrus as South Florida's most common fruit tree (most likely—official ballot numbers are still pending). Identifiable by their long, oval-shaped leaves and reddish new growth, they were first introduced to Florida in 1861, and many people now have a cherished mango tree growing in their backyard. There are dozens of horticultural varieties, with some being sweeter and others having a softer texture. If you're looking to harvest a few mangos, the best practice is to wait until the fruits naturally fall off the tree. Set the fruits aside until they adopt shades of orange, red, and yellow. Too much green on the fruit can be an indication of underripeness, which compromises the fruit's sweetness.

Mangos are in the family Anacardiaceae, or the cashew family, which also contains poison ivy, poison oak, and poisonwood. A lot of "poison" in there! Members of Anacardiaceae often contain a chemical called urushiol, which causes a rash in humans. Mangos have minimal amounts of urushiol in their skins, but people who are more sensitive to the irritant can still get rashes and swelling—if someone is kind enough to peel the skin off for them, they can eat the fruit safely. One thing you should never do is burn mango wood, leaves or branches; the vaporized urushiol can cause some uncomfortable and potentially dangerous respiratory irritation.

Marlberry

Ardisia escallonioides

NATIVE

WHERE TO FIND THEM: All Camino 305
Field Trips

South Floridians would do well to incorporate marlberry more in the urban landscape. Typically a common subcanopy element within hardwood hammocks, this versatile species can grow to be a large, columnar shrub, making it a perfect choice for a native privacy hedge. It can also be maintained as a low border and even trained into a small specimen tree. With its clusters of dainty, sweet-scented flowers that mature into small inky-black fruits, marlberry is attractive to both the aesthetic-seeking homeowner and the hungry pollinator or bird.

Unfortunately, it is easy to confuse marlberry with the closely related and physically similar shoebutton ardisia (*Ardisia elliptica*), a native to tropical Asia and one of South Florida's most dastardly invasive species. Though it is listed as a noxious weed in Florida and is illegal to grow and sell, it has already encroached into a variety of terrestrial ecosystems. It is not enough to not plant any more shoebuttons. Its fruits are as attractive to birds as marlberries, which means they end up dispersing the seeds and increasing the plant's spread.

Narrowleaf Yellowtops

Flaveria linearis

NATIVE

WHERE TO FIND THEM: All Camino 305
Field Trips

A road trip down to the Florida Keys in spring and summer presents plentiful patches of deep yellow all along the side of the road. If you safely pull your vehicle over for a closer inspection, you can meet one of South Florida's most lively wildflowers. With linear leaves, average height of about a foot, and characteristic clusters of dainty yellow flowers that sit above the foliage, narrowleaf yellowtops beautify roadsides as well as the homes of many native plant enthusiasts. The lemon-colored flowers attract a variety of pollinators seeking sugary nectar, most especially smaller butterfly species such as skippers and blues. This makes them an essential plant for native butterfly gardens.

Orange Tree

Citrus sinensis

NON-NATIVE

WHERE TO FIND THEM: Not found at any Camino 305 Field Trips

Orange groves are symbols of the Sunshine State, on par with plastic pink flamingos and palm trees. They are the poster child of Florida's agricultural legacy. Anyone visiting the state's welcome centers may even be offered a free cup of orange juice. Oranges have been grown here since the mid-1800s and quickly turned into a booming industry that, today, generates upward of $9 billion annually. Though oranges are the most known citrus variety grown here, our climate is also suitable for limes, tangerines, and grapefruits. In fact, Florida grows more grapefruits than any other place in the world.

Citrus trees do not tolerate below-freezing temperatures, so southern and central Florida are the only parts of the state that can support them. Though people still grow citrus in South Florida, the industry is not what it used to be. The number of citrus trees here has diminished as a result of a tumultuous battle with citrus canker. This bacterial disease causes lesions on a leaf's surface, harming the tree enough to potentially kill it. The most recent serious outbreak happened in the 1990s, and nowadays, it's usually only individuals at home who grow citrus trees in South Florida.

A particularly productive backyard citrus plant is the Key lime, whose juice is commonly used in making Florida's world-famous Key lime pie. If you have yet to try a slice, we hereby declare that you are not allowed to leave until you do. Just make sure to wash it down with a fresh glass of Florida orange juice. Otherwise, can you really say you visited?

Poisonwood

Metopium toxiferum

NATIVE

WHERE TO FIND THEM: All Camino 305 Field Trips

To the untrained eye, nothing about the deceptively ordinary-looking poisonwood tree would rouse alarm. However, as anyone with the unfortunate first-hand experience of brushing through the tree's foliage can tell you, you really want to keep your distance. A member of the poison ivy family, Anacardiaceae, all parts of the poisonwood plant contain high concentrations of the skin-irritating compound urushiol. Exposure to this chemical, say from accidentally touching some poisonwood leaves, can lead to a severe rash and blistering. Depending on how swiftly your immune system responds, you might not see signs of a rash for up to a week after exposure.

Poisonwood is one tree everyone in Miami should know how to identify. Though it blends in well with other trees and shrubs growing on the edges of hammock and pineland forests, it is easy to pick out if the tree has a wound on its smooth trunk. The sap that oozes from poisonwood bark oxidizes to an inky black, looking like something the Wicked Queen would serve to Snow White. If that indicator is absent, look to its leaves, which are composed of five leaflets—two opposite pairs and one at the end—that have a thin, yellow margin and often small, black splotches.

Though hazardous to humans, poisonwood doesn't bother the threatened-within-Florida white-crowned pigeon, which will happily eat its fill of poisonwood fruits.

Fun fact

The family Anacardiaceae also includes cashews and mangos. Like poisonwood, these popular tropical foods contain urushiol. Cashews picked and eaten fresh off the tree can be deadly. Since heat destroys the irritating compound, all store-bought nuts are cooked, including those labeled as raw cashews, which are steamed before being packaged.

Privet Senna

Senna ligustrina

NATIVE

WHERE TO FIND THEM: Camino 305 Field Trips 3, 18–21, and 23

One of the most beautiful butterfly species in Florida, the cloudless sulphur butterfly uses the privet senna as one of its host plants. In fact, several sulphur butterflies use sennas as larval hosts. If you have a privet senna at home, take a closer look at the leaves from time to time. The caterpillars adopt the color of the parts of the plant they consume, in the same way that the skin of a person who *really* loves carrots will gain an orange hue (fortunately, this doesn't happen with every food, otherwise our partners and roommates would always know who ate all the red velvet cookies from the cookie jar).

The privet senna tries to defend itself from nibbly caterpillars by symbiotically recruiting ants. It entices the insects with a sugary liquid secreted from glands at the base of the leaf called extrafloral nectaries. In return for the sweet treat, the ants will attack and kill the very hungry caterpillars.

Royal Poinciana

Delonix regia

NON-NATIVE

WHERE TO FIND THEM: All Camino 305 Field Trips, Except 14, 19, and 20

Few trees can match the blazing beauty of the royal poinciana while in full bloom. In spring and summer, Miami's poinciana trees produce hundreds of large, deep-red flowers. So numerous are the flowers that red becomes the dominant color of the tree's canopy. Unfortunately, royal poinciana is not native to South Florida, but rather to Madagascar, where it is classified as an endangered species. It was introduced to Miami by David Fairchild (of Fairchild Tropical Botanic Garden fame), who reportedly campaigned to spread the tree across the county.

In our natural areas, royal poinciana has been known to be somewhat aggressive, with each of its giant seed pods releasing nearly two dozen seeds. But it's unlikely that this tree will disappear from Miami's urban canopy, as local affection for it runs deep. So beloved is the poinciana that it even inspired the annual Royal Poinciana Fiesta in Coral Gables, which has been running since 1938 and is Miami's longest running festival.

 Fun fact

For its popularity, history, and illustrious beauty, royal poinciana is Miami-Dade County's official flowering tree.

221

South Florida Slash Pine

Pinus elliottii var. *densa*

NATIVE

WHERE TO FIND THEM: Camino 305 Field Trips 4, 9, 11, 12, 15, 17, 20, 21, 22, and 23

Before it held towering office buildings and condominiums, downtown Miami used to house towering pine trees. Hundreds of years ago, Miami-Dade County hosted an expansive stretch of pine rockland forest, which was concentrated along the Miami Rock Ridge, a geologic formation of exposed limestone well above sea level. The only canopy species in that ecosystem was the South Florida slash pine. If it weren't for the millions of these readily accessible trees, Miami wouldn't have had the raw materials necessary to grow as rapidly as it did. Slash pine wood is very dense, making it incredibly resilient to damage, decay, and termites. Buildings constructed with their lumber more than a century ago retain a solid character to this day, essentially looking new. Unfortunately, only about 1.5 percent of the original pine rockland forests exist outside of the Everglades today, and the pine rockland ecosystem is imperiled.

Spanish Needles

Bidens alba

NATIVE

WHERE TO FIND THEM: All Camino 305 Field Trips

If you've spent any amount of time walking around Miami, from natural areas to the hustle and bustle of downtown, chances are good you have seen this daisy-like flower. The ubiquitous Spanish needle is one of Florida's most common native weeds. It is the definition of resilience, growing through cracks in the sidewalk and even from almost four-century-old seeds!

Famed treasure hunter Mel Fisher recovered the latter from the *Atocha* shipwreck in 1985 and scientists were able to get them to germinate even after centuries underwater.

Someone unfamiliar with this plant may worry upon hearing its name, maintaining a distance due to fear of cactus-esque spines or thorns. Fret not. The name refers to the plant's

thin, elongated seeds, which are safe to handle barehanded. A microscope reveals two pointed spikes at one end of these "needles," armed with opposite-facing spines. This is where the genus name comes from. *Bidens* means "two-teeth." The backward-facing spikes help the seed latch onto passing animals or clothing, which then carry them to new locations.

Spanish needles grow and spread exceptionally fast, allowing them to outcompete other native plants. On the flip side, they are one of the most reliable sources of nectar for pollinators in the entire state, flowering year-round. Because of these two competing factors, most native gardeners hold strong opinions about whether or not to keep this plant around.

Strangler Fig

Ficus aurea

`NATIVE`

WHERE TO FIND THEM: All Camino 305 Field Trips

Marjory Stoneman Douglas gave what's probably the most apt description for a strangler fig tree in her landmark book *Everglades: River of Grass*. In it, she said, "Its long columnar trunks and octopus roots wrap as if they were melted and poured around the parent trunk, flowing upward and downward in wooden nets and baskets and flutings." This unusual shape is the result of a unique life cycle, which begins when a bird eats the tree's fruits (though small, they are quite delicious). After eating its fill, the bird flies away and may perch on a cabbage palm or oak tree and excrete the strangler fig seeds that have passed through

its digestive system. The seeds germinate high up in the tree, and, if conditions are favorable, the plant will establish itself as an epiphyte (plants that grow on other plants). Over time, the strangler fig sends out tendrils that work their way down the host tree's trunk and into the ground. After reaching the soil, it's growing time! With access to nutrients that promote its growth, the tendrils swell up and become trunks. As the strangler fig grows, it sends down even more tendrils. Eventually, the host tree will become fully encapsulated in a tangle of throttling trunks. Despite this arguably violent life strategy, strangler figs grow in balance with the many native hammock species and also serve as a year-round source of nutritious food for birds and other animals.

Tropical Milkweed

Asclepias curassavica

NON-NATIVE

WHERE TO FIND THEM: All Camino 305 Field Trips

In recent years, milkweeds have become a hot-ticket item among butterfly enthusiasts because they host the beautiful monarch butterfly. However, take a closer look at many butterfly gardens and you won't find native milkweeds but a South American species called tropical milkweed, which is characterized by clusters of star-shaped, fiery red, orange, and yellow flowers. Sold by nurseries throughout southeast Florida and planted heavily in Miami, tropical milkweed does serve as a host for monarch caterpillars, but it's true conservation value is debatable. Milkweeds are naturally toxic. One class of chemical compounds that make them toxic are called cardenolides. Monarch caterpillars are typically able to withstand these compounds, but research has shown that under hotter conditions (like the ones climate change is bringing), tropical milkweed can produce them in concentrations high enough to kill the caterpillars. Additionally, monarch butterflies can carry a type of parasitic protozoan called *Ophryocystis elektroscirrha*, which they unintentionally deposit on milkweed leaves upon landing. On native milkweeds, which die back over the winter, this isn't much of a problem, but tropical milkweed grows year-round, allowing the protozoans to accumulate until the monarch caterpillars hatch. The caterpillars then eat the protozoans and get sick. Finally, tropical milkweed can spread into natural areas and supplant populations of its native cousins by competing for limited resources, reducing the supply of high-quality caterpillar food. Our love for the

monarchs may be causing more harm than good, but the remedy is simple—plant native milkweeds from locally derived stock or seeds.

Virginia Live Oak

Quercus virginiana

NATIVE

WHERE TO FIND THEM: All Camino 305 Field Trips

A mainstay of South Florida landscaping, Virginia live oaks can be found throughout urban Miami, casting shade over houses, schools, and sidewalks. With trunks reaching a diameter of six feet and long branches that both bend down toward the ground and reach up for the sky, few trees can match the regal majesty of a full-grown live oak. The word *stately* is often used to describe them. Miami Lakes and Coral Gables are known for having many beautiful oak specimens and some of the densest canopy cover in Miami.

While many species of oak are deciduous (losing their foliage in fall before going

dormant in winter), this tree is named live oak because it is evergreen and keeps its leaves year-round. Virginia live oaks are a great habitat for epiphytes (plants that grown on other plants), like airplants, orchids, and the resurrection fern. Garlands of Spanish moss (*Tillandsia usneoides*), which is actually a species of airplant, can give a live oak a truly ancient appearance. Rambunctious eastern gray squirrels are often seen zipping about in the tree's branches. Because what do squirrels like? Acorns, of course! People can eat acorns, too, if they're processed correctly (they are poisonous raw), and live oak acorns are apparently tastier and less astringent than those of other oak species.

West Indian Mahogany

Swietenia mahagoni

NATIVE THREATENED

WHERE TO FIND THEM: All Camino 305 Field Trips

Another staple of Miami landscaping is the West Indian mahogany, identifiable by its grayish-brown bark, pairs of oblong leaves, and pear-shaped capsular fruits. Coveted for its hard, reddish wood, mahogany is used in luxury furniture and flooring, but there is a strong argument for stopping or limiting its use. West Indian mahogany was once the dominant source of the wood, but big-leaf mahogany, whose native range extends from Mexico to Brazil, has grown more popular recently. Both species are currently listed as threatened, due to unsustainable harvesting practices. Compounding the danger for West Indian mahogany in Florida is its small natural range, which is mainly limited to rockland hammocks in the upper and middle keys and a few locations on the mainland. Fortunately, its popularity as a street tree helps support its continued presence in our state.

White Stopper

Eugenia axillaris

NATIVE

WHERE TO FIND THEM: All Camino 305 Field Trips

If you ever happen to be walking through one of the many hammock trails in South Florida and suddenly perceive a foul smell in the air, don't automatically blame one of your friends. Some liken the smell to diluted skunk spray, others to a person smoking something other than tobacco. But what you're smelling is likely not a nearby skunk nor a cannabis

aficionado, but rather a white stopper tree. A common understory plant within hardwood hammocks, the white stopper gets its name from a tea steeped from its leaves that makes a remedy for diarrhea. As one of four native *Eugenia* species, white stopper is distinguishable by its rhomboid leaves and fruits nestled in the leaf axil (the point where the leaf meets the stem). These fruits are highly sought after by birds.

Whitemouth Dayflower

Commelina erecta

NATIVE

WHERE TO FIND THEM: Camino 305 Field Trips 9, 11, 12, 15, 17, 18, and 23

If you observe it at the wrong time of day, you might dismiss whitemouth dayflower as just another weedy-looking plant. Its long, lance-shaped leaves and spreading growth habit make it look like a species of grass. But this wildflower holds a secret. Have you ever heard the phrase "the early bird gets the worm"? Well, only those enjoying the beach dunes or pinelands during the morning hours can appreciate the whitemouth dayflower's ephemeral beauty. Shortly after sunrise, the plant's flower buds unfurl into quarter-sized blooms with two showy, royal blue petals pointing skyward and one smaller white petal pointing toward the ground. Much like ice cream in Miami, the dayflowers cannot handle the brutality of the afternoon sun and quite literally begin to melt as the day progresses. By midafternoon, the once-beautiful petals will have fully disappeared, and sleepy-headed morning snoozers will be none the wiser.

Wild Coffee

Psychotria nervosa

NATIVE

WHERE TO FIND THEM: All Camino 305 Field Trips

The name "wild coffee" can serve as quite the attention grabber for someone unfamiliar with this common forest understory shrub. "Wait, Florida has its own native coffee? Is it any good?" In a word, no. Though its scientific name, *Psychotria nervosa*, certainly sounds like it could produce a jitters-inducing brew, and it does bear physical similarity to its Ethiopian relative enjoyed the world over, it turns out "nervosa" simply refers to the deep veins on the shrub's shiny leaves. On more than one occasion, folks have experimented with drying,

roasting, grinding, and steeping our native wild coffee seeds in an attempt to make a coffee substitute, but, alas, the resulting drink is not very pleasant in taste, is wholly lacking in caffeine, and acts as a mild laxative. You may not want to try this at home! The best reason to grow wild coffee isn't for a morning pick-me-up, but rather to support wildlife. Bees and butterflies love sipping nectar from its spring flowers and birds enjoy the bright red fruits.

Wild Cotton

Gossypium hirsutum

`NATIVE` `THREATENED`

WHERE TO FIND THEM: Camino 305 Field Trip 18

Wild cotton is one of the four primary species of cotton grown commercially, mostly to produce clothing. The wild form of this species is a South Florida native, occurring as a five-foot tall shrub with bright yellow-and-white cup-shaped flowers that develop into cotton bolls (not cotton balls). These fluffy masses are fibers connected to the plant's seeds; they are meant to help disperse the seeds by catching currents of wind. Wild cotton, also known as Mexican or upland cotton, has a unique reason for its threatened status. While most species disappear by the broadscale and indiscriminate destruction of habitat, upland cotton was intentionally targeted for elimination due to fear that it was aiding the spread of the boll weevil (*Anthonomus grandis*), which wreaked havoc on commercial cotton fields by feeding on immature bolls. Fortunately, though millions of plants were destroyed, the eradication efforts did not totally succeed. Still, it remains illegal to grow wild cotton in Florida.

Freshwater Wetlands

When you think of South Florida, you don't think of mountains or rolling hillsides but of flat, leveled beaches and freshwater marshes. This long, flat peninsula stores vast amounts of rainwater, especially during the wet season, accumulating much of it in low-lying areas. South Florida's freshwater ecosystems are everywhere, the largest being the federally protected Everglades National Park. One of the most important aspects of Florida's wetlands is a term you may not be familiar with: a hydroperiod. It refers to the depth and duration of water at a site, and it ebbs and flows with the wet and dry seasons. Hydroperiods determine the species that occupy a space. In the flat Everglades, even an inch of elevation difference can affect whether an organism is exposed to water during most of its life cycle or not.

Soil is an often overlooked aspect of ecology. South Florida soils are sandy and often littered with clay and limestone. Differences in soil composition and moisture affect the species of plants able to grow within certain areas, sometimes limiting the varieties to a few sturdy species such as sawgrass and cocoplum. In fact, huge stretches of the Everglades are covered in just sawgrass, which can tolerate being submerged in freshwater during the wet season and then exposed during the dry.

▼ Baby American Alligators

▲ Snowy Egret

South Florida wetlands dominated by herbaceous plants such as grasses and sedges are called marshes. Marshes come in a variety of forms, including prairies and sloughs, and provide habitat for wildlife during times of both flood and drought. Sloughs are the deepest type of marsh habitat, with moving water that lasts about eleven months of the year, making them suitable for many fish and aquatic plants. In these marshes, submerged plant roots remain saturated enough to survive during the driest of periods and can even quickly regrow after the above-ground tissues are burned by fire. Here the American alligator is a keystone species, which means it provides equilibrium for the entire ecosystem. As an apex predator, they maintain the food web from the top down just as a lion does on the Serengeti. As the winter dry season approaches and water levels begin to drop, these territorial reptiles dig deep holes to maintain a supply of water and reproduce. Once the rains cease, usually around November, these deep holes are some of the only areas remaining with access to freshwater, and they become a refuge for a variety of wildlife. Be warned: these freshwater refuges have toothy landlords.

Forested wetlands, or swamps, such as those found in South Florida's Big Cypress National Preserve, are dominated by dense vegetation, usually monopolized by one or two predominant tree species such as bald cypress and pond apple. Stands of these trees grow in areas where water is directed through a shallow limestone depression across a flat landscape. Forested wetlands can only occur where soil is suitable for tree growth. Within them, the microclimate is suitable for many epiphytes (plants that grow on other plants) and understory plants, such as ferns. Unlike in marshes, fire is not a critical process within forested wetlands.

Wetlands are important for a variety of flora and fauna, but we humans also rely on the groundwater for our own needs. The porous limestone bedrock beneath wetlands help to purify and filter water as it seeps into aquifers, huge underground basins that store water. In Miami, we mainly rely on the Biscayne Aquifer, which provides the majority of our drinking water. Though it is vast, it is not inexhaustable. At the moment, there is concern that we are using water faster than the aquifer can replenish itself. As sea levels continue to rise, saltwater may begin to intrude, creeping up through the limestone from the ocean. This is already happening in Broward and Palm Beach counties, where freshwater drawn from wells in some coastal areas is coming up salty. Draining the Biscayne Aquifer wouldn't just deplete our drinking water, it would be devastating for freshwater wetland habitats.

▼ During a drive on Loop Road, be sure to stop often and enjoy the freshwater views.

South Florida's Water Management District is tasked with managing this crucial resource and ensuring land and water areas are maintained and used safely by humans.

Alteration of the natural water flow through the construction of canals, roads, and other development, along with the suppression of fire, which marshes rely on, has disrupted wetland communities. To make matters worse, these ecosystems face other threats as well. The introduction of invasive species has imperiled native plants and wildlife through direct, heavy competition, altering the sensitive ecosystem balance. The long-term effects of climate change, particularly in relation to longer droughts and more severe weather events, are still unknown. Still, conservation organizations are putting their best foot forward. In this next section, you will learn about the plants and animals in South Florida that rely on our unique freshwater wetlands, as well as individuals and organizations working tirelessly to protect them.

Mammals

Cotton Mouse

Peromyscus gossypinus

NATIVE

WHERE TO FIND THEM: Camino 305
Field Trip 25

Florida is home to many different species of mice, but the one most likely to be encountered by humans (unless you're in Orlando visiting Mickey and Minnie) is the cotton mouse. With tan-colored fur and large ears and eyes, these little critters prefer to live in forested wetlands. They eat mostly nuts, berries, seeds, and insects, and, unfortunately for them, they are on the dinner menu for a lot of predators.

Although the cotton mouse is common to Florida, there is a subspecies, the Key Largo cotton mouse (*Peromyscus gossypinus allapaticola*), which is extremely rare. Inhabiting hardwood hammocks and nesting in hollow trees, the Key Largo cotton mouse is federally endangered due to habitat loss and fragmentation, which have isolated its populations and reduced genetic diversity. If you ever get the opportunity to see the cotton mouse and Key Largo cotton mouse side by side, you'll notice they are slightly different colors, with the Keys mouse having a more hazel to reddish-brown fur and a white underside.

Everglades Mink

Neovison vison evergladensis

NATIVE   THREATENED

WHERE TO FIND THEM: Camino 305 Field Trip 20

The American mink is native to the majority of North America, from Alaska and Canada down to Central and Northern Florida. Here in South Florida, we have a subspecies, the Everglades mink, which only resides in the Everglades, Okeechobee, and Big Cypress basin regions. These minks are semiaquatic mammals living in salt and freshwater marshes. Although they are related to otters, they are much smaller by comparison, usually maxing out at around twenty-five inches long. They have dark brown, silky fur all over their body, sometimes sporting white spots. Their heads are round and flat with tiny disk-shaped ears. Weighing in at a relatively light four pounds, they are still tough predators, and have been documented attacking mammals and reptiles much larger than themselves.

Moles

Eastern Mole

Scalopus aquaticus

NATIVE

Star-Nosed Mole

Condylura cristata

NATIVE

WHERE TO FIND THEM: Camino 305 Field Trip 20

Unless you're looking for (or more realistically, digging for) a mole, you have a slim chance of encountering one. However, we would be remiss to not mention these unique underground mammals. Because they spend a majority of their time underground, vision is

Conservation Connection

The Everglades mink is state-threatened and faces a handful of human-made threats, mostly habitat loss from development and waterway construction, pesticides, and invasive-species encroachment, especially by the Burmese python. They are susceptible to the canine distemper virus, which is deadly to many animals, including puppies who aren't vaccinated. Having an accurate estimate of how many Everglades mink live in an area can help scientists know how to manage and protect them. However, tracking these little mammals has proven difficult due to their small size, quickness, and stellar hide-and-seek skills. Florida Fish and Wildlife Conservation Commission (FWC) is looking for citizen scientists to report sightings of both the Everglades mink and its cousin, the long-tailed weasel (*Mustela frenata*), to gather more information on these species.

▲ Eastern mole

▲ Star-nosed mole

not their strongest sense. As the eastern mole digs in search of food, leaving tunnels and molehills in its wake, it can create up to 1.5 feet of tunnel per minute. With its grayish fur, sealed eyelids, and webbed feet, it looks like it might be a good swimmer, and its scientific name, *Scalopus aquaticus*, suggests so too. Alas, the eastern mole doesn't fare particularly well in an aquatic environment. Fortunately, that's where the star-nosed mole thrives. Excellent swimmers, star-nosed moles live in soft-soil environments near wetland streams where they hunt crustaceans and fish. When not partaking in a seafood diet, they enjoy a "seefood" diet, happily eating insects, snails, and worms. The star-nosed mole has one obvious, unique characteristic that differentiates it from its eastern mole counterpart: that schnoz. Twenty-two finger-like appendages surround their nostrils, and the moles use them to investigate and explore their surroundings in much the same way we humans use our eyes. Their special noses can also detect prey through electrical impulses. Let's see your eyes do that.

North American River Otter

Lontra canadensis

NATIVE

WHERE TO FIND THEM: Camino 305 Field Trips 14, 19, and 20

Not many people are aware that Florida is home to one of the most adorable animals, the North American river otter. This furry, semiaquatic mammal can be found in waterways all over Florida, except for the Florida Keys. Although they prefer freshwater habitats like rivers, lakes, and ponds, these strong swimmers have been known to pop up in brackish and coastal waters, and sometimes even on land. If you do see them on land, you might notice they look pretty awkward as they attempt to maneuver as a terrestrial mammal. This is because their bodies are built for the water, with webbed toes and a strong tail for swimming. They have the ability to close their ears and nostrils underwater, allowing them to submerge for several minutes at a time and have specially adapted whiskers and snouts for underwater hunting. As members of the Mustelidae, or weasel family, they are omnivores that spend much of their time looking for crustaceans, plants, mollusks, fish, and other small critters to eat. If you're lucky enough to see one, there is most likely another nearby, as they tend to travel in pairs or familial groups. River otters are considered a top predator in Florida, doing their part to keep ecosystems in check, but they do have to worry about a few larger species, like alligators and, of course, humans, who hunt them for their pelts during the state-regulated hunting season.

Rabbits

Eastern Cottontail Rabbit

Sylvilagus floridanus

`NATIVE`

Marsh Rabbit

Sylvilagus palustris

`NATIVE`

WHERE TO FIND THEM: All Camino 305 Field Trips

Two species of rabbit live in South Florida, the eastern cottontail rabbit and the marsh rabbit. Contrary to what many believe, rabbits are not rodents; they belong to their own separate order, Lagomorpha. Our two Florida species look similar, but the marsh rabbit is slightly smaller, darker, and has stubbier ears than its cousin. Another visual difference to look for is the white fluffy tail on the cottontail rabbit compared to the small gray-brown tail of the marsh rabbit. It also helps to know that they behave quite differently. The cottontail, like many rabbits, uses a hopping technique to

▲ Eastern Cottontail Rabbit

▲ Marsh Rabbit

get around, usually in heavily vegetated areas such as fields and forests. The marsh rabbit walks and can also often be observed swimming around their preferred watery habitats of brackish marshes or wet prairies.

Raccoon

Procyon lotor

`NATIVE`

WHERE TO FIND THEM: All Camino 305 Field Trips

Although they don't get much credit, raccoons are one of most intelligent species in South Florida, especially when it comes to creative foraging methods. Sometimes called trash pandas, because of their nighttime garbage-bin dining habits, raccoons can make a meal of almost anything. Unfortunately, these cunning omnivores have also been known to dig up threatened sea turtle nests to eat the eggs and hatchlings. Raccoons have a unique appearance and are easy to identify, with a black band across their eyes, that make them look like masked bandits. Their bodies are mostly gray, and their fluffy tails are banded with black stripes. Although they look cute and cuddly, it's important to exercise caution around them and to keep your distance from wildlife. Raccoons are known to carry a variety of diseases and have a nasty bite. Their sharp, multipurpose teeth are used for hunting, chewing, tearing, and grinding. Their population in South Florida is thriving to the point where they may seem to be a nuisance until you remember that they keep rodents and insects in check.

Wild Hog

Sus scrofa

NATURALIZED

WHERE TO FIND THEM: Camino 305 Field Trips 14, 19, and 20

Yes, South Florida has wild hogs. Florida has everything (except for meerkat sidekicks). The wild hog (or feral hog) is an exotic species that naturalized here after being introduced in 1539 by Spanish explorer Hernando de Soto, who arrived in Florida in search of gold with a sounder of pigs in tow (*sounder* is the term for a group of pigs). Descended from wild boar but also possessing traits from domesticated pigs, they now are found in every county in Florida. Although their appearance may vary, they generally have a shaggy coat, long legs, and a lean snout. Males can have tusks and weigh more than 150 pounds. Hogs are ungulates, which means they have hooves, and these help them trot around swamps, forests, and other habitats.

Reptiles and Amphibians

American Alligator

Alligator mississippiensis

`NATIVE` `THREATENED`

WHERE TO FIND THEM: Camino 305 Field Trips 14, 19, and 20

Emblematic of the south, the American alligator resides from Texas to North Carolina, but Florida has one of the largest alligator populations and is closely associated with this prehistoric reptile. The abundance of freshwater wetland habitat in Florida, particularly within the Everglades, provides them with a vast habitat.

Alligators can measure up to fifteen feet long and weigh nearly 1,000 pounds. Although they're burdened with a reputation for attacks on humans and pets in urban areas, it doesn't happen often, and usually only during times of drought when alligators go in search of

Fun Fact

While alligators live in freshwater, recent research shows that large males in the southern end of the Everglades will move into saltwater habitats to hunt for big fish and crustaceans. But they can't be in saltwater for long, and once they get back home, scientists believe they gulp large amounts of freshwater to flush the salt from their system.

accessible water and wind up in man-made ponds or swimming pools. Unless you venture into their natural habitat, you're most likely to see alligators when they're sunning themselves along the banks of canals, giving us a wonderful chance to observe them from a safe distance.

The American alligator, now common, was once on the verge of extinction due to habitat destruction and hunting. In 1967, the species was placed on the endangered list, but continued poaching led to its near collapse only a decade later. Soon after, a program to raise alligators in farms successfully filled the demand for leather and meat while diminishing demand on the black market. In addition, some of the farmed alligators were released into the wild, strengthening those populations. The American alligator is the beneficiary of one of the first massively successful conservation programs; its success shows that when we work together to bring a species back, anything is possible. Today, over a million American alligators live in the Florida wild.

Burmese Python

Python bivittatus

`INVASIVE`

WHERE TO FIND THEM: Camino 305 Field Trips 14, 19, and 20

The Burmese python is the stuff of nightmares. Setting aside its massive size of up to eighteen feet, its method of slowly asphyxiating its prey before swallowing it whole is terrifying to contemplate. With a pattern of irregularly shaped, dark brown spots overlaying a light brown body (similar to a giraffe), this snake can easily blend into its surroundings. At some point (probably in the 1980s or 90s), some overwhelmed pet owners couldn't handle their snakes anymore and released them into the wild. They have been wreaking havoc ever since. Currently an invasive powerhouse in the Everglades, this introduced apex predator only has competition from the American alligator—and compete they will. In 2005, the National Park Service released a memorable image of a thirteen-foot python attempting to swallow a six-foot alligator. Talk about biting off more than you can chew, or in this case swallow.

Declining mammal populations reveal the impact of the Burmese python in the Everglades ecosystems. Raccoons, though increasingly common in Miami's urban areas, are rare in the Everglades.

Conservation Connection

Hosted by the Florida Fish and Wildlife Conservation Commission (FWC), python removal programs such as PATRIC (Python Action Team Removing Invasive Constrictors) are encouraging experienced anglers, hunters, and enthusiasts to join the team in the battle against python expansion. Although only FWC contractors and staff can be paid for removing pythons, they are making it easier for more people to get involved in this ever-growing dilemma. Methods continue to evolve, and one of the most effective has been focused around telemetry, which tracks adult pythons to their nests so conservationists can locate and remove the nesting females and their eggs.

Florida Cottonmouth Snake

Agkistrodon conanti

`NATIVE`

WHERE TO FIND THEM: Camino 305 Field Trips 14, 19, and 20

Beware the cottonmouth. Also known as a water moccasin, because it swims on the water's surface, it is Florida's only aquatic viper and has even been observed swimming in the ocean. As luck would have it, it's also relatively common and often aggressive. If threatened, the cottonmouth will open its jaws to reveal fangs nestled in a large white mouth, hence its common name. As with all vipers, it is venomous and can be easily distinguished by its triangular head. Measuring up to thirty inches long, it is often mistaken for Florida's other venomous snake, the feared eastern copperhead (*Agkistrodon contortrix*). You can tell them apart by the dark stripes that extend from a cottonmouth's eyes along the side of its head, but since both snake species are venomous, we don't recommend approaching either to confirm proper identification. Luckily these snakes are hardly ever found in urban environments, but you should always be cautious when wandering near the water's edge in South Florida.

Common Snapping Turtle

Chelydra serpentina

NATIVE

WHERE TO FIND THEM: Camino 305 Field Trips 14, 19, and 20

This is not your average turtle. While maybe not as impressive as a sewer-dwelling, pizza-eating crimefighter, snapping turtles do have some pretty incredible defense mechanisms. The force of their bite, measured in pounds per square inch, is around 1000 psi, on par with that of hyenas, lions, and tigers. (Humans average a psi of 150–200, and saltwater crocodiles are the world champs, with a bite force up to 3,700.) They can reach body lengths of up to eighteen inches and can weigh well over thirty pounds. Happily, they're not usually aggressive toward humans, but they will absolutely defend themselves with an impressive chomp if ever captured or cornered out of the water.

Despite being somewhat awkward on land, snapping turtles are very agile within their preferred freshwater habitats. Their diet consists of fish, frogs, snakes, small mammals, and birds, and they sometimes venture into brackish (mixed salt and fresh) water for a meal. While they are of minimal conservation concern at the moment, consistent habitat loss due to the continued development of freshwater wetlands may pose a threat to future populations.

Florida Softshell Turtle

Apalone ferox

NATIVE

WHERE TO FIND THEM: Camino 305 Field Trips 3, 9, 12, 14, 17, and 19–23

The Florida softshell turtle is quite an odd-looking species found only in the southeastern United States. Although it lacks the hard keratin carapace (shell) most commonly associated with turtles, it does have a cartilaginous carapace that's covered in thick, leathery skin. Measuring roughly two feet in length, the body of this turtle varies in color from brown to olive with a cream-colored underside. Females can be three times larger than their male counterparts, sometimes weighing up to fifteen pounds. While most of the turtle seems somewhat typical in appearance, their elongated neck, tapered snout, and slim, two-nostril nose makes softshell turtles easy to identify. These features make them look like a cross between a turtle and a pig. Their ideal habitat is freshwater with mild currents, but they can also tolerate brackish water, which makes them very comfortable in Florida. Ectothermic (cold-blooded) and almost entirely aquatic, the Florida softshell turtle only emerges from the water to lay eggs or bask in the sunlight. While they may look adorable, they are a fast, agile predator that sits atop the trophic pyramid (food chain). As adults, their only predators are large alligators or birds of prey. They sometimes even eat ducks.

Southern Dwarf Siren Salamander

Pseudobranchus axanthus

NATIVE

WHERE TO FIND THEM: Camino 305 Field Trips 19 and 20

The tiny southern dwarf siren is a species of salamander with incredibly small, three-toed front feet and no rear legs, a body type that often causes people to confuse them with snakes. Their preferred habitat is shallow swamps and highly vegetated ponds, and though they have occasionally been found in both southern Georgia and southern South Carolina, they mostly live in Florida. Nocturnal and aquatic, these slow-moving amphibians survive on a diet of small invertebrates. During droughts, southern dwarf sirens are able to surround their bodies in a protective cocoon of mucus. Immersed in minimal water or mud, they can survive until water levels increase.

Florida has two subspecies of southern dwarf siren, but the one you're most likely to see in South Florida is the Everglades dwarf siren (*Pseudobranchus axanthus belli*).

 **Conservation Connection**

The southern dwarf siren's range might have gotten a lucky boost because of its association with a non-native, ornamental floating plant called water hyacinth (*Eichhornia crassipes*). This South American intruder forms a floating layer of dense vegetation that has become a primary habitat for the southern dwarf siren. It's a common conservation conundrum—is it better to benefit a native species by enhancing a non-native, or restrict the non-native expansion and negatively impact the native?

Birds

Bald Eagle

Haliaeetus leucocephalus

`NATIVE`

WHERE TO FIND THEM: All Camino 305 Field Trips

The official animal emblem of the United States of America, the bald eagle dominates all forms of Americana, from coins to flags to the official seal of almost every federal agency. It's probably the most identifiable bird on this list, with its white-feathered head, large yellow bill, and dark-ish brown mantle. Young eagles require around five years to grow this iconic plumage; through-out the first few years of life they are various shades of spotty brown. Obviously, the bald eagle is not only found in South Florida, but their population here is important. Florida has one of the highest concentrations of bald eagles in the continental United States, with an estimated 1,500 nesting pairs. People are often surprised to learn bald eagles exist in the tropics, because they're most often depicted in the colder, north-western states. But it's really the presence of tall trees and nesting cliffs near coasts, rivers, or lakes, rather than climate, that makes a suitable habitat for them. During breeding season, bald eagles primarily hunt for fish, but they aren't above scavenging for an easy roadkill meal.

 Fun Fact

There's a myth that Ben Franklin pro-posed the wild turkey as our country's national symbol instead of the bald eagle. Unfortunately, it's not true. Although he was quoted praising the wild turkey's behavior in comparison to the bald eagle, he never formally pro-posed the turkey as our national bird.

 Conservation Connection

Prior to the 1970s, populations of bald eagles were in precipitous decline as a result of hunting and dichlorodi-phenyltrichloroethane (DDT), a toxic chemical insecticide commonly used at the time to curb mosquito populations.

Since DDT was outlawed by the federal government in 1972, bald eagles have made a dramatic comeback and are a testament to what consumer-based, national conservation plans can do for a species in crisis.

Everglades Snail Kite

Rostrhamus sociabilis plumbeus

NATIVE ENDANGERED

WHERE TO FIND THEM: Camino 305 Field Trips 19 and 20

The snail kite is an endangered species of raptor (bird of prey) only found in the subtropical climate of Southern Florida. The disruption of water flow from wetlands that have been drained for development has hurt surrounding habitats and the snail kite populations that depend on them. Belonging to the family Accipitridae, which also includes hawks and eagles, the snail kite (like most members in this family) has a thin, deeply hooked bill it uses for eating meat. It can be found near lakes and freshwater canals, specifically in wet prairies or sugarcane fields. Males and females are physically similar, but differently colored; males are a blackish-gray from the legs up and females are brown. Unlike other species in their family, these birds aren't known for speed—their primary food source is, of course, slow-moving snails. Everglades snail kites specifically eat applesnails. As long as the kites focus on both the native and non-native applesnail species, then South Florida can knock out two birds with one stone. Or two snails with one bird.

Florida Sandhill Crane

Grus canadensis pratensis

NATIVE THREATENED

WHERE TO FIND THEM: Camino 305 Field Trips 17, 19, and 20

Not to be confused with the greater sandhill crane (*Grus canadensis tabida*), a migratory bird that winters in Florida but nests in the northern Great Lakes region, the Florida sandhill crane is a year-round resident here. It can reach heights of just under four feet, with a wingspan well over six feet, and is typically gray with a distinguishable red cap above its eyes. From a distance, the red spot looks like red feathers, but it's actually a bald spot exposing red skin underneath.

Sandhill cranes are also often confused with herons, but the tail feathers (called tertials) that hang over their rear end to form a sort of feather bustle are a dead giveaway for proper identification. Florida sandhill cranes can be spotted in and around freshwater sources and marshes, foraging and hunting for a wide variety of food including berries, seeds, insects, small mammals, and reptiles.

Common Gallinule

Gallinula galeata

NATIVE

WHERE TO FIND THEM: Camino 305 Field Trips 4, 9, 12, 14, and 16–20

With a definitive red shield on its head and a red bill seemingly dipped in yellow at the tip, common gallinules are fairly easy to identify. Year-round residents of Florida and many other southern states, they are omnivorous, eating everything from seeds, berries, insects, and snails to carrion (decaying meat). As their wetland habitat diminishes, they have declined in number. They live in marshes, ponds, and other forms of slow-moving freshwater, and as cities continue to develop in such areas, it's unlikely the common gallinule population will be increasing any time soon.

Purple Gallinule

Porphyrio martinica

NATIVE

WHERE TO FIND THEM: Camino 305 Field Trips 14, 19, and 20

Unless you're an ornithologist or an avid bird watcher, it's unlikely you've ever heard of the purple gallinule. Which is a shame, because they are stunningly beautiful birds. From their blueish-purple heads to their greenish mantle, to their yellow-and-red bills and vibrantly yellow legs, these migratory birds are a walking crayon box. Found year-round in South Florida, Cuba, and parts of Central America, they also spend their breeding season in the states surrounding the Gulf of Mexico.

In addition to being a particularly vocal bird, they also have the comical habit of dangling their legs while flying, giving the impression that they have forgotten how to bird. These omnivores prefer slow-moving shallow water such as lagoons and swamps with heavy vegetation where they can find plenty to eat. You'll often see them walking on the pads of spatterdock lilies (*Nuphar advena*), giving the impression they are walking on water. Though not officially listed as threatened, their populations are at risk due to water diversion and loss of wetlands.

Great Blue Heron

Ardea herodias

NATIVE

WHERE TO FIND THEM: All Camino 305 Field Trips

This huge wading bird is the largest species of heron, growing to fifty-four inches tall. Its winding neck curls into an S shape while flying. It has long yellow legs and a thick, sharp bill. Its bluish-gray wings are broad, and it has a wide black stripe over its eye. Often seen moving slowly or standing motionless in the water while stalking prey, great blue herons are mostly solitary animals. They aren't the pickiest of eaters and will eat just about anything and everything, from fish, amphibians, and crustaceans, to insects, birds, and mammals. A white subspecies of the great blue heron, the great white heron (*Ardea herodias occidentalis*), was once considered a separate species but is now known as a subspecies that primarily lives in the Florida Keys.

Yellow-Crowned Night Heron

Nyctanassa violacea

NATIVE

WHERE TO FIND THEM: Camino 305 Field Trips 1, 2, 6–8, 16–18, and 21–25

Florida has two species of night heron, the yellow-crowned and the black-crowned (*Nycticorax nycticorax*), but they aren't too difficult to tell apart. The crowns help; the yellow-crowned night heron's has a yellowish stripe, while the black-crowned night heron's is all black. Additionally, the yellow-crowned night heron has a black face with a white stripe on the cheek beneath the eye. It can grow to twenty-five inches tall and tends to remain in South Florida most of the year but has also been known to travel slightly north for breeding.

Yellow-crowned night herons typically live in salt marshes and mangroves and have sturdy bills that help them prey on their favorite foods: crabs and crayfish. Often solitary, when they mate, both the male and female build the nest and share incubation responsibility for their three to four blue eggs. Despite their name, and unlike their black-crowned counterparts, they aren't nocturnal.

Ivory-Billed Woodpecker

Campephilus principalis

NATIVE **EXTINCT**

WHERE TO FIND THEM: Not Found at Any Camino 305 Field Trips

Extinct or not extinct? Though it's officially labeled as critically endangered by the International Union for Conservation of Nature (IUCN), the last sighting of this bird in the United States occurred in 1969, and all indicators suggest it's extinct. Once common to most of the eastern United States in lowlands and forested wetlands, it lived throughout Florida's panhandle. A separate population, or potential subspecies, was once found in Cuban tropical forests, but after those areas were cleared and logged, potential habitat decreased so dramatically that it's presumed they are extinct there too. Some hopeful bird enthusiasts have claimed to have heard or seen them after the last documented observation occurred, even as recently as a few years ago, but the claims remain unverified. When ivory-billed woodpeckers did live in the United States, they were one of the largest woodpeckers in North America, measuring over twenty inches tall. If humans are ever fortunate enough to encounter this woodpecker again, we could recognize it by its black plumage, a prominent crest with a red crown (on males only), and, of course, its ivory-colored beak, which it used to tap into trees to find beetle larvae.

Limpkin

Aramus guarauna

NATIVE

WHERE TO FIND THEM: All Camino 305 Field Trips

If you spend enough time in Florida, you're bound to spot one of these large, slender birds wading alone through swamps and wetlands (or even a grass field after a heavy rain). Everything about this bird is long. From their long, down-curved bills, to their extended necks, to their even-lengthier legs, the limpkin has an anatomy perfectly suited to hunt for snails and frogs in wet environments. If you come across a grim graveyard of empty applesnail shells, a limpkin may be nearby, as they tend to discard the remains of their meals within a relatively small space. Limpkins rarely venture outside of Florida and live here year-round, but occasionally somebody will spot one that has ventured too far up the eastern seaboard.

Their name comes from their unusual walking method, which makes them look like they are injured and limping. A success story for legal action and proper wildlife management, limpkins are comeback kids in Florida, having been hunted close to extinction in the beginning of the twentieth century. Their recovery is still underway, and continued action is needed to ensure their populations can increase to healthy levels.

Roseate Spoonbill

Platalea ajaja

NATIVE THREATENED

WHERE TO FIND THEM: Camino 305 Field Trips 14, 19, and 20

At first glance, you might think you've spotted a flamingo, but if you take a closer look at the beak of this pink-plumaged bird, you'll notice a specialized bill—flattened and widened at the tip, just like a spoon. This adaptation helps spoonbills to locate prey like small fish, crustaceans, and aquatic insects in muddy wetland environments. Instead of using visual cues to find their food, roseate spoonbills swing their special bill side to side, detecting prey by touch. You can imagine how useful this method is in areas with heavy vegetation or murky water. Like the flamingo, their pink coloring comes from their food, which contains carotenoids (red, yellow, or orange pigments produced by plants and algae). In addition to their bright pink feathers and funny-shaped beak, their bald head, red legs, and white chest, neck, and mantle can all help you confirm identification.

White Ibis

Eudocimus albus

WHERE TO FIND THEM: All Camino 305 Field Trips

It's all about the U! The most famous (infamous?) white ibis is probably the University of Miami's mascot, Sebastian. Outside of campus, you can recognize white ibises by their stark white plumage, reddish pink legs, and distinctly downward-hooked bill. They have black-tipped wings, and some have a unique marbled brownish-white coloring.

Often flying in large groups, these birds will commonly pitstop in wetlands or even rain-soaked front yards to feed. Their diet consists of crustaceans, fish, insects, reptiles, and amphibians. The non-native scarlet ibis (*Eudocimus ruber*) is relatively rare, but you'll sometimes see them intermixed with their white cousins. These two species sometimes interbreed, producing an adorable pink hybrid. Like many southern birds, they were subject to plume hunting in the late nineteenth century. Today, habitat loss is their most serious threat.

Wood Duck

Aix sponsa

WHERE TO FIND THEM: Camino 305 Field Trips 14, 19, and 20

Although this native duck was once common throughout eastern North America, overharvesting and destruction of forested wetland

habitats almost drove it to extinction in the early twentieth century. Male wood ducks are very colorful, with iridescent and intricate green, blue, red, and black plumage on their crested head and back. Their chests are a brilliant chestnut with unique white markings. These vibrant colors are believed to attract females, which tend to have more toned-down colors by comparison. Wooded areas are typically a safer habitat for such brightly colored ducks than open marshes with less natural protection. Fortunately, thanks to the Migratory Bird Treaty Act of 1918, the wood duck is no longer on the verge of extinction. This treaty, along with other conservation efforts, lead to mass installation of wood duck nest boxes throughout their known habitats, helping their population recover.

Wood Stork

Mycteria americana

NATIVE THREATENED

WHERE TO FIND THEM: Camino 305 Field Trips 14, 19, and 20

One of the largest wading birds in Florida, the wood stork is easy to identify due to its sheer size, but also its bald, grayish black, scaly head, and black legs, bill, and wing feathers, which contrast with the white plumage that covers its body. Like most wading birds, it feeds on aquatic organisms like fish, crustaceans, reptiles, and amphibians. However, its hunting strategy is unique: as it walks through shallow water, it uses its feet to sift mud on the bottom, swiftly snatching up any prey it finds.

The wood stork is the only stork species that nests in the United States. In South Florida particularly, it nests in high trees near water during the dry season. Though federally and state protected, the South Florida population is declining rapidly due to agricultural expansion and human disruption of naturally flowing water throughout the state. Wood storks need normal hydrocycles (wet periods) to increase their access to food and protect themselves from predators.

Conservation Connection

The wood stork helps scientists and environmentalists determine the well-being of wetlands based on how successful their nesting season is each year. Abnormal hydrocycles with too much water or drought result in failed nests and indicate problems in the overall health of wetlands. The National Audubon Society calls the wood stork "the barometer of the Everglades."

Insects and Arachnids

Band-Winged Dragonlet

Erythrodiplax umbrata

NATIVE

WHERE TO FIND THEM: All Camino 305 Field Trips

The band-winged dragonlet is one of the most common species of dragonfly you can find in South Florida. Its body is grayish-blue, and each of its four wings have a bold, black stripe running perpendicularly along its length. Dragonflies may look intimidating but are harmless and even beneficial to humans. These insectivores specialize in catching prey midflight, acrobatically maneuvering through the air like fighter pilots. Mosquitoes are among their targets, making dragonflies an effective natural control for those disease-carrying bloodsuckers. Their ability to orient each of their wings independently allows dragonflies to perform complex aerial feats, swiftly flying vertically,

side to side, back and forth, and also hovering in place. This multidirectionality is more sophisticated than any current, human-made flying machine.

Everglades Sprite

Nehalennia pallidula

NATIVE

WHERE TO FIND THEM: All Camino 305 Field Trips

The Everglades sprite is a species of damselfly, which are related to and look like miniature versions of dragonflies. Damselflies are distinguishable from dragonflies because they generally fold their wings back while at rest, whereas dragonflies keep their wings pointed out. The United States has many species of damselfly, but only the Everglades sprite is endemic to Florida and Texas. Its thin, black abdomen is punctuated by tiny blue stripes, with larger blue spots appearing at the club-like tip. Though the species does not currently have any state or federal conservation designations, its limited range and the slow disappearance of its freshwater wetland habitats has caused the International Union for Conservation of Nature (IUCN) to list it as near threatened.

Yellow Fever Mosquito

Aedes aegypti

NON-NATIVE

WHERE TO FIND THEM: You don't have to look for these, they will find you.

What animal kills more people on an annual basis than any other species? Sharks? Not even close. How about panthers? Nope. No, the deadliest killer is the seemingly harmless (though insanely annoying) mosquito. Responsible for over one million annual deaths worldwide, mosquitoes far surpass other animals in deadliness. And it's not about the blood they take out of you (though it'd be fantastic if they wouldn't do that), it's about what they put in you. Mosquitoes carry many kinds of diseases; the yellow fever mosquito spreads Zika and dengue fever. These mosquitoes are small, around 0.2 inches, and have white bands on their legs and a violin-shaped white border on the top of their heads. They were introduced into Florida a century ago, and we have been trying to control them ever since. Broadcasting insecticide has been the most effective strategy, but the practice is a double-edged sword; mosquito populations may be reduced, but the chemicals are poisonous to people and to many non-target insects (many of them beneficial and even endangered), which end up dying as well, potentially unbalancing ecosystems. A program is underway in the Florida Keys that experiments with releasing genetically modified, sterile male mosquitoes into the environment, in the hopes that their unsuccessful mating with females will lead to smaller and smaller generations over time. The verdict is out on whether these controversial modified mosquitoes will do their intended job or cause more harm than good.

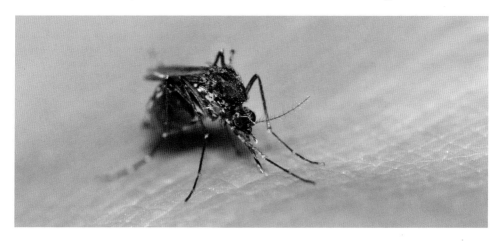

Black Salt Marsh Mosquito

Aedes taeniorhynchus

NATIVE

WHERE TO FIND THEM: Camino 305 Field Trips 2, 3, 6, 7, 8, 14–18, and 22–25

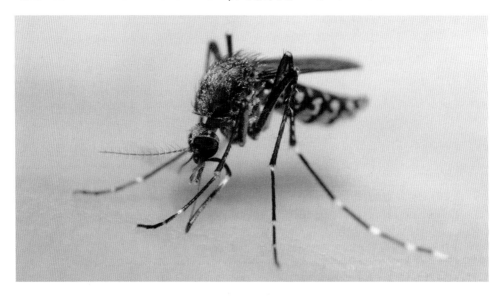

The most common mosquito in the Florida Keys, the black saltmarsh mosquito is relatively benign compared to the yellow fever mosquito, but it still has the potential to transmit disease. It is found throughout Florida and along the coasts of eastern North, Central, and South America. If you look closely, you will notice its characteristic narrow wings and white bands along the abdomen. Though they're less of a threat to humans, they're still a vector for eastern and Venezuelan equine encephalitis (a rare disease) and dog heartworm, which affect horses and dogs. Not to mention that unchecked swarms of them can render a place unlivable. Much of the aerial insecticide deployed throughout Florida is aimed at reducing the population of this incredibly pesky species.

 **Fun fact**

The fourteenth Dalai Lama, Tenzin Gyatso, is credited with saying, "If you think you are too small to make a difference, try sleeping with a mosquito." Every Floridian can understand this on a personal level.

Fish

Asian Swamp Eel
Monopterus albus

NON-NATIVE

WHERE TO FIND THEM: Camino 305
Field Trip 14

Introduced from southern China as a food source and through the aquarium trade, these shallow-water inhabitants share a number of similar features with our native eel species, such as an elongated body and tapered tail, but they don't have scales, pectoral fins, or even the caudal fins commonly associated with the American eel (*Anguilla rostrata*).

In areas where they're unable to breathe underwater efficiently, Asian swamp eels can breathe air through specialized gills. This feature also allows them to burrow in mud bottoms and survive in moist areas with a minimum amount of slow-moving water. They are nocturnal and sequential hermaphrodites, which means they can switch sexes from female to male later in life. Thankfully, due to their poor vision, ineffective swimming capabilities, and small mouths, Asian swamp eels have had minimal effect on native fish populations and freshwater ecosystems in Miami.

Bluegill
Lepomis macrochirus

NATIVE

WHERE TO FIND THEM: Camino 305 Field Trips 14, 19, and 20

Bluegills do possess some blue on their gills, but not enough to say it's their most distinguishing characteristic. For that, you'd be wiser to focus on the black spot at the back of their dorsal fin, plus their long and pointed pectoral fins. A member of the sunfish family, bluegills are a commonly caught freshwater fish in South Florida (and the United States in general). Because of this, they're intentionally stocked in popular fishing locations and are heavily managed by humans. Native to Miami, bluegills are opportunistic feeders; you'll find them in creeks, channels, lagoons, lakes, and ponds.

Bowfin

Amia calva

NATIVE

WHERE TO FIND THEM: Camino 305 Field Trips 14, 19, and 20

Eerily similar in appearance to the invasive bullseye snakehead, the native bowfin can be distinguished by its short anal fin. They have an elongated shape with a dorsal fin running the length of their bodies. Mature males have an orange-ringed, black spot on their upper caudal fins, while females do not. They're sometimes referred to as a living fossil because they possess some primitive traits modern fish lost long ago, but that doesn't mean they're behind the times—they simply found a system that works and are sticking to it. One example is their air bladder, which allows them to breathe in either water or air. This means that they can live in low-oxygen areas where other fish can't survive. They also have armored bodies that drastically limit the number of fish willing to hunt them.

Their preferred habitat is lakes and streams with clear water, minimum current, and high vegetation, and their diet is mostly fish. Bowfin are commonly caught by anglers aiming for tastier targets. Bowfin flesh has received mixed reviews from critics, and most people don't eat it.

Bullseye Snakehead

Channa marulius

INVASIVE

WHERE TO FIND THEM: Camino 305 Field Trips 14, 19, and 20

Bullseye snakehead is the invasive counterpart to our native bowfin. The most distinguishing feature to differentiate the two is the long anal fin on the underside

of the bullseye snakehead's body. Limited in range by temperature and a few conveniently restricted canals in South Florida, the bullseye snakehead sounds more like a comic book villain than an actual species. Red-eyed and torpedo-shaped, with an orange eye shape at the base of its tail, the bullseye snakehead uses an ambush technique to hunt for everything from small fish to reptiles in a wide variety of habitats. It was first documented in South Florida in the early 2000s, but really gained notoriety when scientists confirmed that the fish could breathe air and navigate across small patches of land. Rather than using gills to collect dissolved oxygen in the water, this fish uses a specialized organ called a suprabranchial chamber to breathe air at the water's surface.

Butterfly Peacock Bass

Cichla ocellaris

NON-NATIVE

WHERE TO FIND THEM: Camino 305 Field Trips 14, 19, and 20

In the 1980s, the butterfly peacock bass was introduced to Miami from the Amazon River in South America with the goal of managing non-native fish species, specifically the spotted tilapia. This is one of many attempts throughout Florida's history of mitigating a fluctuation in an ecosystem by introducing a new species. Fortunately for Miamians, this introduction seems to have been favorable, although there is still debate as to its effectiveness. This golden-colored member of the cichlid and tilapia family has three black bars on its backside and the golden outline of an eye near the base of its tail. With the ability to lay up to 10,000 eggs during spawning season, this species acclimated well to the Sunshine State and its new tilapia-based diet.

Fun Fact

Butterfly peacock bass fishing generates more than $8 million annually in South Florida. Because of their effectiveness at removing exotic fish species, Florida Fish and Wildlife Conservation Commission (FWC) actually recommends releasing any fish longer than fourteen inches

Flagfish

Jordanella floridae

NATIVE

WHERE TO FIND THEM: Camino 305
Field Trip 19

Endemic to Florida, flagfish are nonmigratory, predatory killifish that prefer to hunt for small crustaceans, worms, and insects in heavily vegetated, subtropical fresh and brackish water. Males come in a variety of vibrant reds and greens, while females are a light brown with an array of darker spots across their bodies. Both sexes have a signature dark spot about halfway down each side of their body, and the spot tends to be larger on females. There's no evidence one way or another about how patriotic they are, but flagfish are members of the pupfish family, which are found throughout the Americas.

 Fun Fact

The flagfish currently holds the Guinness world record as the fish that lays the fewest number of eggs—over the course of multiple days it can lay as few as twenty.

Florida Gar

Lepisosteus platyrhincus

NATIVE

WHERE TO FIND THEM: Camino 305 Field Trips 14, 19, and 20

Florida gars are definitely one of the more unique-looking freshwater species in Miami. Their fins are positioned way back on their elongated body, which tapers sharply toward their snout, eventually becoming a thin, toothy jaw. They look somewhat like a brown barracuda with black spots, especially near the top of the head, and are typically three feet long but have been found to grow over four feet. Their nostrils are located at the tip of their snouts, and they can use an air bladder to breathe surface air in locations with low-oxygenated water like warm, slow-moving canals and mud-bottom springs with heavy vegetation.

Aggressive predators, Florida gar wait at the surface of the water for opportunistic

moments to ambush unsuspecting prey. Their long and narrow bodies, in combination with their subtle swimming behaviors, help them camouflage as floating debris until suitable prey comes within range. After a successful strike, Florida gars will shift their prey to eat it headfirst. Throughout their lives, their hunting preferences will transition from zooplankton and insect larvae to crustaceans and fish. But they shouldn't get too confident, as they themselves could be a meal to larger birds, fish, and alligators.

Found in streams and lakes, this native species is not commonly caught for eating but is known to put up a worthy fight when hooked via rod or bowfishing. Edibility wise, they're rated below average, and their roe (eggs)

Fun Fact

Florida gar scales are classified as ganoid scales, which lack flexibility due to their peg and socket joint but more than compensate with sturdiness and protection. Diamond-shaped and composed of bone, dentin, and inorganic bone salt called ganoine, they cover the gar's whole body. Only its throat lacks these scales.

contain ichthyotoxin, a type of protein highly toxic to humans.

Florida Largemouth Bass

Micropterus salmoides floridanus

NATIVE

WHERE TO FIND THEM: Camino 305 Field Trips 14 and 19

The largemouth bass is arguably the most well-known recreational fish species in the United States and is the official state freshwater fish of Florida. The bass industry has expanded to become an international, multibillion-dollar industry, and populations are stocked worldwide in lakes, rivers, and ponds outside their native range.

They are named for their incredibly large mouths, specifically how the corner of the mouth is situated behind the eye. Those large mouths are used to feed on everything from insects to crayfish to amphibians and crustaceans, and rarely in waters deeper than twenty feet. They have a distinct stripe that runs from their snout, through the eye, to the base of their tail, and they can reach lengths up to two feet. Once at that size, they don't have many predators besides humans, but as juveniles, they can fall victim to a number of fish and bird species. Be mindful of telling any secrets around freshwater habitats in Miami. These fish do have big mouths after all.

Fun Fact

Largemouth bass are not bass at all. They're actually members of the sunfish family.

Jaguar Guapote

Parachromis managuensis

NON-NATIVE

WHERE TO FIND THEM: Camino 305 Field Trips 14, 19, and 20

The jaguar guapote's teeth, leopard-like spots, and protrusible (thrusting) mouth helped earn this species its common name. This non-native cichlid has a very nonspecific diet that includes fish, insects, lizards, worms, and small fish. During spawning season, a single female can lay more than 4,000 eggs, and, as with most cichlid species, both parents are extremely protective of their young.

Like the Mayan cichlid, the jaguar guapote is native to Central America, where it has a high edibility rating. They were first reported on three separate occasions in South Florida in 1992.

Today, they're common in canals and can tolerate poorer quality water, but colder temperatures limit their spread. When trying to identify them, look for the multiple black blotches all over their bodies and the darker, squarish markings along their sides. If you're trying to level up your fish identification skills, look for a broken, two-part lateral line running along the sides of the body and ending at the base of the caudal fin. A lateral line is a system of sensory organs located on the side of a fish's body that's used to detect movement and pressure change and helps schooling fish stay together.

Mayan Cichlid

Mayaheros urophthalmus

NON-NATIVE

WHERE TO FIND THEM: Camino 305 Field Trips 3, 4, 9, 14, 19, and 20

First recognized as a resident of South Florida in the early 1980s, the Mayan cichlid has a wide omnivorous diet and qualifies as a euryhaline fish, meaning it has an incredible tolerance for salinity. Such adaptable characteristics, combined with parents who protect their young for the first six weeks of life, have allowed these Central American visitors to flourish here, especially in Shark River Slough within Everglades National Park. Fortunately, these nonindigenous fish are not only edible, but also great for fishing. There are no bag or size limits on them.

If you're ever unsure of an ID, the six to eight widely spaced, vertical dark bars, combined with their bright red chins (especially on breeding males) are a dead giveaway you've encountered a Mayan cichlid. They also have a blue-ringed eyespot near the base of the caudal fin to confuse predators, which earns them their species name, *urophthalmus*, Greek for "tail eye."

Pike Killifish

Belonesox belizanus

WHERE TO FIND THEM: Camino 305 Field Trips 14, 19, and 20

Killifish is a general term applied to a number of freshwater fish in the Cyprinodontiformes order, also known as toothcarps. This particular killifish, with its maximum length of eight inches, could almost pass as a juvenile Florida gar; it has an elongated jaw, fins located on the back one third of its body and black spots all over. Or, with all those sharp teeth, and a lower jaw that's longer than the upper, it could also be a cross between a minnow and an alligator. An effective piscivore known to affect native populations, the pike killifish has an unpicky diet and ability to bear live offspring; both traits have allowed them to become quite successful since their introduction into South Florida in the 1950s. They prefer slow-flowing bodies of water with excess vegetation and are able to start hunting at one day old.

 ## Conservation Connection

This species was first introduced into South Florida canals as part of medical research on how they might reduce mosquito populations. Since then, other introductions from farms and aquarium releases have helped make them permanent residents of the 305. Of all invasive species, fish can be the most damaging, because they can travel long distances and their eggs can be moved indiscriminately into new areas by currents and tides. Never release unwanted fish into local water bodies.

Spotted Sunfish

Lepomis punctatus

`NATIVE`

WHERE TO FIND THEM: Camino 305 Field Trips 14, 19, and 20

A sunfish in the Sunshine State? Obviously. This native species is related to the bluegill and the oft-mislabeled sunfish, the Florida largemouth bass. Despite its name, it's commonly found far away from the sunshine, in swamps with dense vegetation, or even within submerged logs or debris as it hunts for insects and snails. The easiest way to identify the spotted sunfish is to focus on its eyes, specifically the blue, half-moon-shaped line that outlines the under-eye area. They also have a black spot near the gills and a number of smaller black spots on their back.

Fun Fact

For their habit of spending most of their time around underwater logs they have earned the nickname "stumpknockers."

Spotted Tilapia

Pelmatolapia mariae

`INVASIVE`

WHERE TO FIND THEM: Camino 305 Field Trips 14, 19, and 20

Since their introduction from West Africa in the 1970s, spotted tilapia have become one of the most abundant species in the Miami-Dade County canal systems. These omnivorous, bottom-feeding fish are yellowish colored with six to nine spots or bars located on the sides of the body. They're edible, but if you're out fishing for dinner, be prepared to put these fish on ice right away. Due to their aggressive breeding behaviors, possession or transport of live spotted tilapia is prohibited in Florida without a specialized permit. It's also worth noting the edibility of a fish is not always as important as the water quality of the location in which they are caught.

A few decades ago, spotted tilapia represented as much as 25 percent of the fish by number and weight in the Miami canal systems. Their population growth was so fast, that some argued the only way to combat their expansion was the introduction of another exotic species: the butterfly peacock bass. What could possibly go wrong?

Walking Catfish

Clarias batrachus

NON-NATIVE

WHERE TO FIND THEM: Camino 305 Field Trips 14, 19, and 20

Between the bullseye snakehead and the walking catfish, apparently non-native fish of Miami did not receive the memo about fish living and breathing underwater. Another air-breather, the omnivorous walking catfish can use its pectoral fins to hold itself upright and rhythmically wiggle across short distances on land in search of better habitats. Originally from Southeast Asia, it was first discovered in the late 1960s and has subsequently been reported in most South Florida environments. They have a preference for the Everglades, or any shallow, slow-moving, vegetated area, but these opportunistic feeders can survive in areas with minimum water and even minimum oxygen. Combine that with a protective mucus

 Fun Fact

The barbels, the catlike whiskers that give them their name, surrounding their mouth allow them to locate food in environments with poor visibility and minimum light.

that shields their skin from drying out and you have a fish capable of withstanding the toughest of environments.

Invertebrates

Applesnails

Florida Applesnail

Pomacea paludosa

NATIVE

Channeled Applesnail

Pomacea canaliculata

INVASIVE

WHERE TO FIND THEM: Camino 305 Field Trips 14, 19, and 20

Though we try not to think of animals as "evil" for just doing what they do, it's hard not to think of the channeled applesnail as the evil twin of the Florida applesnail. This non-native gastropod has been labeled as a devastating invasive species as a result of its effect on aquatic fruits, vegetation, and various wetland crops. There are three other exotic snails of this genus found in Miami: the spike-topped applesnail (*Pomacea diffusa*), titan applesnail (*Pomacea haustrum*), and island applesnail (*Pomacea maculata*), which vary in size, shape, and color. In addition to being difficult to distinguish from the native species, they are more effective at reaching reproductive age—some can do so twice as fast as the native Florida tree snail. So how can you help? For now, the channeled applesnail is well established in South Florida, so the best option for any non-gastropod expert is to avoid buying exotic snails and never release them into the wild.

▲ Florida Applesnail

▲ Channeled Applesnail

Cuban Brown Snail

Zachrysia provisoria

NON-NATIVE

WHERE TO FIND THEM: All Camino 305 Field Trips

Sometimes it's anyone's guess as to how a non-native species arrived in South Florida. Was it the aquarium trade? Ballast water from a ship? Did it hitch a ride on the back of a brown pelican? Honestly, for this species, any one of those options could be true, since its native range is an island just 330 miles south of Miami.

Cuban brown snails have, you guessed it, brown shells. Their shells are about the size of a quarter and the apex (the tip) is not very pointy. The key feature that will help you identify this gastropod correctly is on the bottom (ventral side) of the shell; most snails have an umbilicus, a hole or depression formed in the center of the shell's spiral, but the Cuban brown snail shell lacks this feature.

You can spot these common snails on all kinds of leaves, but they especially love the ornamental plants that decorate many Miami homes. Their big appetite for such plants can become quite a nuisance for gardeners.

Florida Tree Snail

Liguus fasciatus

NATIVE

WHERE TO FIND THEM: Camino 305 Field Trips 13, 14, 19, 20, 22, and 23

Florida has three native genera of the land snail family Bulimulidae. The genus *Liguus*, which includes the Florida tree snail, is perhaps the most well-known, usually found on the trunks and branches of hardwood hammock trees feeding on lichens, fungi, and algae. Florida tree snails have brilliantly colored shells that can be a combination of yellow, pink, brown, or green. This variety makes color a poor indicator for identification; instead look for an aperture (shell opening) that is less than half the shell's overall length. You'll spot them in wild native shrubs, hardwood hammocks, backyard vegetation, and groves. They are hermaphroditic, meaning they possess both male and female sex organs.

A number of factors, including but not limited to habitat loss and the introduction of invasive competitors, pose a threat to Miami's population of Florida tree snails.

Giant African Snail

Lissachatina fulica

INVASIVE

WHERE TO FIND THEM: Camino 305 Field Trips 19 and 20

Another invasive snail? Why are so many invaders so slow? Nicknamed GAS, the giant African snail may move slowly, but it reproduces often, laying nearly 1,200 eggs per year. These hermaphrodites possess both male and female reproductive organs and, after one mating session, can reproduce multiple times without the need to mate again. They've earned the *giant* in their name with their conical-shaped, brown shells that can grow up to eight inches long and nearly four inches wide.

Efforts to reduce their population in South Florida have been ongoing since the 1960s, but because the snails eat at least 500 different plants, success has proven difficult. The original removal plan cost Miami roughly $1 million and took nearly ten years. Unfortunately, the snail was rediscovered again in 2011, and eradication has had to begin again. On top of their invasive qualities, GAS can also carry a nematode worm that leads to meningitis in humans.

Plants

Airplants

Tillandsia species

NATIVE

WHERE TO FIND THEM: All Camino 305 Field Trips

Plants in the genus *Tillandsia* are known as epiphytes, meaning they grow on other plants rather than directly in the soil. Florida has thirteen native tillandsia species that grow in a variety of ecosystems, but they're particularly concentrated in swamps and hammocks and usually grow on oaks, buttonwoods, and cypresses. In Miami (but also in Central and North Florida), Spanish moss (*Tillandsia usneoides*) is the most common species in the genus. It festoons trees of all kinds with its long foliage strings. Gather enough of them, and you can make one unique wig. Also common is ball moss (*Tillandsia recurvata*), which often grows in unusual places like on power lines or chain link fences. Among the airplants that grow throughout the Everglades are large cardinal airplants (*Tillandsia fasciculata*), named for their deep-red pointed flower spikes. Sometimes high winds or wildlife knock airplants from their trees. If you come across one of these, please leave it where you found it. Most of Miami's native airplants are threatened or endangered, and a culture of removing them from their environment (even the fallen ones) makes their conservation much trickier.

Conservation Connection

One of the strongest voices in the state for native species preservation is the Florida Native Plant Society (FNPS), a nonprofit founded in 1980. Many chapters exist throughout Florida, including Miami's Dade Chapter (DCFNPS), which has adopted the emblematic tillandsia, specifically a cardinal airplant, as its symbol. DCFNPS works to promote policies and land use that put the conservation of native plants and their associated ecosystems at center stage, while also fostering public appreciation for native plants and their use in home landscaping. They offer field trips to local natural areas and monthly educational programs that are free and open to the public.

American Elderberry

Sambucus canadensis

NATIVE

WHERE TO FIND THEM: Camino 305 Field Trips 3, 4, 9, 12, 14, 19, 20, 22, and 23

American elderberry is a large shrub that typically grows in moist, freshwater soils. It has serrated, compound leaves and clusters of small white flowers with yellow anthers. It has an incredibly large range in North America, growing from Florida, north to Canada, and west to California. Many are familiar with elderberry for its medicinal benefits, sold in stores in the form of cough drops and syrups and touted for its ability to treat mild cold symptoms. They may not, however, be aware that this plant in its raw form is extremely toxic. Every part of the plant, including its leaves, stems, and unripe fruits, contain chemical compounds called glycosides, which the human body processes into cyanide. If you cook the ripe berries, which are jet black, properly before eating, the heat destroys the glycosides and renders the berries safe to eat.

Bald Cypress

Taxodium distichum

NATIVE

WHERE TO FIND THEM: Camino 305 Field Trips 4, 14, 15, 20, and 22

Cypresses are a kind of coniferous tree that thrive in areas flooded by freshwater. In Florida, bald cypress is joined by a second native species, pond cypress (*Taxodium ascendens*), and both grow across the state. Together, they serve as guardians of the swamp forests, gigantic sentinels that form the structure in which countless species of plants and animals make their homes. Though both grow large, the bald cypress is a veritable colossus; with a maximum height of 120 feet, it is one of Florida's tallest native tree species. The tree

achieves such height slowly, over many years of growth. Just how many? The oldest bald cypress alive today may have germinated around the same time the Ancient Greeks were forming their civilization. The character of these giants is heightened by the many epiphytes that usually grow on them, including mosses, airplants, and orchids.

Cypress swamps carry a sense of mystery and spark our imaginations as we wonder what creatures may lurk in their dark, damp depths. Many ghost stories have used swamps as their setting, and, in fact, ghosts do hide among the branches. Not phantoms from the spirit world, but a beyond-rare species called the ghost orchid (*Dendrophylax lindenii*). Only in Florida's cypress swamps, growing on the branches of cypress trees, can you hope to encounter this pale white specter, an achievement on the bucket list of most of South Florida's plant enthusiasts.

Brazilian Peppertree

Schinus terebinthifolius

INVASIVE

WHERE TO FIND THEM: All Camino 305 Field Trips

Like many plants now invasive in Florida, Brazilian peppertree, commonly referred to as Brazilian pepper, started its ill-fated journey as a seemingly innocuous ornamental. A native to South America, it has oval-shaped, compound leaves that smell peppery when crushed. (Interestingly, this species is not related to black pepper (*Piper nigrum*), which is in the Peperomia family). It was once commonly available in South Florida nurseries and was marketed as Florida holly because of its dark-green leaves that are seasonally accented by clusters of small, red fruits. Those complementary colors appealed to many, and the tree became widely planted.

Birds were also attracted to the trees, eating the small fruits and dispersing their seeds far and wide. Soon, Brazilian pepper began showing up in pinelands, coastal uplands, and prairies. Today, it is one of Florida's most invasive plants, and the cycle only continues, with each female tree producing thousands of fruits annually and birds happily gobbling them up.

Unfortunately, no native animals consume its leaves, leaving the tree to grow unchecked in natural areas. But in the tree's native range, there are two insects that may be able to help us turn the tides of this battle. These are the Brazilian peppertree thrips (*Pseudophilothrips ichini*) and the yellow Brazilian peppertree leaf-galler (*Calophya latiforceps*). The thrips consume the soft new growth of the tree, while the immature leaf-gallers feed on the

269

sap. But approval to introduce a foreign biological control organism is not given lightly. After all, history is full of cases where biological control species end up becoming an even worse invasive (looking at you, cane toad). Both insects had to be studied for more than fifteen years, until scientists were confident they wouldn't interact with any native species. As Brazilian pepper specialists (they feed on that tree and *only* that tree), the thrips and the leaf-gallers have received the green light for introduction.

 **Fun Fact**

If you are allergic to mangos, steer clear of Brazilian pepper. Both are related to poison ivy and contain minute amounts of the same irritating compounds. Most people, however, can safely handle exposure to this tree.

Broad-Leaved Paperbark

Melaleuca quinquenervia

INVASIVE

WHERE TO FIND THEM: Camino 305 Field Trips 4, 14, 19, and 20

Commonly just called melaleuca, broad-leaved paperbark trees are one of the greatest threats to the Everglades ecosystem. Forests of these fecund trees are replacing sawgrass prairies and cypress swamps and supplanting the wildlife that require those habitats. Mainly identified by its pale, papery bark that peels off in thick sheets, the tree's other characteristics include sickle-shaped leaves possessing five parallel veins and white, bottlebrush-shaped flower clusters. When in full bloom, these flowers make it appear as if fresh snow has fallen on the tree.

Paperbark was introduced to Florida in a shortsighted attempt to dry out wetland soils. Early settlers ascribed little value to the prairies and swamps, viewing them only as impediments to development. The idea was to broadcast melaleuca, an exceedingly thirsty tree, in wetlands to suck up all the water. The experiment was too successful, and now millions of dollars have been spent in the gargantuan task of curbing its spread. As we as a society continue to adopt a more ecological mindset, hopefully nefarious attempts at broad-scale land modification become relics of the past.

Cocoplum

Chrysobalanus icaco

NATIVE

WHERE TO FIND THEM: All Camino 305 Field Trips

Cocoplum is a popular native plant in Miami's urban landscape, primarily used to make formal hedges in homes, parking lots, and alongside buildings. There are three main varieties: red tip, green tip, and horizontal. In nature, these inhabit different types of ecosystems, with the red and green tip varieties usually growing in freshwater wetlands and the horizontal variety growing in coastal uplands. In contrast to their neatly tended cube shapes in urban areas, cocoplums grow as large shrubs or small trees in nature. They produce a fruit ranging in size from grape to golf ball that is palatable to people and wildlife. Some people don't appreciate the fruit's fluffy consistency and occasional astringency, but with a bit of luck, you'll be plum-surprised to bite into a perfectly ripe specimen with a mildly sweet, pudding-like taste.

Cowhorn Orchid

Cyrtopodium punctatum

NATIVE ENDANGERED

WHERE TO FIND THEM: Camino 305 Field Trip 20

It is a lucky treat for any flower appreciator to come across a full-blooming cowhorn orchid in the wild—they are as rare in Florida as they are magnificent. A wetland species, cowhorn orchids are also sometimes referred to as bee swarm orchids. You'll usually find them growing on buttonwood and cypress trees, living or dead. The vibrant red and yellow of their blooms makes a full-grown plant look like a blazing fire in the landscape. The orchids were very sought after in the 1900s for their intense beauty, and overharvesting made Florida's remaining population exceedingly precarious. Today, the state lists it as an endangered species.

Cowhorn orchids are now being grown by Fairchild Tropical Botanic Garden's Million Orchids Project. The organization is using its research muscle and expansive facilities as part of its Micropropagation Laboratory. Here, staff and volunteers are propagating native orchids for reintroduction to urban landscapes and natural parks throughout South Florida. Their goal is to help the orchids eventually self-propagate in the wild, and their scientists are providing lectures at local schools to engage more residents and volunteers in the micropropagation efforts.

Crenulate Lead-plant

Amorpha herbacea crenulata

`NATIVE` `ENDANGERED`

WHERE TO FIND THEM: Camino 305 Field Trips 9, 15, and 21–23

Before the construction of South Florida's complex canal drainage system, some of the water flowing from the Everglades used to flow eastward through Miami's once-extensive pine rockland forest to discharge into Biscayne Bay. At the interface between the pine rocklands and freshwater prairies were the transverse glades, essentially long stretches of moist soil that supported a diversity of herbaceous plants. Among these is the Miami-Dade endemic crenulate lead-plant. This small shrub with no showy characteristics beyond spikes of small white and purple flowers is easy for an untrained eye to miss in the field. It is one of the rarest plants in the state, with only a few hundred individual plants scattered across roughly six locations. The partial reestablishment of the Everglades' historical flow, coupled with ongoing pine rockland restoration and fire management practices, is probably the only way this species will bounce back from the brink of extinction.

Giant Leather Fern

Acrostichum danaeifolium

NATIVE

WHERE TO FIND THEM: Camino 305 Field Trips 2, 3, 4, 9, and 12–23

The giant leather fern looks like it doesn't belong in this time period. Able to grow to a whopping twelve feet tall, with thick, leathery leaves, it appears to have come straight from a Mesozoic jungle brimming with dinosaurs. Florida is the only state that hosts this primeval-looking plant—ironic considering that dinosaurs had already been extinct for tens of millions of years before the landmass that is now Florida emerged from the ocean. This towering fern enjoys moist soil and is a common feature of shallow freshwater or brackish wetlands outside the city. A related species, the golden leather fern (*Acrostichum aureum*), can be found in similar environments, but as a state-threatened species, it is much less common. The two are physically similar, so it takes a trained eye to tell them apart.

Florida Royal Palm

Roystonea regia

NATIVE   ENDANGERED

WHERE TO FIND THEM: All Camino 305 Field Trips

Dwarfing most other palm species, royal palms are true behemoths; their royal title is not granted lightly. These seventy-foot giants have thick, pale-gray trunks and broad, feather-like leaves. In nature, they usually grow in the shallow freshwater wetlands of the Everglades and Big Cypress, so it's a little peculiar to see them as such a common ornamental within Miami's relatively high-and-dry landscape. Once you can identify them, you'll notice them everywhere, from home fronts to roadsides. Ironically enough, despite their prevalence in the urban landscape, their numbers are sufficiently low in natural areas to warrant their state-endangered status.

Sabal Palm

Sabal palmetto

NATIVE

WHERE TO FIND THEM: All Camino 305 Field Trips

What is South Florida without its palm trees? Our sunshine-filled, tropical paradise would seem incomplete without them. These Florida icons go far beyond their aesthetic value, playing an important role within the ecosystem. Though dozens of palm species grow in the state, only twelve are native. Of these, the most common is the sabal palm. It has hand-shaped leaves and a jutting rib cage that grows along the trunk. Plentiful throughout the state's hammock forests, pinelands, mangrove fringes, swamps, and prairies and extensively utilized in the urban landscape, the sabal palm is so ubiquitous, it earned the designation of Florida's official state tree, a title it has proudly held since 1953.

Common names for the sabal palm include cabbage palm and swamp cabbage, which refer to the tree's edible interior, or "heart of the palm." This soft, edible heart, known botanically as the apical meristem, is delicious in a variety of dishes such as stews and salads. Sabal palms were once the main commercial source of store-bought hearts of palm, but they are no longer as common on grocery shelves. Today, it's frowned upon to harvest these trees from natural areas, and flat-out illegal in protected lands. Better to leave them as food for wildlife. Keen black bears make a meal of palm hearts, using their strong, sharp claws to rip the trees open. In fact, in some areas of South Florida, sabal palms grow a bit more densely than they did historically partly because bear populations have declined so much.

Pond Apple

Annona glabra

NATIVE

WHERE TO FIND THEM: Camino 305 Field Trips 2, 4, 9, 15, 17, 19, and 20–23

Closely related to the delicious soursop fruit (*Annona muricata*), known as guanabana among Spanish-speakers, pond apple is one of the most characteristic trees of South Florida's

freshwater swamps and sloughs. Though its fruit is not as sweet and tangy as soursop, it is still tasty when eaten at peak ripeness (you can tell it's ripe when the skin changes from green to a light orange). The fruit certainly is a favorite for wildlife, consumed by everything from raccoons to birds and reportedly even alligators, hence its second common name: alligator apple.

Two historical Florida populations of pond apple are particularly noteworthy. One was an extensive pond apple forest that grew south of Lake Okeechobee—it covered over 30,000 acres and was essentially the Everglades' starting point. It didn't take long for settlers to realize that, if only the water could be drained, the rich soil of this forest would be great for

agriculture. So, drained it was, and today in place of a majestic pond apple forest we have primarily sugar cane plantations. The other population grew where the Miami River empties into Biscayne Bay—it contained what were perhaps the tallest pond apples in the state, up to sixty feet tall! Thankfully, even without these great stands, pond apples are still pretty common. Big Cypress National Preserve contains some particularly beautiful specimens.

Sawgrass

Cladium jamaicense

NATIVE

WHERE TO FIND THEM: Camino 305 Field Trips 14, 19, and 20

Sawgrass prairies are the defining feature of the Everglades, which comprise, for the most part, wide expanses of this one species. Botanically speaking, sawgrass is not a true grass but a sedge, a grass-like plant with subtle flowers and triangular stems that is commonly found in wetlands. However, sawgrass got its common name for two reasons: One, it looks like grass to the casual observer, and two, the name *sawsedge* would be a confusing homophone with the word *sausage*. Imagine watching a nature documentary and hearing the sentence "The Everglades are one vast sawsedge prairie." What's next, sauerkraut streams?

The long blades of the sawgrass plant are armed with sharp serrations, making it extraordinarily difficult for us humans to walk through without enduring multiple papercut wounds. Some people actually think that the presence

of so much sawgrass in South Florida is one of the reasons why it took so long for the state to be colonized by Europeans.

275

Coastal

Our first line of defense against storms, South Florida's array of coastal eco-systems start well offshore beneath the waves and provide protection, food, recreational opportunities, and other benefits to local residents and wildlife. They form a tropical trifecta of associated habitats: corals, seagrasses, and mangroves. Each habitat supplements the others in providing nutrients, migratory corridors, and shelter for fish, marine mammals, and invertebrates in all phases of life.

Florida's Coral Reef off South Florida's coast is the only coral reef system in the continental United States. Healthy coral reefs have been found to reduce wave energy by 97 percent, which is important considering Miami's extreme weather, especially during hurricane season. This natural barricade, home to eighty species of coral and thousands of other aquatic species, reduces physical damage to the mainland and barrier islands where humans reside. You can access the reef anywhere from the St. Lucie Inlet just north

▼ Gray angelfish on Florida's Coral Reef

► Coconut
Palms

of West Palm Beach to the Dry Tortugas, an island in the Gulf of Mexico, seventy miles west of Key West. Setting aside the environmental benefits, the reef acts as a centerpiece for recreational activities such as fishing, scuba diving, and snorkeling, supporting billions of dollars in economic benefits in southeast Florida.

Next in the coastal defensive arsenal are seagrass meadows, which grow in shallow waters between coral reefs and the shoreline. Often overlooked, or considered unpleasant to beachgoers attempting to wade through them, seagrasses are essential to the coastal ecosystem and South Florida. During storms and hurricanes they prevent erosion by stabilizing coastlines with their roots. They also provide essential nursery habitat to many juvenile fish and crustaceans that humans rely on for food. Aquatic herbivores, including our beloved sea turtles and manatees, rely on seagrass for shelter and sustenance. Carnivores like the charismatic barracuda also utilize the seagrasses, patiently waiting in a shroud of green for an unsuspecting meal to present itself. Healthy seagrasses filter coastal waters and store carbon in their blades, roots, and underlying sediment, reducing the amount released into the atmosphere.

Moving from the water to the shoreline, other habitats prevent erosion and protect against strong weather-induced damage. Mangroves are known worldwide for their astonishing ability to absorb carbon dioxide from the atmosphere, storing an estimated four times more than rainforests. Like coral reefs and seagrasses, they provide essential habitat for many organisms. Their underwater root systems act as nurseries for juvenile fish, crustaceans, and various invertebrates, and above the waterline they play host to reptiles, mammals, birds, and more.

Farther up the shore, beach dunes are essentially living sea walls. The dense root systems of their primary plant, sea oats, are the glue holding our coastline in place, while simultaneously acting as a windbreak during strong storms. They also provide habitat for a myriad of reptiles, birds, and invertebrates.

▼ Purple sea fan

▶ It's estimated that roughly 1 in 1,000 loggerhead sea turtle hatchlings survive to adulthood.

All of South Florida's coastal habitats face a variety of threats. One of the biggest is habitat loss due to coastal development. Living in a subtropical, rapidly growing city on the coast brings many benefits, including the ability to live and work with an ocean view, but there is a limit on available land. Construction on the coast displaces the effective defense of mangroves and dunes and replaces them with concrete sea walls, which, once breached by rising waters, cannot protect the buildings.

Every day, our South Florida environment is facing new threats with lasting impacts. Dredging and beach-nourishment projects dump sediment on corals and seagrasses, suffocating them. Construction and new development force wildlife to adapt to smaller, sometimes completely different habitats, reducing their numbers. Pollution from trash, fertilizers, and sewage systems pours into the oceans from land, diminishing water quality. South Florida needs our natural coastal barriers to combat the threats of climate change, including sea level rise, ocean acidification, and stronger storms, which have already begun to wreak havoc on the plants and animals, including humans, that reside here.

In this next section, you will learn about many of the creatures that can be found in South Florida's coastal ecosystems and the roles they play in making this environment so unique. There are thousands of local heroes volunteering their time to help protect and preserve these truly unique habitats for future generations. We will highlight a few of the many local organizations fighting for conservation, coastal resilience, and resource protection through volunteering events, coastal management, and activism.

Mammals

Caribbean Monk Seal

Monachus tropicalis

`NATIVE` `EXTINCT`

WHERE TO FIND THEM: Not Found at Any Camino 305 Field Trips

Though the last official sighting of the Caribbean monk seal occurred in 1952 on the isolated Serranilla Bank in the Colombian Caribbean, scientists still held out hope of finding a surviving population. Unfortunately, in 2008, this species was officially declared extinct, making it the first species of seal to be extirpated due to human activity. In Florida, the last individual was killed off Key West in 1922. At the time of European conquest in the Caribbean, estimates suggest the monk seal population surpassed 300,000 individuals in thirteen major colonies throughout the vast Caribbean Sea and Gulf of Mexico. They were an easy target for the first Europeans, who hunted them for oil and meat. By the nineteenth century, their populations were so fragmented that only small, isolated groups remained. Soon enough, those disappeared as well.

The Caribbean monk seal is a sad example of poor timing. In the northeast Pacific Ocean, the northern elephant seal was also targeted for meat and blubber, but it was only hunted for fifty years before a hunting ban was implemented in 1911, effectively saving the species; today more than 175,000 individuals live off Alaska, Canada, and the western US coast. Had a ban on monk seal hunting happened just a little sooner, Florida might still host these warm-weather seals.

Common Bottlenose Dolphin

Tursiops truncatus

NATIVE

WHERE TO FIND THEM: Camino 305 Field Trips 1, 2, 6–8, 16–18, 24, and 25

Arguably the most well-known species of dolphin in the United States, bottlenose dolphins can be found cruising in coastal waters throughout the Atlantic Ocean, Gulf of Mexico, and our very own Biscayne Bay. Often seen in nearshore habitats or playing in boat wakes, bottlenose dolphins are also the most common species encountered in human-run sanctuaries and aquariums, and their intelligence and trainability have contributed to their fame through their time on the big and small screens. (The television show Flipper, which ran from 1964 to 1967 and made people all over the country fall in love with dolphins, was filmed right here in Miami, at Miami Seaquarium.) Although there's no arguing with bottlenose dolphin lovability as measured by media influence, we still have much to learn and discover about these cetaceans (members of the order Cetacea, which includes whales, dolphins, and porpoises). Here in South Florida, we have *Tursiops truncatus*, the common bottlenose dolphin, which can be identified by

Conservation Connection

Even though bottlenose dolphins aren't considered a threatened species, they are still protected under the Marine Mammal Protection Act of 1972 (MMPA), which prevents humans from any form of marine mammal harassment. In South Florida, teams from the National Oceanic and Atmospheric Administration (NOAA) and other research institutions consistently monitor their population through a process called photo-identification, which catalogs images of wild dolphin's dorsal fins. Like a human fingerprint, each dolphin's dorsal fin is unique, and the photographs allow scientists to capture each distinctive notch, nick, or color pattern and use them for identification and, more importantly, for monitoring their population numbers to be sure they are safe and thriving.

MAMMALS

its large and usually darkish gray body, pinkish white underbelly, tall and centrally located dorsal fin, and stout medium-length beak. The shape and curve of their beak often makes these dolphins appear as if they're smiling—another reason people love them.

Author Story: Shannon C. Jones

If it weren't for the acrobatic, seemingly smiley, fish-devouring bottlenose dolphins at SeaWorld Orlando, I wouldn't be where I am today. When I was seven years old, my parents took me on my first trip to Orlando to visit the big theme parks. It was a life-altering trip; I remember the pure joy and awe I had watching these magnificent marine mammals soar through the water. I daydreamed about having a bond with a dolphin the way those trainers did, giving them love and care. Over the years, I returned many times and visited other facilities, like the Dolphin Research Center in Key Largo, and I would ask the trainers advice on how to become one of them. As I continued my studies, I learned about all the threats facing these and other organisms around the world and how many humans, even with good intentions, were harming marine life. I made it my life's mission to educate people about marine conservation and to stimulate passion in my community for protecting our planet. If I can inspire even just one person to find something like the intense love I had for dolphins as a seven-year-old and help them learn to make the world a better place, I'm doing my job.

Florida Manatee

Trichechus manatus latirostris

`NATIVE` `THREATENED`

WHERE TO FIND THEM: Camino 305 Field Trips 1, 2, 6–8, 16–18, and 22–25

Is that a giant potato suspended in the water? Nope, it's the Florida manatee, a slow-moving marine mammal known for its plump figure and habit of munching on seagrass all day. Their short snout, flexible upper lip, and sensitive vibrissae (whiskers) allow them to locate food, while their large, flat teeth are perfectly adapted for chomping on aquatic vegetation. As vegetarians, they spend a large portion of their day eating, eventually growing to more than 1,000 pounds and twelve feet long. Rounded flippers and large paddle-shaped tails help them maneuver through the coastal waters in South Florida.

A subspecies of the West Indian manatee, the Florida manatee is the largest surviving member of their order, Sirenia. Legend has it that the name sirenian originated from

fishermen who spotted these animals while they were out at sea and mistook them for enormous mermaids. In Greek mythology, sirens were creatures who lured sailors to their deaths with their beautiful singing.

Although we have yet to hear a manatee sing, unfortunately they do have their fair share of interactions with boaters. Vessel strikes are one of the biggest threats to Florida manatees, including direct hits from boat hulls and propellers. Although they can hold their breath for up to twenty minutes, they usually surface much more often. Spending this much time at the surface makes them incredibly vulnerable to boats cruising by— their gray complexion provides camouflage in the water, and boat drivers often don't see them until it is unfortunately too late. During your time in Biscayne Bay and the Florida Keys, you're likely to encounter signs stating "No Entry" or "Manatee Zone Slow Speed Minimum Wake" to indicate areas protected for mating or feeding manatees. These signs are testament to the power of collective conservation efforts; once listed as a federally endangered species, the Florida manatee has now been downgraded to threatened due to successful legal protections and rehabilitation programs.

Conservation Connection

Florida Fish and Wildlife Conservation Commission (FWC) oversees a network of manatee rescue and rehabilitation facilities in Florida, including Miami Seaquarium and Dolphin Research Center in the Florida Keys. These organizations are equipped with talented veterinary teams who are trained to care for injured and sick manatees until the animals can be successfully reintroduced into the wild. These efforts, along with education, waterway signage, and legal acts such as the Endangered Species Act, Marine Mammal Protection Act, and Florida Manatee Sanctuary Act of 1978 have contributed to an increase in healthy manatee populations in Florida.

Key Deer

Odocoileus virginianus clavium

NATIVE ENDANGERED

WHERE TO FIND THEM: Not Found at Any Camino 305 Field Trips

Key deer are a unique subspecies of the white-tailed deer. They are only found in the southern Florida Keys, specifically Big Pine Key and the surrounding islands, and can swim from island to island. Much smaller than white-tailed deer, males can reach eighty pounds, while females only weigh up to sixty-four. They are usually reddish brown to gray in color.

When males are ready to breed (at roughly fifteen years old), they can become very aggressive and compete with other males. Two males will charge at each other, locking antlers and sometimes fighting to the death. Like humans, deer usually have only one baby, but on rare occasions they can have twins. Fawns are usually born in spring and weigh about four pounds.

Historically, the Key deer's range was throughout the entire archipelago of Southern Florida, but in the 1940s their numbers fell to less than 50 individuals due to hunting and development. Almost twenty years later, the establishment of the National Key Deer Refuge and installation of fences along roadways have proven successful and are credited as turning the tide toward species survival. Additionally, local government increased speed limit enforcement and enhanced educational signage, and now Florida can proudly boast more than 700 thriving individuals. Although the population is stable, scientists monitor it constantly. The biggest threats they face now are to the habitats they rely on.

Key deer are known to use all the habitats in their range, including mangroves, hardwood hammocks, pinelands, and freshwater wetlands, but diminishing habitat and continued development of roads and fences increasingly harm Key deer populations.

Although it may be tempting to channel your inner Snow White and feed the Key deer, it's illegal to interact with these endangered animals because this increases their comfort with humans, potentially altering the deer's natural behaviors such as foraging, migration, and rearing young. Human interaction can also make it easier for parasites and disease to spread in deer populations. Looking toward the future, the deer are likely to face increased threats from climate change, including stronger hurricanes and sea level rise.

North Atlantic Right Whale

Eubalaena glacialis

NATIVE ENDANGERED

WHERE TO FIND THEM: Camino 305 Field Trip 24

The North Atlantic right whale is one of the most endangered species of cetaceans on the planet; only about 350 individuals remain. Seeing one off the shores of South Florida is rare, but not impossible. Each winter, North Atlantic right whales travel to the Sunshine State to breed from as far north as the Labrador Sea, where they spend the summer feeding.

These large marine mammals are baleen whales, which means instead of teeth lining their mouths, they have large, tightly knit bristles made of keratin. To eat, they take a large gulp of water and use their giant tongues to push the water out through the bristles, trapping small fish, krill, and other small critters in their mouths. Think of draining pasta: you dump your full pot into a colander and all the water flows into the sink leaving your pasta behind for you to enjoy. It is ironic that baleen whales, some of the largest animals on the planet, eat some of the smallest species out there. They need to eat a lot of them to sustain themselves on long migrations.

Right whales got their name from whalers who used to hunt them for their high blubber content (which produces high yields of valuable whale oil). They are quite docile and slow and spend time close to shore, which makes them easy targets—the *right* whales to hunt. Though whale hunting is much rarer today, their slow-moving nature still plays a huge role in their endangered status, and their near-coast habits make them vulnerable to getting struck by ships, the most common cause of death for these large mammals. Their frequent proximity to areas of large-scale fishing also leads them to becoming entangled in derelict fishing gear.

As marine mammals, North Atlantic right whales must come to the surface to breathe air. They have two blowholes located at the top of their head that act as their nostrils and connect to their lungs, allowing them to breathe. You might notice that unlike other cetaceans such as dolphins, they don't have a dorsal fin. They are usually grayish in color, with white callosities (thick, hardened parts of the skin) around their heads.

Reptiles and Amphibians

American Crocodile

Crocodylus acutus

`NATIVE` `THREATENED`

WHERE TO FIND THEM: Camino 305 Field Trips 2, 16–18, 24, and 25

Florida is the only place in the world where both alligators and crocodiles coexist in the same geographic range. Although both species share the 305 area code and belong to the same order, Crocodilia, you're unlikely to find them dwelling together, considering the alligator's preference for freshwater and the crocodile for saltwater. The American crocodile's range extends from Florida all the way south to Peru. It is a bit smaller than the alligator and much more timid (quickly entering the water with a splash if frightened). Often the two can look alike, but the telltale difference is that crocodiles have thinner snouts that end in a rounded bulge, while alligators are generally darker, with a snout that is flat and paddle shaped. Also, when a crocodile's mouth is closed, its bottom teeth (specifically the fourth tooth on the lower jaw) are exposed, while an alligator in the same position will only show its upper teeth.

Little Bahama Curly-Tailed Lizard

Leiocephalus carinatus armouri

INVASIVE

WHERE TO FIND THEM: All Camino 305 Field Trips

A native to the Bahamas, this species was introduced to Florida during the 1940s as a combatant against pests in sugar cane fields. A half century later and this lizard might as well be called "Florida's lizard." One glance is enough to explain how the name curly-tail might have stuck. Though their tail is their most distinguishing characteristic, you can also recognize them by their speckled-brown bodies and wide bellies. They have strong rear legs and like to eat insects, smaller lizards, and the native railroad vine. Though they are nowhere near as big as a green iguana or giant ameiva, at six inches, they're significantly larger than the green anole or brown anole, with whom they tend to share common space.

These ectotherms (animals that depend on external sources for body heat) prefer full sun and rocky or sandy areas. They also frequent buildings, seawalls, and any piece of man-made architecture that also has cracks and crevices where they can quickly hide for protection. When frightened, the curve in their tails become more pronounced, alerting any would-be predators that the game has now become quite serious.

Loggerhead Sea Turtle

Caretta caretta

NATIVE THREATENED

WHERE TO FIND THEM: Camino 305 Field Trips 1, 16–18, 24, and 25

Once land dwelling reptiles, these turtles made the transition back to a life at sea when dinosaurs roamed the land. Having evolved little during the past 200 million years, they

remain extremely well adapted to their ocean environment. There are seven different species of sea turtle around the world, five of which can be found in Florida waters. Of those, the loggerhead, green (*Chelonia mydas*), and hawksbill (*Eretmochelys imbricata*) are the ones you're most likely to spot while you're boating, snorkeling, or scuba diving.

The loggerhead is the largest of the hard-shelled sea turtles and is named for its large head. Its carapace is massive, heart shaped, and, in older adults, often covered in sponges and mollusks. Adults generally weigh around 200 to 400 pounds, but it's not uncommon to see a mature adult tipping the scales at over 700 pounds. Most males have longer tails and claws, a slightly shorter carapace, and larger heads, but overall, it's difficult to tell males from females. Like most sea turtles, loggerheads have a cosmopolitan distribution, meaning they live in all the world's warm and temperate oceans. They also have extremely long migratory routes. In the Pacific, loggerheads have been tracked swimming from Japan to Mexico.

The loggerhead is one of Florida's most iconic species and the most common nesting turtle on our beaches. Florida is one of the

 ## Conservation Connection

There are a multitude of organizations working to protect loggerheads. Research institutions such as the Marine Order for Research and Action through Environmental Stewardship (MORAES) and the Miami-Dade County Sea Turtle Conservation Program are responsible for monitoring nesting efforts. Lighting ordinances are in effect on most nesting beaches throughout the county to avoid disorienting nesting females or hatchlings. Technology is also helping coastal homeowners put screens on their lights. If you're visiting Miami, please practice proper beach etiquette. If you're interested in seeing hatchling releases, contact the Miami-Dade County Sea Turtle Conservation Program. Supporting MORAES and other environmental nonprofits helps keep sea turtles thriving.

most important nesting areas in the world for loggerheads—in some years, around 60,000 nests have been documented. Females lay clutches of about 100 eggs in the sand and are very selective about where they choose to lay their nests, often returning to the beach where they themselves were born. Some major turtle nesting beaches in Miami include Fisher Island, Haulover Beach, Miami Beach, Key Biscayne, and Virginia Key. Unfortunately, coastal development and sea wall construction have negatively impacted turtle nesting.

When a female does manage to successfully lay eggs, her hatchlings are still in danger from both natural and anthropogenic (human caused) threats. After emerging from their eggs on shore, hatchlings need to reach the ocean; they use the brightest light on the horizon, which, on a dark night, is the moon reflecting on the water, to know which way to go, but artificial beach lighting from streetlights, hotels, etc. can lead them astray, causing them to actually head away from the water. On top of all that, sea level rise and storms are reducing the size of our beaches, with higher tides now flooding more nests. Because the sex of sea turtles is determined by the temperature of the nest (common in reptiles), our warming planet is creating a phenomenon in which many more females are born than males, lowering reproductive rates. Despite everything, loggerhead nests are common during summer and are highly protected by state and federal law. Keep your eye out for yellow signs and taped-off stakes on the beach. These are used to mark nests and protect them from getting trampled.

Reef Gecko

Sphaerodactylus notatus

NATIVE

WHERE TO FIND THEM: Camino 305 Field Trips 6–8, 16–18, and 22–25

Although geckos are not generally cockney-accented car insurance representatives, they are known globally as the only lizards that vocalize. They also have sticky feet that allow them to adhere to almost any surface, even glass. Surprisingly enough, Florida is not exactly a gecko hotspot. There are invasive geckos such as tokay and tropical house geckos, but for local species, Florida has only one. Florida's reef gecko, which is also found in the Bahamas, Cuba, and Central America, is a two-inch-long, brown dwarf gecko with darker spots, a stocky body, and pointy tail. Some believe it was introduced more than a hundred years ago from Cuba, but for now, most scientists simply consider it a native. Its shyness and preference for damp ground beneath leaf litter make this species incredibly hard to find. Keep your eyes open and be careful where you step. Studies at the University of Miami have shown that, due to their small coastal range, these Florida residents may be the US reptile most vulnerable to sea level rise.

Birds

American Flamingo

Phoenicopterus ruber

NATIVE

WHERE TO FIND THEM: Camino 305 Field Trips 2, 14, 15, 19, 24, and 25

This pink wading bird, also known as the Caribbean flamingo, has become a symbol of summertime and relaxation. Genetic evidence, coloring, and behavior have distinguished it from the greater flamingo (*Phoenicopterus roseus*), and the American flamingo is now considered its own species. They have distinctive, pink and black feathers, and the average adult is about five feet tall. Their famously long necks and legs help them feed on algae, seeds, and aquatic invertebrates such as shrimp and mollusks as they wade in shallow waters. These social birds often gather in flocks of hundreds, and, though over 95 percent of sightings are in the Florida Keys, Biscayne Bay, or the Everglades, there have been increasing reports of them on the northern fringe of South Florida's wetland habitats. This is good news, since Florida's population was nearly demolished by the start of the twentieth century due to overharvesting.

 Fun Fact

Hialeah has its own breeding population of American flamingos descended from imported birds that were once pinioned (had their wings clipped so they can't fly). Subsequent generations created a free-flying colony, but if you spot a wild flamingo there, it may be related to the original flightless population.

Belted Kingfisher

Megaceryle alcyon

NATIVE

WHERE TO FIND THEM: All Camino 305 Field Trips

This large, stocky bird averages about a foot in length and is named for its ability to hunt and impale fish with its long, sharp beak. Males are slightly smaller than females, with a blue body, white and orange chest, and a shaggy blue crown. Females have orange bands on their chest and tend to be more gray than blue. Found throughout most of North America and as far south as Central America, this species lives in lakes and streams and prefers water-side habitats with clearer water. They like to perch up high and dive headfirst into the water while hunting. In South Florida it has a plethora of water habitats to choose from but is mostly a coastal species, where it perches on everything from tree branches to power lines, waiting for an opportunistic moment to catch an unsuspecting fish.

Black-Necked Stilt

Himantopus mexicanus

NATIVE

WHERE TO FIND THEM: Camino 305 Field Trips 1, 16–18, 24, and 25

The black-necked stilt looks like an awkward teenager that never fully developed into an adult. Its long, spindly legs appear as if they grew first, while the rest of the body, including the bill, are still waiting to catch up. Despite this awkward silhouette, they are actually quite graceful and proficient at hunting insects and assorted crustaceans in marshes and shallow lakes. They have reddish legs, a black mantle, a black head, and white feathers underneath. Above their eye, they have a white patch of feathers that looks like an eyebrow. You'll find them year-round in South Florida, Mexico, and California, and their breeding areas are spread across the central and western parts of the United States. This native species also seems to be expanding its range and growing in number.

 Fun Fact

Not one to waste an opportunity, the black-necked stilt will quickly adapt to artificial habitats such as dams and sewage lagoons. Set up a back-yard pond and you might just receive some visits from a curious new feath-ery neighbor.

Boat-Tailed Grackle

Quiscalus major

NATIVE

WHERE TO FIND THEM: All Camino 305 Field Trips

Many mistake this bird for the American crow, and honestly, it's an easy mistake to make—they have similar colors, plumage, and dispositions. But pay close attention, and it's not too hard to pick out the fanned tail and bluish hue that sets the grackle apart. Up until the 1970s, boat-tailed grackles were thought to be the same species as the great-tailed grackle (*Quiscalus mexicanus*), but when scientists confirmed that the birds don't interbreed even though they live in overlapping areas along the Gulf Coast, they declared the two separate species. Boat-tailed grackles aren't seabirds, but they do tend to live near the ocean or mudflats. They live more inland, but these locations still tend to orbit lakes or marshlands. Unsurprisingly, their diet is focused around prey commonly found in the water, but they are omnivorous and won't pass up food scraps, insects, or seeds if available. Other birds, especially herons, should think twice about asking these grackles to babysit—they have a reputation for feeding on unguarded eggs.

Brown Pelican

Pelicanus occidentalis

NATIVE

WHERE TO FIND THEM: Camino 305 Field Trips 1, 2, 6–8, 16–18, 24, and 25

In *Finding Nemo*, the loveable large-mouthed pelican Nigel helped rescue Nemo and reunite him with his father. In real life, it's Nigel and his fellow pelicans who need rescue, having faced many threats in the United States since the early 1900s. First, plume hunting decimated pelican populations along with many other birds. At the same time, the fishing industry viewed them as a nuisance, and thousands of

Conservation Connection

It's a dangerous world out there for wildlife. Many species not only have predators constantly looking to eat them but also additional, unnatural hazards from living near people. Thankfully, some people are ready and able to help. What began with taking in and caring for a single injured pelican in 1980 has since broadened to become one of Miami's most dedicated team of wildlife doctors. The Pelican Harbor Seabird Station accepts and treats injured wildlife, nursing them back to health until they are ready to be reintroduced to the wild. Though they primarily focus on treating brown pelicans and other species of marine birds, they don't turn away other species, such as small native mammals and reptiles. To date, over 300 species and tens of thousands of individual animals have received tender attention from the folks at Pelican Harbor.

pelicans were killed to avoid competition. By the mid 1900s, pesticides, like the now-banned DDT, began ravaging pelican populations. Even though the first National Wildlife Refuge was created on Pelican Island in the Indian River Lagoon in 1903, brown pelicans weren't listed as federally endangered until 1970. In recent years, the species has bounced back, and it's been delisted across the nation, but Florida still catalogues it as a species of special concern.

Brown pelicans are most identifiable by their huge bill and its extending pouch, which can hold double the contents of its stomach. The pouch can even act as a fishnet when scooping up prey. Their brown bodies are roughly fifty inches long, and they have a white neck and yellowish head.

Diving Birds

Double-Crested Cormorant

Phalacrocorax auritus

NATIVE

Anhinga

Anhinga anhinga

NATIVE

WHERE TO FIND THEM: Camino 305 Field Trips 1, 2, 4, 6–9, 12, and 16–25

▲ Double-Crested Cormorant

▲ Anhinga

When exploring a Miami coastal area, you're likely to see certain birds perched motionless upon telephone poles or dock pilings with their wings spread wide. It's almost as if they're getting frisked at airport security. Don't worry about them. They're not acting strange and they're not in trouble—they're just drying off. Both the double-crested cormorant and anhinga are diving birds who hunt underwater for small fish and invertebrates. They use the spread-wing method to dry out their feathers after swimming. Unlike other waterfowl, they aren't equipped with a preening gland (the feature that helps keep water off a duck's back), so they've had to adjust. Sun-tanning isn't the worst adjustment to make.

If you want to be able to differentiate between cormorants and anhinga, a couple tips can help. To start, double-crested cormorants have a narrow, hooked bill that helps them hunt. Combine that with an expandable throat, a jet black body, an orange neck, and a height of about thirty-five inches, and you should be able to pick them out. While anhingas are also black, the males have a cluster of silverish white feathers on their wings and females have tan feathers on their neck. Additionally, each bird species has a different hunting style. Double-crested cormorants dive headfirst into the water after their prey. Rumor has it, they swim faster than many fish, which is good, considering they are awkward fliers. Anhingas swim with their heads above water, diving down to stab their prey with their sharp bills before flipping it into their mouths at the surface like a skilled juggler.

Killdeer

Charadrius vociferus

NATIVE

WHERE TO FIND THEM: Camino 305 Field Trips 1, 2, 16–18, and 22–25

The award for the bird that least lives up to its name goes to the killdeer. With just that description your mind might conjure a large-taloned eagle, hovering above the forest, waiting for an opportunistic moment to strike at large terrestrial mammals. What you're not expecting is a small brown-and-white bird with a maximum wingspan of ten inches. Even the tiny endangered key deer would laugh at the less-than-menacing killdeer. In fact, these plovers eat mostly insects. Their name comes

from the sound of their calls during flight—a high, plaintive *kill-deer* they repeat over and over. They're easy to identify by the double black-and-white bands across their chest and their orange rumps. Their preferred habitat is at ground level, either in fields or on shorelines, and they typically create their nests on open ground.

 Fun Fact

Killdeer are good actors. If a predator is threatening its nest, a killdeer will pretend to have a broken wing, fluttering on the ground and dragging its wing while moving away from its nest in a bid to lure the threat away from its eggs or chicks.

Laughing Gull

Larus atricilla

NATIVE

WHERE TO FIND THEM: Camino 305 Field Trips 1, 2, 16–18, and 22–25

A fixture on beaches across the United States, this species is commonly called the seagull. There actually are many kinds of seagulls that live near or are associated with the ocean, but this species seems to have monopolized the term for the foreseeable future. For those who live in Miami Beach, this is probably one of those species you can recognize by ear; their ubiquitous squawk is one most people automatically associate with the ocean (especially when they're excited about beachgoers mistakenly feeding them). In terms of diet, they don't solely eat dropped Doritos but will also gobble up insects, fish, horseshoe crab eggs, and even juvenile birds. A dark gray mantle, white underparts, a black head, and black primaries are their common features, but over the course of this bird's first few years of life, it will go through multiple phases with distinct characteristics. Florida laughing gulls tend to stay close to the beach, rarely venturing inland, and essentially living year-round on the southeast coast.

 Fun Fact

Excellent food thieves, laughing gulls are known to be opportunistic feeders who take advantage of unsuspecting passersby. They have even been known to land on the heads of brown pelicans and steal fish right out of their pouches.

Magnificent Frigatebird

Fregata magnificens

NATIVE

WHERE TO FIND THEM: Camino 305 Field Trips 1, 2, 6–8, 16–18, and 22–25

Magnificent is a good way to describe this unique, large bird. Frigatebirds have the largest wingspan in proportion to weight of any bird. This coastal species has a wingspan of 7.5 feet and is equipped with a long, hooked bill and a deeply forked tail, which increases their agility and ability to make quick turns. Both males and females have black feathers, but males stand out with their bright red gular sacs (throat skin), which they use to attract mates. They usually nest in mangroves throughout the Florida Keys, Dry Tortugas, and Marquesas Islands, and when it's time to lay eggs, the female only lays one at a time. Their diet consists of marine life such as fish, jellyfish, squid, crustaceans, and young turtles or birds.

Mangrove Cuckoo

Coccyzus minor

`NATIVE`

WHERE TO FIND THEM: Camino 305 Field Trips 1, 2, 7, 16–18, and 22–25

Limited mostly to South Florida—specifically the Florida Keys—the mangrove cuckoo occasionally makes it as far north as central Florida, but only for breeding. It has a brown mantle and a black-and-white pattern on its tail feathers, but it's the black masklike blotch behind its eye that confirms identification. Commonly found in mangrove trees or deep inside tropical hardwoods, these birds prefer to perch near the center of a tree as opposed to on outlying branches, making them difficult to view. Combine that with a general shyness and a preference for areas associated with high heat, high humidity, and dense vegetation, and, well, if you're able to get one, you'll have yourself a well-earned photograph. If you somehow get close enough to see a mangrove cuckoo's feet, you'll notice they only have two toes on each foot, a common feature of those in the cuckoo family, Cuculidae.

Osprey

Pandion haliaetus

`NATIVE`

WHERE TO FIND THEM: All Camino 305 Field Trips

One of the most common raptor species found in Florida's coastal waters is this huge, bulky bird that rules the coastline. Twenty-two inches from beak to tail, osprey are counter-shaded, like many marine animals, with dark brown feathers on their mantle and white feathers on their belly. This is a method of camouflage that helps the predator blend into the bright sky when viewed from below by potential prey. They are some of the best fishers in the business, earning the nickname fish hawk. Their diet consists strictly of fish, so their talons are equipped with four piercing toes and spiky toe pads for gripping scaly prey, and they can soar high above the water before diving down to grasp unsuspecting surface swimmers.

Your best chance of spotting an osprey in Miami is via boat. Look for them perched on navigational signs and mile markers, scanning for prey. As with many fish-eating coastal birds, pollution from DDT devastated their populations. Since the banning of this chemical pesticide, their numbers have been on the rise, but they're still listed as a species of special concern in Florida due to continued threats of habitat loss and degradation.

Willet

Tringa semipalmata

NATIVE

WHERE TO FIND THEM: Camino 305 Field Trips 1, 16–18, 24, and 25

Willet? Or won't it? The willet is in the family Scolopacidae along with sandpipers and phalaropes. For the amateur birder, this species can be quite difficult to properly identify since it looks like any other common shorebird. Its coloring is rather bland, usually grays and browns, but its plumage can change depending on the season. There are even two subspecies, eastern and western willets, with the eastern counterpart being darker and smaller than its western cousin. When these birds open their wings, however, identification gets easier. Look for a white band on the middle wing feathers (called greater primary coverts). Willets mostly eat aquatic insects and crustaceans but have been known to dabble with fish and vegetation.

Insects and Arachnids

Eastern Cicada Killer

Sphecius speciosus

NATIVE

WHERE TO FIND THEM: Camino 305 Field Trips 1, 6–8, 16–18, and 22–25

Cicadas are a type of winged insect that look like big, inflated grasshoppers. Even if you've never seen a cicada, you've almost certainly heard one. In spring and summer, adults emerge from underground pupae, climbing high up into trees where swarms of them begin to chirp loudly in an effort to attract a mate. They can be maddeningly loud, sometimes forcing people to abandon camping spots. But campers have an unlikely ally: wasps.

Poor, underappreciated wasps have the unfair reputation as the psychopaths of the insect world. Though many species can sting, they usually only do so if they or their nests are

threatened. Like the ladybird beetle, wasps are incredibly beneficial predatory insects who keep the populations of pests in balance. The eastern cicada killer is one such predatory wasp. They are tricky to identify on color alone, since they share their amber, yellow, and black color scheme with many other species. But cicada killers are diggers, so if you see a wasp emerging from or digging a burrow in sandy soil, you've got your ID. Female adult wasps eat nectar from flowers, but they hunt cicadas for their young. Once a female catches a cicada, she paralyzes it with venom and drags it into her burrow. She then lays her eggs in the cicada's carcass so her larvae will have a nutritious meal when they hatch. Wasps may seem scary, but at least the cicada killer helps keep the noise down.

No-See-Ums

Culicoides species

NATIVE

WHERE TO FIND THEM: All Camino 305 Field Trips

No-see-ums are always in competition with mosquitoes over who can make an outdoor trip more unpleasant for humans. Also known as biting midges, these miniscule flies received their colloquial name because, whether they're flying around or actually landing on you, they are really hard to see! You wouldn't think something so small could give such a noticeable bite, but you sure do feel them. Female no-see-ums, like mosquitoes, suck blood from other animals before laying their eggs. Their bite can be compared to a tiny but noticeable pinprick, not necessarily the most painful experience, but definitely irritating. Couple that with the fact that no-see-ums like to swarm, and suddenly your kayaking trip involves a lot more arm and leg slapping than you might have hoped for. Remember that these flies are most active in the early morning, evening, and on overcast days, so if you're hanging around a coastal area at those times, we recommend you plan accordingly.

Fish

Atlantic Needlefish

Strongylura marina

NATIVE

WHERE TO FIND THEM: Camino 305 Field Trips 1, 2, 6–8, 16–18, and 22–25

Let's get one thing straight (pun intended if you've ever seen one of these fish), Atlantic needlefish don't have needles. Their family name, Beloniformes, comes from the Greek word *belone*, which means "needle." Long and thin, with a forked tail, this indigenous, aquatic species uses its flexible body and pointed, equal-length jaws full of tiny teeth to hunt for smaller fish near the surface. Their ability to control salinity within their bodies allows them to move from ocean to coastal streams and various bodies of freshwater. If you look at the surface of the water in shallow bays, marinas, or calm open ocean out of the surf zone, you might see what looks like a highly reflective, silver pen cutting through the water. Chances are, you're looking at the Atlantic needlefish.

 Fun Fact

Sailfish have been known to swim at the surface with only their dorsal fin breaching the water.

Atlantic Sailfish

Istiophorus albicans

NATIVE

WHERE TO FIND THEM: Not Found at Any Camino 305 Field Trips

The title of Florida's state saltwater fish belongs to the fastest fish in the ocean.

Conservation Connection

Sailfish are protected under the management of the National Marine Fisheries Service (NMFS), through the Magnuson-Stevens Fishery Conservation and Management Act (MSA), and all US commercial fishing vessels are prohibited from selling, retaining, or purchasing them. MSA arranges fisheries into regions that meet regularly and use catch data and full participation from fishers to determine catch limits for certain species. Implemented by the US Congress in 1976, the legislation has been amended twice—in 1996 and 2007—and continues to undergo revisions to ensure it is effective in managing fish stocks.

A member of the billfish family, the carnivorous sailfish gets its name from the large, sail-like dorsal fin that stretches from its head to the base of its caudal fin. Reaching up to eleven feet and more than 200 pounds, sailfish have an elongated, spear-like upper jaw. They prefer open water, where they can swim at nearly seventy miles per hour while hunting—you're not likely to encounter one while snorkeling in the shallows. Sailfish are not particularly valued for their meat, but they promise a thrilling catch for sport fishers seeking a big offshore battle.

Blue Chromis

Chromis cyanea

NATIVE

WHERE TO FIND THEM: Camino 305 Field Trips 24 and 25

This common reef dweller is a beautiful, brilliant blue. The dorsal portion of its body and the top and bottom of its deeply forked caudal fin are black, making it look as though the fish has been outlined with a black marker. It's a common aquarium fish for a reason: it's very pretty. At a maximum size of four inches, it prefers to remain inshore near the ocean floor in areas associated with rocks and coral reefs and can live at depths of up to ninety feet. A planktivore, this damselfish is often found hovering above reefs picking plankton out of the water column.

Bluestriped Grunt

Haemulon sciurus

NATIVE

WHERE TO FIND THEM: Camino 305 Field Trips 1, 2, 6, 7, 16–18, and 22–25

So numerous are these schooling grunts that they make up a significant portion of Florida's Coral Reef biomass. Their bright, horizontal blue stripes make them well deserving of their common name, but this pattern, and their iridescent yellow base color, are shared with several other species of grunt, so to identify the bluestriped grunt correctly, look for their black caudal fin and rear dorsal fins.

Grunts have special teeth, called pharyngeal teeth, deep within their throats. When the teeth grind together, the sound is amplified by their air bladder and is so noticeable it earns the whole group of fish their name. In general, grunts have deeper forked tails than snappers and lack canine teeth. Bluestriped grunts are likely to be found schooling together with other grunt species in mangrove forests, coral reefs, or seagrass beds, foraging for bivalves, crustaceans, and smaller fish.

Bonefish

Albula vulpes

NATIVE

WHERE TO FIND THEM: Camino 305 Field Trips 24 and 25

If its name filled your head with images of swimming skeletons, the bonefish might disappoint you. Its name comes from its high number of bones plus its silver skin that displays parallel, sort of bony-looking streaks along the body—in short, a normal-looking fish with a spooky name. Bonefish hang around sandy bottoms and mangroves, preying on shrimps, crabs, snails, and various fish species they find in shallow flats on rising tides. Their inferior mouths (a mouth that is pointed downward) are typical of bottom feeders, and their conical noses that extend beyond the mandible (lower jaw) make them easy to identify.

They are considered a prized sportfish among local anglers because of their elusiveness and ghostlike appearance. However, a 2013 regulation passed by Florida Fish and Wildlife Conservation Commission (FWC) now prohibits keeping any bonefish caught.

Checkered Puffer Fish

Sphoeroides testudineus

NATIVE

WHERE TO FIND THEM: Camino 305 Field Trips 1, 2, 6–8, 16–18, and 22–25

Also called toadies, these puffer fish are common to the shallow bays, inlets, and canals of South Florida, but their native range extends along the coastline of the eastern United States and south to Brazil. They have a high tolerance for changes in salinity, so any body of saline or brackish water with a grassy or sandy bottom can host these common, black-spotted locals. The checkered puffer can employ a nifty defensive strategy—inflating its body with either water or air to dramatically increase its size and become sphere shaped, which usually deters any would-be predator. Combine that with an aggressive, predatory behavior of its own and a strong beak-like mouth capable of crushing the shells of crabs, bivalves, and barnacles, and you have a marine species built to survive in the 305. Rhyme intended.

Fun Fact

Anglers be wary. Although its flesh is edible, this puffer contains tetrodotoxin in its reproductive organs, intestines, skin, and liver, which makes it highly poisonous if prepared improperly.

Cobia

Rachycentron canadum

NATIVE

WHERE TO FIND THEM: Camino 305 Field Trips 24 and 25

If a shark and a catfish decided to mate, the end result might resemble a cobia. With a maximum length of six feet, they are another of the larger fish species found in South Florida waters. Cobia are characterized by a long, shark-like, torpedo-shaped body with triangular fins that rigidly extend while swimming. As a result, they're commonly mistaken for juvenile sharks. However, it's not actually difficult to distinguish these fish from their cartilaginous cousins. First, their bottom jaw extends beyond the upper jaw, a trait uncommon to most shark species. Next, they have two darker bands extending from their snout to the base of their crescent-shaped caudal fin and a depressed head. When handling cobia, be careful of the row of sharp spines in front of their dorsal fins.

Little is known about species that hunt cobia for food (other than humans, of course), and beyond a few large species found with juvenile cobia in their stomachs, adult cobia don't seem to be a preferred lunch for other predators. Cobia themselves are incredibly efficient and opportunistic hunters with a wide variety of prey. They patrol near offshore reefs, docks, and even boats, and sometimes hunt in groups composed of dozens or more fish.

Common Snook

Centropomus undecimalis

NATIVE

WHERE TO FIND THEM: Camino 305 Field Trips 16–18 and 22–25

South Florida anglers consider the common snook a top-tier fish, both in their ability to fight when hooked and overall taste when cooked. Officially labeled as a gamefish, snook cannot be sold in the state of Florida and have a number of regulations that protect them, including slot limits (size range of caught fish), bag limits (number of fishes per person per day), and even seasons when they can't be fished at all. Large fish that can grow up to four feet long, common snook have a flattened, depressed forehead and a yellow-colored body with a black lateral line running from the head to the base of the caudal fin. They typically hang out in small groups in or around mangroves or in isolated locations near reefs. A common prey species for dolphins and large bird species, they act as predators themselves. Younger snooks feed on copepods (small crustaceans) before moving on to larger fish and shrimp at maturity.

 **Fun Fact**

Common snook are known as protandric hermaphrodites, which means they change sex after maturation; born male, they transition to female with age and size. Basically, the larger the fish, the higher likelihood of it being female.

Crevalle Jack

Caranx hippos

NATIVE

WHERE TO FIND THEM: Camino 305 Field Trips 24 and 25

Like most species in the jack family, the crevalle jack has a thin, streamlined body with silvery sides and large eyes. Two other distinguishing features can help you identify it. The first is the prominent black spot at the base of the pectoral fin and near the top of the gill cover. The second is a lack of scales on the chest, with the exception of one small patch in front of the pelvic fins. Crevalle jack is the only species of jack in the western Atlantic with this particular scale pattern. As a juvenile, it has dark, vertical bars along its sides, but those eventually fade away as the fish matures. As a pelagic hunter, the crevalle jack preys upon smaller fish, invertebrates, and crustaceans in the open ocean. Its small tail base and deeply forked caudal fin allow for quick bursts of speed. Unfortunately for the crevalle, speed often piques the interest of avid fishers, and this species is absolutely a draw for Miami's sport fishing world.

Doctorfish

Acanthurus chirurgus

NATIVE

WHERE TO FIND THEM: Camino 305 Field Trips 24 and 25

Unfortunately, unless there's an underwater medical university unknown to us, the doctorfish is not a licensed medical practitioner. It

gets its name from a sharp, scalpel-like spine located behind its caudal peduncle (the thin part of a fish's body just before the caudal fin). Biologists believe the fish use this spine as a defense against predators and other doctorfish when establishing territory or dominance. Inexperienced anglers attempting to handle this reef fish should exercise caution to avoid being nicked.

Despite their advanced weaponry, these otherwise peaceful vegetarians feed by grazing algae off hard reef surfaces all day long. This habit serves an incredibly important ecological function by limiting algae growth on corals. Though edible to humans, doctorfish are probably best left at the reef, as they've been known to cause ciguatera poisoning, which involves gastrointestinal issues and weakness for whoever is unlucky enough to contract it. Their typical coloring is a grayish blue with dark, vertical stripes along the sides of the body and several short light stripes trailing behind the eye. They are commonly confused with surgeonfish, which belong to the same taxonomic family, Acanthuridae, but lack the vertical bars. In the end, medical professionals do seem well represented on Florida's Coral Reef.

Dwarf Seahorse

Hippocampus zosterae

NATIVE

WHERE TO FIND THEM: Camino 305 Field Trips 1, 16–18, 24, and 25

You can lead a horse to water, and when you do, it will live there in the shallow seagrass beds of Miami. Pretty sure that's the phrase, right? The body of the dwarf seahorse (and seahorses in general) are unique from other fish. Vertically oriented, with an elongated, tubular snout and curled tail, the seahorse silhouette is a popular marine image. The dwarf seahorse's overall size is its best feature for identification. It's the third smallest seahorse in the world, growing to a maximum length of two inches. With an average lifespan of one year, *el caballito de mar* is not listed as endangered or threatened, but it still faces threats associated with habitat loss, oil spills, and energy exploitation.

Goliath Grouper

Epinephelus itajara

NATIVE

WHERE TO FIND THEM: Camino 305 Field Trips 24 and 25

The goliath grouper, or *guasa* in Spanish, is the largest fish on Florida's Coral Reef. Capable of growing more than seven feet long and over 700 pounds, the goliath grouper is a premier reef resident. As an apex predator, it maintains the ecosystem balance and is an indicator of a healthy reef. Though not typically aggressive toward divers, there have been a few documented occasions in which these giants have stolen the catch from both angler and spearfisher, highlighting the importance of maintaining an awareness of your surroundings during underwater activities. If you're ever unsure if a goliath grouper is uncomfortable around you during an encounter, listen for a low, almost rumbling noise created from the swim bladder and focus on body language tension.

In addition to rivaling David's biblical foe in size, the goliath grouper is also longer-lived. Reaching up to fifty years old under ideal conditions, the goliath grouper tolerates a variety of habitat conditions, including a depth of up to 150 feet and also brackish waters. Through a process called osmoregulation, it can maintain an ideal salt and water concentration within its body, regardless of external environmental conditions. Meanwhile, South Florida residents need a hat and boots if temperatures drop below 70 Fahrenheit.

Usually found looming in solitude near the ocean floor, goliath grouper are typically only social during the breeding season, between the warm months of July and September. Using the lunar cycle as a guide, these fish employ broadcast spawning, in which up to 100 males and females simultaneously release their sperm and eggs into the water column. Fertilized eggs casually drift with the current until they hatch. The goliath grouper is hermaphroditic; they begin life as female and transition to male as they mature.

As newly hatched groupers grow, their diet includes basically anything they can suck into their comically large mouths. They generate enough suction power to pull prey in whole—crustaceans, fish, and octopi are all on the menu—and any individual with the strength to try and escape the vacuum will be caught instead in thousands of grate-like teeth.

Once fully grown, goliath groupers are easy to identify by size alone, but there are other useful distinguishing characteristics for younger fish. To start, they possess small, distinctive, dark spots that resemble chicken pox across their body. Those, in combination with its blotchy coloring should suffice for identification.

Conservation Connection

Despite their massive size and seemingly untouchable apex predator status on the reef, goliath groupers nearly went extinct in South Florida's waters due to over-fishing. They take a long time to grow and mature, so fishery management councils moved to protect them from harvesting in Florida (and the rest of the southeast United States) in 1990. The International Union for Conservation of Nature (IUCN) currently lists them as vulnerable. Today, South Florida is one of the last reliable locations on the planet to see wild goliath groupers, and we as humans—their most formidable predator—need to continue preserving their populations through scientifically supported fishery management, habitat preservation, pollution reduction, and educational awareness.

Great Barracuda

Sphyraena barracuda

NATIVE

WHERE TO FIND THEM: Camino 305 Field Trips 1, 2, 6–8, 16–18, and 22–25

Great barracuda have quite the fearsome reputation. They have a habit of following snorkelers and, though it's rare, they will occasionally attack a human. They're not actually hunting humans—their behavior is natural curiosity combined with an innate attraction to shiny objects like jewelry that look like silvery fish. While at rest, they tend to rhythmically open and close their jaws, contributing to their threatening appearance, but this is merely a technique they use to help circulate water through their gills. Great barracuda are not listed as either vulnerable or endangered and occur worldwide in tropical waters. In addition to their slender body, large protruding teeth, and jutting lower jaw, it's the roughly twenty darkened bars along their sides that confirm identification. They frequent reefs and seagrass beds, often appearing to drift effortlessly, seeming not to swim at all.

Fun Fact

Great barracuda battle admirably when hooked on a fishing line but are often released when caught because eating them (specifically larger adults) could cause ciguatera poisoning. By preying on reef fish that have accumulated ciguatoxins through their plankton diet, apex predators such as the great barracuda can build up large amounts of the toxin in their flesh. Effects of ciguatera poisoning on humans can last for weeks and have been known to cause stomach pains, weakness, and sensation confusion.

Hogfish

Lachnolaimus maximus

NATIVE

WHERE TO FIND THEM: Camino 305 Field Trips 16, 17, 18, 24, and 25

Between the porkfish, hogfish, and cowfish, those in charge of naming fish seem to have been inspired by farm life. A member of the wrasse family, the hogfish earned its name for its elongated snout, its habit of digging in the sand for food (mollusks and crustaceans), and the three spines on its back that somewhat resemble the mane of its terrestrial warthog counterpart. Prized in the world of spearfishing, they are commonly served in restaurants. (Try a hogfish sandwich when you're in the Keys.) Protogynous hermaphrodites, they are born female and change to male later in life. Their color can vary, and though they sometimes have a black spot near the end of the dorsal fin, it can disappear as the fish matures.

For a clear-cut identification feature, focus on the eyes, specifically the iris, which remains red throughout a hogfish's life.

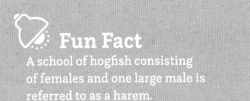

Fun Fact
A school of hogfish consisting of females and one large male is referred to as a harem.

Lookdown

Selene vomer

NATIVE

WHERE TO FIND THEM: Camino 305 Field Trips 16, 24, and 25

Lookdown seems like more of a command than a fish name, but it makes sense once you see how these fish can hover in a forward-tilting position while swimming, which makes them appear to be looking down. These iridescent, coastal-water fish live within estuaries, where they hover above sandy bottoms hunting for crustaceans, mollusks, and smaller fish. While snorkeling, you're most likely to spot them around docks and bridges, but you'll have to look carefully because they have the ability to camouflage themselves through a manipulation of polarized light. The physics are somewhat complex, but essentially, lookdowns can create a sort of mirror effect with available sunlight, which helps them blend into their watery surroundings.

Lookdowns are a kind of jack, a group that includes crevalle jacks, blue runners (*Caranx crysos*), and yellow jacks (*Carangoides bartholomaei*). They have thin, silvery, almost circular bodies just under a foot in length, which earned their genus the name *Selene*, a Greek word for "moon," but their enormous, steep head and extended dorsal and anal fins distinguish them from other similar species within the jack family.

Mahi-Mahi

Coryphaena hippurus

NATIVE

WHERE TO FIND THEM: Camino 305
Field Trip 24

¡Es un dorado! If you've ever seen a dorado in person, you'll immediately understand how its name, Spanish for "golden," perfectly describes one of Florida's most well-known species. Other common names include mahi-mahi or dolphinfish. To be clear, mahi-mahi are in no way related to the marine mammal. The origins of the name dolphinfish are somewhat vague, but there are a few theories, one of which points out the high-pitched noises both species make while underwater. The name mahi-mahi, on the other hand, is easy to trace—it translates directly from the Hawaiian language and means "strong strong," a reference to their incredible ability to reproduce.

Mahi-mahi's elongated body, forked tail, and dorsal fin that essentially runs the length of its body enable this open-water predator to reach speeds just under sixty miles per hour and depths of up to 300 feet. This is ideal considering that their preferred prey of flying fish, juvenile tunas, jacks, mackerel, and various species of cephalopods are super speedy. Given their preference for open water, it's incredibly unlikely, though not completely impossible, that you'll hook a dolphinfish from the shores of South Beach. These high-speed hunters are highly valued in the

Fun Fact

Mahi-mahi is one of only two species within the family Coryphaenidae. Its cousin, the pompano dolphinfish (*Coryphaena equiselis*), has similar features but is much smaller. With shorter pectoral fins and a maximum length of 2.5 feet, pompano dolphinfish are commonly mistaken for juvenile mahi-mahi. Pompano Beach, Florida is said to be named after the smaller dolphinfish.

fishing industry for both their taste and prize sport fishing status—adults are an impressive catch, with the potential to reach lengths up to six feet. Their annual monetary value to the state of Florida is measured in the hundreds of millions. Fortunately, mahi-mahi are one of the fastest-growing fish in the ocean, which, combined with their short lifespan (no more than five years) has allowed their population to remain relatively healthy despite the numbers harvested each year. Various studies have concluded that these fish remain a sustainable option, and the same characteristics that make them good for sport fishing also make them a strong candidate for fish farming.

As for the beautiful blues and striking greens for which dolphinfish are famous, they are a little more complicated than you might realize. In a natural setting, these fish are quite colorful, catching the sunlight and reflecting it into multiple eye-catching colors, but when the fish is stressed, especially after being hooked, the colors change dramatically, becoming more vibrant before eventually fading away to silver. Mahi-mahi are sexually dimorphic, meaning the sexes have different physical characteristics. Males have large, blunt heads, while females have smoother, less dramatically curved heads.

Mutton Snapper

Lutjanus analis

NATIVE

WHERE TO FIND THEM: Camino 305 Field Trips 1, 2, 16–18, and 22–25

If you have dined anywhere in South Florida that serves locally caught fish, you've seen mutton snapper on the menu. It, along with the heavily fished red snapper (*Lutjanus campechanus*), is highly sought after by anglers and spearfishers. Commercial-level fishing operations caused the population to decline, so in 2021 the International Union for Conservation of Nature (IUCN) listed this species as near threatened.

Snappers in general tend to have several features in common: a triangular head, single dorsal fin, and upturned mouth. The mutton snapper's most identifiable feature is a distinctive black spot on its upper back. They also have a blue line underneath their eyes positioned similarly to the eye black that football players wear to reduce glare. Though mostly a nocturnal hunter, mutton snappers can still be seen during the day; they're usually solitary as opposed to in schools.

Fun Fact

Ever wonder how snappers got their name? When hooked on a line, they will aggressively snap their jaws open and closed, showing their large, canine teeth.

Porkfish

Anisotremus virginicus

NATIVE

WHERE TO FIND THEM: Camino 305 Field Trips 1, 2, 16–18, and 22–25

With its snout-like nose and pink curly tail, the porkfish. . . No, wait. Erase that image from your mind. Although entertaining to imagine, the porkfish doesn't actually look like a piggy—it just sounds like one, making the characteristic sounds that earn grunts their name.

Fun Fact

The Spanish name for the porkfish is *arroz con coco*, which directly translates as "rice with coconut." Interesting for a fish that purportedly tastes like ham.

Porkfish are a nocturnal schooling fish with a yellow head and two distinctive, black bands that run vertically over each eye and behind its gill plates. They're the only grunt species in the Atlantic Ocean with this color pattern. Juveniles have two dark lines running parallel to their bodies, but the lines tend to fade away as they mature. A common aquarium fish, they have a higher dorsal profile than other grunts. Porkfish eat mollusks and crustaceans, while larger snappers, groupers, and sharks (and of course humans) consider porkfish a farm-to-table lunch option.

Queen Angelfish

Holacanthus ciliaris

NATIVE

WHERE TO FIND THEM: Camino 305 Field Trips 24 and 25

When you think "queen," do you think Beyoncé, Freddie Mercury, or Elizabeth II? If you're oceanically inclined, your answer may instead involve the vivid sapphire and citrine colors of the queen angelfish. The crown of this aptly named reef monarch is a prominent black spot that's bordered and speckled by brilliant blue scales. The queen angelfish has the graceful trailing fins typical of angelfish in shades of vibrant yellow, striking orange, and sometimes purple, a combination that seems like it could be too loud for the ocean but is actually very effective when it comes to camouflaging on a coral reef. Made up primarily of sponges and algae, the diet of this royal reef-dweller is humbly frugal, however, they will also sometimes feed on corals, jellyfish, and sea fans.

Queen Parrotfish

Scarus vetula

NATIVE

WHERE TO FIND THEM: Camino 305 Field Trips 24 and 25

These colorful reef-dwellers have earned their unique name. With powerful, beak-like jaws and a swimming behavior that relies on their pectoral fins, parrotfish really do resemble a bird in flight. The queen parrotfish, unquestionable ruler of them all (the authors voted), is distinguishable by the vibrant blue and green surrounding her mouth.

More than a dozen species of parrotfish live in South Florida, and it can be difficult to differentiate between them, because they all range in size and display dramatic differences between juveniles and adults. The parrotfish life cycle is divided into three parts: juvenile, initial, and terminal (adults). Depending on the species, the fish may look different at each phase—different shape, different color patterns, different markings. Only sexually mature males reach the terminal phase. Some parrotfish are hermaphroditic—females may choose to enter the terminal phase and thus change sex to male (usually as a result of an environmental cue), others simply remain in the initial phase as the same sex throughout their entire life. It's not uncommon for a parrotfish under suitable conditions to remain in one specific area for its entire life.

 Fun fact

Parrotfish are one of the main producers of sand in tropical waters. The beautiful white beach sand often showcased in resort commercials most likely contains a respectable percentage of parrotfish poop. While nibbling on algae and coral polyps, they often scoop up pieces of limestone, which are then ground up by the fish's bony, plate-like teeth, swallowed, and ... let's just say the rest is sandy.

Red Lionfish

Pterois volitans

INVASIVE

WHERE TO FIND THEM: Camino 305 Field Trips 24 and 25

At this moment, there may not be a more all-consuming invasive marine species in Miami. The lionfish's introduction into Florida has spread misery throughout our ecosystems. Native to the Indo-Pacific and Red Sea, they were first documented around Dania Beach in the 1980s, and their population numbers have skyrocketed over the last few decades as a result of few predators, quick maturity, lots of offspring, and an indiscriminate diet.

Striped with reds and browns on the body and white bands on the head with extended rays on their fins, they are easy to identify. Typically about a foot long, they prefer habitats with crevices and ledges, but have acclimated to most habitats around Florida. These predatory ambush hunters have a big impact on native reef fish and ecosystems. They compete with other predatory fish such as groupers and snappers and eat the fish responsible for removing algae on the reef, disrupting the reef's environmental balance and imperiling its long-term health and sustainability. When hunting, red lionfish outstretch their fins to create a wide "mane" and slowly pursue their prey until they can corner it. They also blow water on their prey in an attempt to disorient it. In South Florida, the red lionfish diet includes as many as seventy marine species. Mature red lionfish females reproduce year-round and can lay as many as two millions eggs per year.

They may not look like something you want on your dinner plate, but lionfish are not only safe to eat but very tasty. If you remove their spines, there is no risk for envenomation and you're left with a delicious, white, flaky fish that can be prepared however you like. The difference between poisonous and venomous can be confusing, but here's a trick to help you remember: Think of a poisonous frog and venomous snake. If you bite the poisonous frog, that's bad, but if the frog bites you, that's safe. If the venomous snake bites you, that's bad, but if you bite the snake, that's safe. Weird, but safe. Don't bite snakes.

Although this fish is edible, you should be very cautious when handling them. The sting from one of their eighteen spines can last for days and has been known to cause paralysis, intense pain, and respiratory difficulty. Their venom is a combination of a neurotransmitter called acetylcholine, a neuromuscular toxin, and a protein. After puncturing the skin, the spines deliver venom through grooves; although it's not deadly, it's definitely a pain most would gladly avoid.

Conservation Connection

If you have the chance to remove these fish from the environment, take it. Whether angling or spearfishing, any opportunity to help mitigate the ever-growing red lionfish population is encouraged. Although there is some evidence of larger shark and grouper species adapting to hunt lionfish, help is desperately needed from anyone willing to lend a spine-resistant-gloved hand. Without intervention, Florida's Coral Reef is likely to be permanently, irreparably damaged. Reef Environmental Education Foundation and other groups organize regular lionfish derbies in which spear fishers can win prizes for the most and the largest lionfish caught. These derbies bring attention to the lionfish epidemic in a fun setting while also encouraging their consumption.

Scrawled Cowfish

Acanthostracion quadricornis

`NATIVE`

WHERE TO FIND THEM: Camino 305 Field Trips 1, 16–18, and 22–25

One quick look at a cowfish—the horns above the eyes, the large-lipped mouth—and the origin of its name is immediately obvious. A member of the boxfish family, this square-shaped seagrass dweller possesses bony armor and the ability to change color to camouflage with its surroundings. Combined with a vibrant yellow body covered in scrawled bluish markings and two sharp spines in front of the anal fin, the cowfish's defenses should give potential predators pause—most just keep moooving on.

Fun Fact

The body armor of the scrawled cowfish is made of hexagonal scales that are fused together to form a protective carapace.

Sergeant Major

Abudefduf saxatilis

`NATIVE`

WHERE TO FIND THEM: Camino 305 Field Trips 1, 16–18, and 22–25

A member of the damselfish family, sergeant major sounds as if it should command all other fish in the sea, ruling the ocean with an iron fist and a circular flat-brim hat. In reality, this fish, like most damselfishes, is quite small, maxing out at around seven inches. But don't let their size fool you. Territorial and known for aggressively defending their nests, they zip to and fro in response to an intruder, regardless of its size. If you happen upon a sergeant major's nest, be careful of any exposed skin, lest you wind up dishonorably discharged from the area with a nibble to your ankle. Very common in most marine habitats in South Florida, the five vertical black bars on their white body make this prison-escapee-looking fish easy to identify. Conveniently, juveniles share a similar coloration and pattern. Sergeant majors (and damselfish in general) possess a single nostril on each side of the snout as opposed to two nostrils like most other fish. Although incredibly difficult to distinguish underwater, that's a detail scientists rely on for correct identification.

Bonnethead Shark

Sphyrna tiburo

NATIVE ENDANGERED

WHERE TO FIND THEM: Camino 305 Field Trips 16–18, 24, and 25

You'd have a hard time finding a more adorable shark species than the internationally endangered bonnethead shark. Their shovel-shaped heads and four-foot length make them look like miniature hammerhead sharks as they school together in shallow estuaries or bays feeding on crustaceans. Essentially harmless to humans, they have a noticeable hierarchy in their schools and tend to follow warmer water with their migration patterns. If you know what to look for, it's not too difficult to tell male bonnetheads from females. The cephalofoils (those wide, flattened heads hammerhead sharks are famous for) are different between sexes; females' are broader and males' have a bulge along the back edge. Take a paddleboard or kayak around the mangroves on a clear day in Miami, and you might get lucky enough to see one zipping quickly throughout the seagrass beds.

Bull Shark

Carcharhinus leucas

NATIVE

WHERE TO FIND THEM: Camino 305 Field Trips 1, 16–18, and 23–25

The bull shark might have one of the most unwarranted reputations of any species in the ocean. Labeled as a vicious predator, this opportunistic hunter's only sin is its affinity for watery habitats commonly frequented by humans. While most sharks are restricted to saltwater habitats, bull sharks can recycle salt in their body through their kidneys and retain additional salt in their tails through the use of specialized glands, allowing them to swim in both salt and freshwater habitats. In the United States, bull sharks have been documented more than 1,500 miles up the Mississippi River. Although only listed as near threatened by the International Union for Conservation of Nature (IUCN), their prefer-ence for shallower, inshore waters makes them vulnerable to human impact. From becoming bycatch in the commercial fishing industry to being targeted for shark fins and leather products, this stout, small-eyed shark has a lot more reason to fear humans than vice versa.

 Fun Fact

The shark responsible for a series of attacks in New Jersey in 1916 is thought to have been a bull shark, making this species the inspiration for the book and eventual block-buster movie *Jaws*.

Caribbean Reef Shark

Carcharhinus perezi

NATIVE

WHERE TO FIND THEM: Camino 305 Field Trips 24 and 25

If someone were to ask you to draw a shark, odds are your sketch would closely resemble this species. Commonly referred to as just *tiburón* in Spanish (the word for shark), this species is simultaneously iconic and also lacking in highly distinguishable features. It has some darkened, dusky coloration on its fins, but that's common on other shark species, too. It's quite common around Florida's Coral Reef, and if you're snorkeling around a reef or scuba diving in the shallows of Miami and you see a shark that isn't a nurse shark, it's probably this species. These bottom-dwellers have been known to lay motionless on the ocean floor when they're not hunting their preferred bony fish prey. They are prohibited from commercial fisheries in US waters.

Lemon Shark

Negaprion brevirostris

NATIVE

WHERE TO FIND THEM: Camino 305 Field Trips 1, 16–18, 24, and 25

These large coastal sharks generally cruise casually through the blue-green tropical shallows of Florida's inshore waters, but they have also been known to inhabit deeper, cooler waters during the day. To identify them, look for a first and second dorsal fin that are similar in size and appearance. Their size (up to ten feet long), teeth, and blunted snouts create a chaotic, somewhat menacing visual, but they're not particularly sour toward humans—they'd rather avoid you in favor of smaller fish, rays, and crustaceans. Though there aren't

any orange or apple sharks, the Pacific Ocean is home to a banana wrasse (*Thalassoma lutescens*) and a pineapplefish (*Cleidopus gloriamaris*) so the lemon shark has good, fruity, company around the globe.

Nurse Shark

Ginglymostoma cirratum

NATIVE

WHERE TO FIND THEM: Camino 305 Field Trips 1, 16–18, and 23–25

Though it may look different from the typical shark shape you're expecting, the nurse shark is likely to be the most common shark you'll encounter in Miami. They belong to a group known as carpet sharks (the same group as whale sharks!), which have a few easily identifiable characteristics: a long upper lobe on their

caudal fin, a dorsal fin situated on the back half of the body, and small eyes set behind the mouth. The nurse shark, specifically, has catlike barbels on its upper lip and two dorsal fins of nearly equal size. A benthic (sea floor) species, they have a preference for shallow water and spend most of the day in groups, basking virtually motionless on the ocean floor (unlike other sharks, they don't need to move to breathe). In the evening, they hunt stingrays, crustaceans, and other critters commonly found in the sand.

Sheepshead

Archosargus probatocephalus

NATIVE

WHERE TO FIND THEM: Camino 305 Field Trips 24 and 25

This fish is named for its teeth, which purportedly resemble those of a sheep. (some have said they look more like they belong in a human's mouth). You probably won't notice the teeth if you spot the sheepshead just

swimming around. One of the easier fish to identify, it has prominent vertical black bars running along the side of its body, earning it a second common name, convict fish, for its similarity to striped prison uniforms. An omnivorous member of the porgy family, sheepshead spend time near sea walls, rocky areas, and dock pilings. A lack of saltwater doesn't deter them; they can be found in brackish waters and lagoons. Though most anglers would be ecstatic to hook this prized fish for dinner, they must beware the spines on the dorsal and anal fins and gill covers.

Smalltooth Sawfish

Pristis pectinata

NATIVE ENDANGERED

WHERE TO FIND THEM: Camino 305 Field Trip 24

Even though it has been protected in Florida since the early 1990s, the smalltooth sawfish

is one of the most endangered species on the planet as a result of overfishing and

habitat destruction. Found in shallow bays or mangroves, they are protected under the Convention on International Trade in Endangered Species of Wild Fauna and Flora (CITES), so trade is illegal and transporting requires special permits. They were also one of the first marine species to be listed under the Endangered Species Act of 1973. Hunted for years for food, liver oil, fins, and prize displays, smalltooth sawfish continue to decline in numbers despite all their protections. Today, reliable numbers are only found in the waters from South Florida to the Bahamas.

One look at the sawfish and its name becomes quite obvious, but before we can discuss that elongated snout we need to talk about its body shape. Although its mouth and gill slits are located ventrally like a ray's, its body and fins resemble a shark. Is it a flattened shark or an inflated ray? Drum roll please. . . It's a ray. Similar in appearance to its cousin the largetooth sawfish (*Pristis pristis*), the smalltooth sawfish has its fins in slightly different spots and about twenty-five teeth on its rostrum. Rostrum is the special name for the sawfish's most obvious feature: its elongated snout lined with teeth. These teeth are actually a type of specialized scale—they don't grow

Fun Fact

Sawfishes are ovoviviparous, meaning their eggs remain within the female's body until hatching, and then the baby sharks are birthed live. To protect the mother during birth, the babies' long rostrums (which are fully formed at hatching) are sheathed in a thick tissue that covers the sharp rostrum scales.

back if lost or removed. Useful for impaling fish, the rostrum also helps sawfish dig in the sand. It contains sensors called ampullae of Lorenzini, which allow these rays to detect electrical fields created by living creatures, helping them find prey.

Smalltooth sawfish can grow up to eighteen feet long, with their rostrum alone exceeding five feet. At first glance, they might look quite intimidating, but considering their current population numbers, any opportunity to encounter such an incredible animal should be met with reverence and admiration.

Conservation Connection

Headquartered at Florida International University, the Tropical Conservation Institute aims to protect imperiled species like the smalltooth sawfish across the world's tropics through scientifically backed projects.

Spotted Eagle Ray

Aetobatus narinari

NATIVE

WHERE TO FIND THEM: Camino 305 Field Trips 1, 16–18, and 23–25

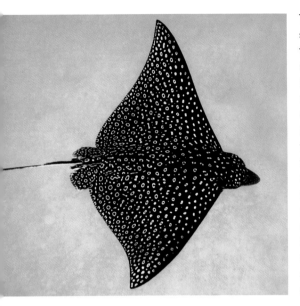

Though they share similar features with stingrays, these diamond-shaped shark relatives have a few obvious differences. Eagle rays have dorsal fins, which stingrays lack. Both have venomous tail spines, but the eagle ray's is located at the base of its tail near the dorsal fin. An eagle ray's tail is more whip-like and can grow much longer than the width of the pectoral fins—no easy feat considering the eagle ray's size. Mature adults can grow up to seventeen feet long, ten feet wide, and over 500 pounds. Their coloring is distinctive, with a light underside and a dark dorsal side scattered with light spots. Though you're most likely to see them in shallow bays or estuaries, they actually spend a majority of their time swimming in open-water schools near the surface of the water.

 Fun Fact

Eagle rays soar through the water like they're flying, but if they need to evade predators, they will actually fly through the air, leaping out of the water as a defense mechanism.

Spotted Moray

Gymnothorax moringa

NATIVE

WHERE TO FIND THEM: Camino 305 Field Trips 24 and 25

Although the green moray eel (*Gymnothorax funebris*) is incredibly common in South Florida, the spotted moray may be even more so. While diving or snorkeling on a reef or bay,

you'll probably come across the spotted moray discreetly poking its head from a crevice or cave while waiting for unsuspecting invertebrates or crustaceans to amble on by. This second largest moray eel is a nocturnal ambush predator with two sets of jaws for successful hunting. The first set grabs prey and the second (located in the throat) pulls the meal into the stomach. Their bodies are long and snake-like, with one, long, continuous fin along its length top and bottom. With no pectoral fins, they rely on a sinuous rhythmic motion to slice through the water.

 **Fun Fact**

Moray eels continuously open and close their mouths, a behavior that appears threatening (especially when it shows off their notable teeth) but is actually just their method of breathing. The movement pushes water through their gills, helping them get enough oxygen.

Striped Mullet

Mugil cephalus

`NATIVE`

WHERE TO FIND THEM: Camino 305 Field Trips 1, 2, 6–8, 16–18, and 23–25

While walking along Miami Beach or one of its many docks or fishing piers, you're likely to notice a school of fish swimming near the surface. Skittish but synchronized, they have dark-colored tails, almost as if each fish has been gently dunked, tail first, into a vat of ink. This is the striped mullet, also called the flathead gray mullet. As juveniles, they school together feeding on algae and tiny marine life just beneath the waves. Adults prefer freshwater and can grow to almost four feet long.

With a high tolerance for salinity changes, mullet live worldwide in tropical and temperate waters and are both a food source for humans and bait for larger fish. They are catadromous, which means they spawn in saltwater but spend a portion of their lives in freshwater. If you're lucky you might see these mullet leaping from the water, something they do both to evade predators and to expose their gills to higher levels of oxygen after swimming in low-oxygen areas.

Sunshinefish

Chromis insolata

NATIVE

WHERE TO FIND THEM: Camino 305 Field Trips 24 and 25

Although the blue chromis and brown chromis (*Chromis multilineata*) are more common in Miami, we had to include the sunshinefish in this guide to the Sunshine State. This planktivorous damselfish earns its glorious name from its appearance as a juvenile. With an illuminating bright yellow on the dorsal side and a bluish purple color on its belly, it looks like a Florida sunrise. As the fish matures, the sun sets on this coloration; greens and browns replace the yellows and purples, and the rear dorsal fin and tail become white, the primary identifying features of the mature sunshinefish. What tends to remain consistent as the fish matures is a bright blue line running from above its eye to its snout, but this feature is not a guarantee. Sunshinefish dwell on deeper reefs, often living in small groups near the ocean floor.

Tarpon

Megalops atlanticus

NATIVE

WHERE TO FIND THEM: Camino 305 Field Trips 1, 16–18 and 22–25

One of the largest fish you will likely encounter in South Florida, with a maximum length of eight feet and a weight pushing 350 pounds, tarpon, colloquially called the silver king, have been known to jump from the water and injure anglers who have hooked them. Mostly inedible due to their high number of bones and strong odor, tarpon are catch and release only in Florida, but that doesn't disqualify them from being a huge pull in recreational fishing due to their fight on the hook. During the day, they school, waiting until nighttime to actively feed. Young tarpon feed by absorbing nutrients directly from the water in a process

Conservation Connection

Both bonefish and tarpon are highly prized sporting fish. Many anglers have come to realize, however, that populations of these fish can only be maintained if their habitats are also maintained. The Bonefish and Tarpon Trust aims to achieve just that, ensuring that the stocks of these fish remain for future generations by advocating for the protection of the seagrasses and corals that they rely on.

called integumentary absorption but transition to eating plankton as they grow, and eventually switch to a completely carnivorous diet at maturity. Thanks to a special type of tissue in their swim bladder and a specialized duct to the esophagus, tarpon can get oxygen directly from air, which allows them to survive in oxygen-poor waters. If habitat conditions are suitable, individual tarpon will reside in one specific location for multiple years. Tarpon are found in a very wide range of habitats, from the deepest areas of a coral reef to mangroves and estuarine areas. Besides their enormous size and large silver scales, their upturned, superior (facing up) mouths are one of their most identifiable features.

Trumpetfish

Aulostomus maculatus

NATIVE

WHERE TO FIND THEM: Camino 305 Field Trips 24 and 25

This long, thin fish looks as though you could snatch it from the water and immediately join a marching band. Color-changing camouflage experts, trumpetfish drift vertically, with their heads facing the ocean floor, to blend in with the sea rod stalks, sea fans, and sea whips of their reef habitat. They are ambush predators who use their wide mouths to suction in prey; any unsuspecting small fish or crustacean that passes beneath on the ocean floor is immediately vacuumed up. Two helpful identifying characteristics are a barbel near the tip of their jaw and a lack of teeth on their upper jaw.

 Fun Fact

Trumpetfish courtship involves an intricate dance and color changes.

Yellow Stingray

Urobatis jamaicensis

NATIVE

WHERE TO FIND THEM: Camino 305 Field Trips 1, 16–18, and 23–25

These yellowish stingrays are commonly found along beaches and near coral reefs hunting for crustaceans, worms, and bivalves. They have a disc-shaped body, no dorsal fin, and a wingspan up to fourteen inches. Though not aggressive toward humans, stingrays do possess a venomous barbed spine on their back near their caudal fin lobes. They spend most of their time in shallow water with sandy bottoms, often burying themselves with a layer of sand while they wait to ambush prey. During mating, male yellow stingrays will bite the pectoral fin of a female so he can swing around and flip himself underneath her. She will have a litter of roughly three to four young called pups.

 Fun Fact

Ever heard of the stingray shuffle? If you spend enough time on Miami beaches you will grow to appreciate it. This method of shuffling your feet along the ocean bottom instead of lifting and stepping is effective at getting stingrays to swim along peacefully instead of defending themselves after you step on them. If you're unlucky and get stung, don't worry; the sting is painful, but not life threatening.

Yellowfin Mojarra

Gerres cinereus

NATIVE

WHERE TO FIND THEM: Camino 305 Field Trips 1, 16–18, 24, and 25

If you're going to read a Miami species guide, then you must learn to pronounce this species properly. Hint, Js sounds like Hs, and don't forget to roll the Rs. The International Union for Conservation of Nature (IUCN) lists yellowfin mojarra status as least concern, which definitely checks out in Miami—it is one of the most common species you'll encounter while swimming at the beaches here. Their bright, compressed bodies with yellow fins can be quite difficult to distinguish in the water, so it's the seven-to-eight faint, darkened vertical bars along the sides of the body that are most useful for identification. They're rarely observed near reefs, instead inhabiting shallow, open flats of sand, seagrass, or rubble. You're likely to see them schooling inshore or digging in the sand as they're foraging for their next meal of small invertebrates such as sea stars and sea cucumbers. They also enter brackish waters on occasion.

Yellowhead Jawfish

Opistognathus aurifrons

NATIVE

WHERE TO FIND THEM: Camino 305 Field Trips 24 and 25

Quick, what color do you think this fish's head is? Red? Purple? I guess we can't get anything past you. It's yellow—but a duller yellow that easily blends in with a sandy background. These five-inch-long diggers are known for endlessly working on their burrows, using their wide mouths to move sand and pebbles. Their burrows tend to be just large enough for their bodies; they provide protection when the fish are feeling threatened and receive vehement defense by the homeowner if necessary. Never too far from their burrow, these fish can be observed hovering above their homes in a vertical position, waiting for tiny meals to come within range. At a moment's notice, yellowhead jawfish can return to their burrow, tail first, until the coast is clear. Sometimes, the only visible thing is their tiny, yellow head suspiciously peeking out of the sand.

 **Fun Fact**

Yellowhead jawfish males protect fertilized eggs by incubating them within their mouths until they hatch. Unfortunately, the males are unable to feed during this time.

Invertebrates

Caribbean Reef Squid

Sepioteuthis sepioidea

NATIVE

WHERE TO FIND THEM: Camino 305 Field Trips 24 and 25

Fun Fact

Squid communicate with each other by using color changes and body gestures.

Unlike their giant cousins 20,000 leagues below, these tiny cephalopods max out at around five inches. Like all squid, they have eight arms, two tentacles, and two fins that extend the length of their mantle, which is the large structure above their eyes that contains all their vital organs. The mantle fins help the squid swim, and each of the arms and tentacles are lined with suckers it uses for hunting. Similar to the common octopus, this squid is capable of altering the colors of its body by using chromatophores (cells that contain pigment or color). Unlike other squids that are typically nocturnal, the Caribbean reef squid is both nocturnal and diurnal (awake during the day), which means its prey (fish and arthropods) must be alert during all hours. While hunting, the Caribbean reef squid uses different poses and color changes to lure prey close enough for its tentacles to seize the meal and bring it to its mouth.

Caribbean Spiny Lobster

Panulirus argus

NATIVE

WHERE TO FIND THEM: Camino 305 Field Trips 1, 16–18, and 22–25

Unlike their Maine-dwelling cousins, spiny lobsters don't have front claws. Despite this "missing" feature, you'll recognize this crustacean from the common tailfan (fan-shaped formation at the end of the tail) typically associated with lobsters. Caribbean spiny lobster (also called Florida spiny lobster), specifically, have two whitish-tan-colored spots on the back of the second portion of their reddish-brown tail.

Their primary defense against predators, other than a reverse propulsion swimming

technique, is their hard carapace and forward-facing spines. During the day, they hide in rock crevices, reef caves, and marine debris; they are particularly fond of discarded car tires. For added protection, their antennae get in on the action—they wave their elongated, horn-esque antennae as a defense, and their smaller, antennae-like features, called antennules, can detect chemical alterations in the water and sense movement, making spiny lobsters hard to sneak up on. And it's a good thing, because there are times when their spines are useless as a defense. Through a process called molting, these lobsters shed their old carapace, absorb water to expand their body size, and begin growing a new protective covering. In the first five to seven years of life, a Caribbean spiny lobster can molt up to twenty-five times. In ideal conditions, they can live as long as fifteen years and weigh up to fifteen pounds.

Nocturnal by nature, they are opportunistic foragers capable of using their mandibles (teeth) to feed on a variety of species, but they

 Fun Fact

A female lobster carrying bright orange eggs under her tail (which will grow duller as they get closer to hatching) is referred to as in berry or berried.

tend to prefer snails and various crustaceans. Younger spiny lobsters eat soft-bodied plankton floating in the water column. Once they reach the juvenile stage, they begin to congregate nearshore for protection and easier access to food, before eventually moving to deeper offshore reefs as adults.

Spiny lobster are an important food source for snappers, octopuses, and sharks. Humans enjoy eating this species, too. And it's an environmentally safe seafood choice based on current sustainable fishery management practices and US regulations. In fact, the spiny lobster fishery is second only to the shrimping industry in Florida in terms of financial profit. According to the Florida Fish and Wildlife Conservation Commission (FWC), the average annual revenue for commercial harvest between 2015 and 2019 was more than $40 million. Roughly a week before the start of the spiny lobster regular season in South Florida, there are two days in which people flock to the oceans in search of them. Commonly referred to as mini season, Floridians and tourists alike mark their calendars for the last Wednesday and Thursday of July to take advantage of the forty-eight-hour open-sport window. The daily bag limit per person is six lobsters in Monroe County and Biscayne National Park (twelve for the rest of Florida) and the carapace of each taken lobster must exceed three inches.

Fun Fact

The brown seaweed (technically an algae) that occasionally accumulates at the tide line on shore is collectively referred to as sargassum. Attached to its branches are oxygen-filled, ball-shaped structures called pneumatocysts that make the plant buoyant and create a floating seaweed island in the middle of the ocean that a variety of species use as a habitat and nursery.

Sargassum Swimming Crab

Portunus sayi

NATIVE

WHERE TO FIND THEM: Camino 305 Field Trips 1, 16–18, 24, and 25

Like trumpetfish, sea turtle hatchlings, and the dozens of other species that use sargassum as a home base, this orange crab relies on its ability to camouflage within the orange and brown, free-floating algae for survival. The excellent swimming paddles on its hind legs and elongated claws make it an effective ambush predator capable of delivering unexpected, lethal stabs to its preferred diet of shrimp, worms, and fish species that share the sargassum habitat.

Mangrove Tree Crab

Aratus pisonii

NATIVE

WHERE TO FIND THEM: Camino 305 Field Trips 1, 2, 7, 16–18, and 22–25

Look for these omnivorous crabs in mangrove trees. Their preferred diet is red mangrove tree leaves, but you're also likely to find them in other mangrove tree species. Though you'll see them in tree canopies during high tide, they must remain close to the water since they can't breathe air. Instead, they use a feature called a branchiostegite, a cover for their gills that retains a thin layer of water and allows for extended terrestrial activities—once the water evaporates, the crabs must return to the water to replenish. Small and greenish brown with a box-like carapace, mangrove crabs are a brachyuran, meaning you can determine their sex by examining their abdomens; females tend to have a wider abdomen to allow for an egg mass. Additionally, males have larger claws that they use in territory defense and mating rituals.

Blue Land Crab

Cardisoma guanhumi

NATIVE

WHERE TO FIND THEM: Camino 305 Field Trips 1, 2, 7, 15–18, and 22–25

After your first encounter with a blue land crab, you might have some questions. Setting aside their intimidating size (up to six inches wide) and the fact that they appear to have one extremely swollen claw; you're probably wondering why you're seeing this crab casually

Fun Fact

A blue land crab's carapace can measure up to six inches—the larger claw can sometimes exceed the length of the carapace.

walking across a Miami intersection a mile away from any significant body of water. Although they prefer coastal areas with a lower elevation,

Florida's largest semiterrestrial *cangrejo* (crab) have been spotted up to five miles from the nearest coastline, typically only returning to the sea to drink or during the peak of the mating season from October through November. They are burrowers and can dig holes up to five feet deep. Shy by nature, they typically retreat into their burrows when approached. Though they're one of the most alarming looking crustaceans you'll encounter in South Florida, you can set any fears aside—they prefer a vegetarian diet focused on fruits and vegetation. Still, don't test their claw strength or reach a hand into any one of their burrows. During peak mating season, hundreds of these crabs crawl over roads, sidewalks, and pathways, making it difficult for vehicles and cyclists to safely navigate coastal areas without injuring themselves (or, more likely, the crabs).

Conservation Connection

Florida Fish and Wildlife Conservation Commission (FWC) enforces both seasonal and bag limit regulations to protect blue land crabs in areas where they are harvested as a food source. Though this has led to a resurgence of the species, urban development has fragmented populations and made their migrations to mate more difficult.

Common Octopus

Octopus vulgaris

NATIVE

WHERE TO FIND THEM: Camino 305 Field Trips 1, 2, 16–18, 24, and 25

One of the most intelligent animals in the sea, the common octopus is a carnivorous invertebrate with a lifespan of only one to two years. Its most famous characteristic are its eight, sucker-covered legs, but it also has a massive head, a flexible body, and an inkjet

defense capable of temporarily dazing even the most cunning of predators. An expert at hide and seek, it's capable of contorting its body to fit in any opening that can hold its small, hardened beak. By using specialized muscles and pigmented cells in its skin, the common octopus can change both color and texture, instantly mimicking its surroundings to completely disappear. It has venomous saliva that helps it subdue prey and if it loses a limb, it can regrow it. There is nothing common about this species.

Massive Starlet Coral

Siderastrea siderea

NATIVE

WHERE TO FIND THEM: Camino 305 Field Trips 24 and 25

This common species of coral found throughout the tropical Atlantic Ocean grows as small round colonies in rocky areas or as large, dome-shaped colonies in reef flats. In more open areas, the domes are quite massive, resembling a boulder and reaching up to six feet in diameter. In 2015, scientists extracted a four-and-a-half-foot core from this species using a specialized drill. Research partners at Woods Hole Oceanographic Institute and the University of Havana off the southern coast of Cuba analyzed the core to reveal the coral was more than 225 years old. For perspective, imagine this coral landing as a tiny polyp on a sandy flat while George Washington was still president of the United States. It grew from there, adding new sheets of tissue year by year. Look for massive starlet corals on snorkeling and dive trips; they are yellow or light brown and covered with dimples.

I was on the team that extracted the core from that 225-year-old massive starlet coral. Spending that afternoon drilling into a coral head was cathartic for me, since I have worked in Cuba since 1998 to study and protect marine resources shared with the US and Mexico. I have committed my career to the field of ocean diplomacy and corals, reminding myself of its importance and the need for governments to respect science and protect marine resources, regardless of maritime boundaries. Nature does not respect human-designated borders put up by nations to protect their interests. Being there underwater during a mass coral spawning that looked like underwater snowfall allowed me to understand that in order to protect our shared resources from common threats such as climate change, mass tourism, or overfishing, we as scientists, conservationists, and human beings need to work together to protect the ocean we love.

Mustard Hill Coral

Porites astreoides

`NATIVE`

WHERE TO FIND THEM: Camino 305 Field Trips 24 and 25

Whether mustard-colored or vomit green, these common Atlantic corals usually appear in small, humble clumps on the reef. In addition to being fast growing and excellent at colonizing new areas, they display rare resilience to bleaching and disease. Able to grow in shallow and deep waters, they display a different morphology (shapes) based on the speed of the currents where they dwell. In shallow water, they appear as small mounds, but on deeper reefs with less flow, their size increases dramatically, resembling more of a hill. As with any coral, they feed on zooplankton using tiny, extendable tentacles, but also make their own food via photosynthesis; mustard hill coral are particularly strong photosynthesizers.

Staghorn Coral

Acropora cervicornis

`NATIVE` `THREATENED`

WHERE TO FIND THEM: Camino 305 Field Trips 24 and 25

This important reef-building coral was once abundant throughout the Caribbean and Florida. Reef-building corals occupy shallow areas and grow in dense clusters that provide a place for other corals to grow. Staghorn coral has lobe-shaped tissues that resemble the young antlers of male deer. These branches provide habitat for a variety of important commercial reef fish while protecting coastal areas from storms. A regional collapse of staghorn and closely related elkhorn coral (*Acropora palmata*) in the 1980s due to white band disease greatly reduced its abundance throughout its entire range. Threats such as bleaching, storms, and new diseases have further reduced current populations. Restoration projects commonly use staghorn corals because lobes can be cut from a healthy specimen without drastically harming the parent. These threatened corals can be grown in laboratory-controlled conditions then planted out in underwater nurseries where they receive more light and circulation creating a sustainable source of healthy coral colonies. New research is increasing the population's genetic diversity and resilience to disease and high temperatures.

Conservation Connection

The University of Miami's Rescue a Reef Program specializes in the emerging field of reef restoration, which gives a leg up to corals that have been decimated by disease, bleaching, or mechanical damage. Traditionally, reef restoration is effective and low cost, but it requires a lot of people power, as one staghorn fragment is just a drop in the ocean bucket. Rescue a Reef takes restoration a step further by offering opportunities for volunteers to help on citizen science field expeditions while learning about the importance of coral conservation.

Fat Sea Biscuit

Clypeaster rosaceus

NATIVE

WHERE TO FIND THEM: Camino 305 Field Trips 1, 16–18, 24, and 25

Members of the family Clypeasteridae are commonly referred to as sand dollars or sea biscuits because their compressed, disc-shaped appearance makes them look just like silver dollar coins or fluffy biscuits—for this species, we have to assume somebody said, "It's kind of fat?" And voilà!

With a habitat preference for turtle grass in shallow water, this thick-bodied sand dollar doesn't burrow in the sand; instead it covers itself with marine rubble such as shells and grass to camouflage with the ocean floor, holding its disguise intact with suctioned tube feet as it crawls across the sand using spines near its mouth. Imagine a pastelito (a Cuban pastry) covered in shells and seaweed slowly moving along the seafloor and you have the right idea. The fat sea biscuit is an infaunal deposit feeder, which means it eats creatures that live within the sandy floor and, through the process of foraging, ingests both living organisms and nonliving particles like sediment.

Giant Caribbean Sea Anemone

Condylactis gigantea

NATIVE

WHERE TO FIND THEM: Camino 305 Field Trips 24 and 25

Anemones are close relatives of corals. While corals form colonies of many polyps, anemones are single predatory organisms that attach themselves to the ocean floor, where they wait for unsuspecting fish to swim into their venomous grasp. The giant Caribbean sea anemone has purplish-pink tips at the ends of its tentacles, which it can retract

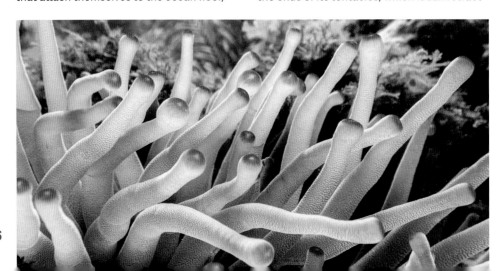

into a digestive cavity, dramatically reducing its overall size. The general anatomy of sea anemones is rather simple and consists of three basic parts: a base (referred to as a foot), tentacles, and a mouth. The tentacles inject a neurotoxin into their prey that causes paralysis, allowing the anemone to guide the subdued catch into its mouth for dinner.

Horseshoe Crab

Limulus polyphemus

NATIVE

WHERE TO FIND THEM: Camino 305 Field Trips 1, 16–18, 24, and 25

The horseshoe crab is a living fossil—its form hasn't evolved much since the Mesozoic era, roughly 200 million years ago. Fossils of horseshoe crabs have been documented as far back as 445 million years ago. Though they are ancient, you could say they are highly evolved, considering they have been around since before the dinosaurs without the need to change. Though this species survived the global cataclysm that killed off a huge percentage of life on our planet, they're currently at risk in the wild due to pollution, overharvesting, and habitat destruction.

Neither crab nor crustacean, horseshoe crabs are primitive arthropods in the phylum Arthropoda, subphylum Chelicerata—they're actually more closely related to spiders and scorpions. Although they do possess claws like crabs, they use them for eating, not protection, tearing off pieces of food and placing them into their uniquely positioned mouth at the base of their five pairs of legs. Their preferred diet is of clams and other bivalves and as they forage, they disturb the ocean floor in a process called bioturbation, which oxygenates the sediment and enhances its biodiversity.

The horseshoe crab's brown helmet provides protection against predators like sharks and seagulls. Their spine-covered tail, called a telson, may look like a weapon or a stinger, but its main purpose is to help the horseshoe crab flip back over if it ends up on its back. It's not super effective for this job either, and you'll often find the arthropods upside down at the shoreline, feet wiggling aimlessly in the air. If you do find one in this state, flip it right side up safely by the shell and return it to the water's edge. Never flip a horseshoe crab over by grabbing the tail, because you could injure the delicate muscle they rely on to control it.

In the past, people used horseshoe crabs as fertilizer and as feed for farm animals. Although that practice is no more, they are still valuable to humans, specifically in the medical field. Horseshoe crabs use copper instead of iron to carry oxygen through their blood, so their blood is blue, not red, and it contains a special clotting agent that reacts to bacteria that are harmful to humans. Doctors and researchers use horseshoe crab blood to test patients for certain diseases. While the practice of bleeding horseshoe crabs has its critics, it continues to this day and threatens wild horseshoe crab populations.

Long-Spined Urchin

Diadema antillarum

NATIVE

WHERE TO FIND THEM: Camino 305 Field Trips 1, 16–18, 24, and 25

With its long, movable, hollow spines that can reach up to eleven inches in length, these circular-bodied sea urchins are a painful foot

Fun Fact

In the Caribbean, if an islander gets a puncture wound from an urchin, they've been known to hammer repeatedly on the affected area to break down the fragile spines left in the skin, which allows the body to remove them faster.

INVERTEBRATES

Conservation Connection

Following a near-complete extinction event that swept through the Caribbean in 1983, these important grazers have yet to fully recover. The Florida Aquarium, the University of Florida, Phillip and Patricia Frost Museum of Science, SECORE International, Force Blue, and the University of Miami are all working on ways to restock this species on Florida's Coral Reef. One technique is relocating individuals from reefs with high density to reefs with low density to promote quicker population growth and genetic enhancement. Another includes raising the urchins in a lab setting with the hope of eventually reintroducing them offshore.

story waiting to happen. If you're unlucky enough to step on one, the poison is manageable with some basic disinfectant. They provide a tremendous service to the local coral reefs. Algae-eaters by profession, they graze reef surfaces, allowing corals to settle and expand. Additionally, their long spines provide protection to juvenile fish and crustaceans, who use these slow-moving urchins as temporary housing. Within the spines, their rigid skeleton is called a test, and they use their numerous tube feet to move around and also for feeding and breathing. Usually jet black, they can also have black-and-white or all-white spines. Unless you're blindly digging your hand into rock crevices along Florida's Coral Reef, you don't have much to fear from these nocturnal herbivores.

Moon Jelly

Aurelia aurita

`NATIVE`

WHERE TO FIND THEM: Camino 305 Field Trips 1, 16–18, and 22–25

The moon jelly (not to be confused with space jam) is an opaque, circular cnidarian found near the surface of the water around coastlines. Due to its ineffective swimming abilities, you'll often find them washed up along the shoreline during enhanced tides or storms. Although the moon jelly's mantra is "go with the flow," that shouldn't take away from its successful hunting technique. It uses its short tentacles filled with cnidocytes (specialized stinging cells) to stun small invertebrates and even small fish. Any frequent Miami beachgoer will inevitably feel the sting at some point and find a red patch of skin where the sting latched

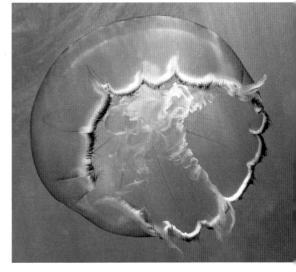

on. If you are stung, don't believe the myth that urine will ease your pain. In fact, urine may actually intensify the sting as it aggravates the stingers into releasing more venom.

339

![Conservation Connection icon] **Conservation Connection**

Plastic bag versus jellyfish? Moon jellies are a common food for leatherback sea turtles (*Dermochelys coriacea*) and ocean sunfish (*Mola mola*), who must eat hundreds of them to obtain enough nutrition. Unfortunately, plastic bags floating in the ocean look a lot like jellyfish and have caused tremendous problems for marine species whose diet is focused on these aquatic invertebrates. As pollution continues to harm moon jelly predators, one resulting consequence is that the moon jelly population increases, further disrupting the ecosystem balance.

Portuguese Man o' War

Physalia physalis

NATIVE

WHERE TO FIND THEM: Camino 305 Field Trips 1, 2, 16–18, 24, and 25

Though it is commonly mistaken for a jellyfish, the venomous Portuguese man o' war is actually a siphonophore, a fascinating kind of organism that's made up of a colony of individual creatures called zooids all working together. The zooids are closely related to jellyfish and there are four types in the colony, each with a specific function related to floating, capturing prey, reproduction, or feeding. The uppermost zooid is made up of an air-filled sack that allows it to float and serves as a type of sail to help the man o' war get around. If needed, it can deflate this sack to sink just beneath the surface and avoid predators. The lower zooid contains the tentacles, which can reach over 100 feet long but average about 30 feet. The tentacles capture and subdue prey and have one of the most painful stings known to humans. Portuguese man o' wars inhabit tropical oceans and tend to wash up on Miami beaches during winter, resembling deflated blue balloons. Look for them on the wrack line, but definitely avoid contact. A general rule to follow while on Miami Beach: unless it's a cocktail, avoid blue on the shoreline.

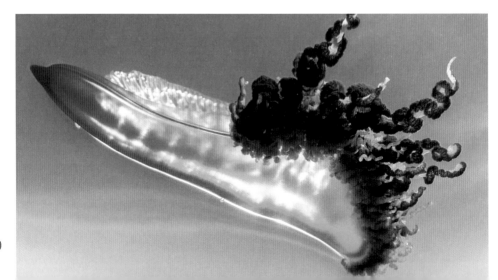

Purple Sea Fan

Gorgonia ventalina

NATIVE

WHERE TO FIND THEM: Camino 305 Field Trips 24 and 25

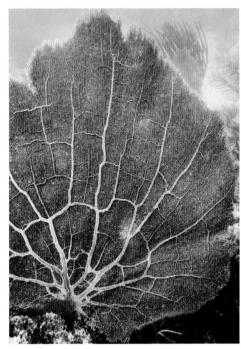

Take a moment to imagine a pharaoh's fan-bearer, rhythmically moving a fan back and forth to cool down the Egyptian ruler. Now take away the bearer and the pharaoh, add the ocean floor, and sprinkle in some purple. You've got the purple sea fan. Gently swaying back and forth with the current, it is a stationary filter feeder, meaning it relies on the current to send it the organic material and nutrients it needs for survival. Typically located on the outer surfaces of coral reefs, sea fans belong to the same phylum, Cnidaria, as jellyfish and corals. It has a slender base that branches out into a single plane made of a supportive substance called gorgonin that helps structure the skeleton. On the outside of the gorgonin, living tissues called zooxanthellae make food for the sea fan through photosynthesis.

Queen Conch

Strombus gigas

NATIVE

WHERE TO FIND THEM: Camino 305 Field Trips 1, 16–18, and 22–25

A conch is a kind of molluscan gastropod—the class of mollusks that includes snails. The queen conch is the largest conch found in the seagrasses of Florida. They have a uniquely large, spiked and coiled shell that is often algae-covered on top and bright pink or orange at the aperture (opening). Their eyes are highly developed and located at the ends of two long stalks. At the base of their eye stalks is a tube-shaped mouth called a proboscis. They can pull both features into their shell to protect themselves when needed. They move along the sea floor with a method known as a strombid leap, in which the conch sort of pole vaults forward using its hardened foot called an operculum. They use this technique to evade predators such as turtles, sharks, and

341

Efforts to mitigate Caribbean fishing pressure on this species have been ongoing since the commercial conch fishery started in the 1970s, with aquaculturists attempting to enhance the populations in multiple territories. According to the National Oceanic and Atmospheric Administration (NOAA), though Caribbean populations are in decline, US wild-caught queen conch is now an environmentally sustainable seafood choice. They continue to monitor and review the species' population status.

rays, and also to scavenge the ocean floor in search of macroalgae, detritus, and seagrass.

There are privileges associated with the queen title, such as indulging your preference for pristine coral sand and warm shallow waters while breeding. During spawning season, males and females (of at least three years of age) mate with multiple partners. Once the eggs are fertilized within the female, she will lay long egg masses, either on seagrass or bare sand, then cover them with sand in an attempt to camouflage them from predators until they hatch roughly three days later. It's estimated queen conches can live as long as twenty-five years, which gives them many opportunities to reproduce.

Ruby Brittle Star

Ophioderma rubicundum

NATIVE

WHERE TO FIND THEM: Camino 305 Field Trips 24 and 25

Slightly nightmarish in appearance, the ruby brittle star looks like a sea star skeleton. It has a small, disk-shaped body and five long, thin arms that host ten to twelve spines per side. Each of the flexible red or purplish arms are ringed with whitish-tan bands. In place of the typical sea star ossicles (calcified material that helps structure their skeleton), brittle stars have scales. They live on reefs and rocky bottoms and are nocturnal, often foraging for food at night.

Sea Sponge

Family Spongiidae

NATIVE

WHERE TO FIND THEM: Camino 305 Field Trips 1, 2, 16–18, 24, and 25

South Florida is home to more than two hundred species of sponges—they surpass the number of coral species by a long shot—and you'll find them in nearly all shallow-water environments surrounding Miami. Sponges are not incredibly complex organisms. With no organs or tissues, or even a front or back, they're really just a system of holes and canals that filter water to feed on plankton, detritus, or bacteria. Because they lack vital organs, they digest food right in their cells rather than in a stomach. They can reproduce either asexually or sexually.

Fun Fact

Your kitchen sponge shares similarities with those found in the ocean because, once upon a time, sea sponges were the only sponges humans had. Today, most household sponges never lived in the ocean and are a blend of synthetic materials.

West Indian Sea Star

Oreaster reticulatus

NATIVE

WHERE TO FIND THEM: Camino 305 Field Trips 1, 16–18, 24, and 25

If you're snorkeling around Miami, especially in the shoal grass (*Halodule wrightii*) or manatee grass beds right offshore, you're likely to happen upon one, or even a dozen, of these sea stars. Also referred to as the red cushion sea star or Bahama sea star, they can't help but catch your eye as you stare down toward the ocean floor on a high visibility day. Bright orange or red in a mess of tan and green, they're the hard-skinned, bony stars laid upon an underwater Christmas tree. The largest of the sea star species found in Miami, they have five thick, stubby arms lined with tiny, tubed feet that steadily move them across the ocean floor (up to twenty-one feet each day) in search

of microorganisms and particulate detritus to eat. Omnivorous and flexible about habitat, they can live in waters as shallow as 3 feet or deeper than 100 feet in the intertidal and littoral (shoreline) zones.

Plants

Australian Pine

Casuarina equisetifolia

INVASIVE

WHERE TO FIND THEM: Camino 305 Field Trips 1, 2, 4, 16–18, 20, and 22–25

Don't confuse this tree with South Florida's slash pine. While slash pine is a native tree in dire need of strong restoration efforts, Australian pine is one of our most aggressively invasive trees. Despite its name, Australian pine is not a true pine. Its branchlets, which resemble pine needles, are an example of convergent evolution, a phenomenon in which two species share similar physical characteristics despite belonging to different taxonomic classes. Think birds and bats—though they're not genetically related, they both evolved wings for flight. Australian pine has a foothold in many of South Florida's coastal areas, where its unfettered growth has allowed it to form dense monoculture forests. In a process called allelopathy, this tree leaches poisonous compounds into the soil that prevent other species' seeds from germinating. These two factors keep a healthy community of native plants from establishing where Australian pines are too numerous.

Native to the South Pacific, it was introduced to Florida in the late nineteenth century because its tall stature and dense growth habit made it an effective windbreak in agricultural areas and tropical fruit orchards. The century-old Australian pines on Miami

Conservation Connection

Despite the harm Australian pines cause to our native ecosystems, many locals prefer the trees be left alone. People have fond childhood memories of sitting in the shade of these trees during family gatherings at the beach, and their branches make a soothing whooshing sound in the wind that many have grown to love. To them, Australian pines are part of Miami's character. But the truth is these trees put South Florida's cherished native species at severe risk. Where Australian pines abound, dozens of species are traded for one. Our hope is to encourage people, especially the next generation, to get acquainted with our indigenous flora and create new meaningful memories with them while understanding the negative impacts of invasive species.

Beach's Pine Tree Drive are remnant protectors of pioneer John Collins' mango and avocado orchard. However, the tree's invasive qualities became apparent not long after its introduction. With no native organisms able to digest its leaves, an incredibly fast growth rate, and the fact that each tree produces thousands of seeds every year, it's no wonder that this species has so effectively conquered our natural areas. Because they have proven to be incapable of coexisting in balance with Florida's native ecosystems, their removal is of the utmost importance when performing ecosystem restoration.

Coastal Sandbur

Cenchrus incertus

`NATIVE`

WHERE TO FIND THEM: All Camino 305 Field Trips

Sandburs test our commitment to the notion that plants and animals can never be "evil." The plant looks innocuous enough, just flat-growing patches of grass on the edges of beach dunes. But step on one of its seeds while barefoot and you are in for some pain. Each seed is armed with several sharp spines that can pierce skin or hook onto clothing and shoes as you brush by. Patches of sandburs tend to have several dozen seeds, so if you find one attached, you're almost certain to find more. Their seeming pack mentality and ability to latch onto surfaces is a dispersal strategy

the parent plant uses to give its offspring a free ride to new locations. However, be warned: removing the seeds can be just as painful as stepping on them. This is a species you definitely want to avoid bringing home, lest you establish a population in your landscape.

East Coast Dune Sunflower

Helianthus debilis

NATIVE

WHERE TO FIND THEM: Camino 305 Field Trips 1, 2, 15–18, 22, 24, and 25

Sunflowers' radiant beauty and brilliant yellow hue, enjoyed in vast golden fields or gifted to someone special in a bouquet, have a particularly strong ability to instantly elevate our mood. The many varieties of the large common sunflower (*Helianthus annuus*) are well known. But did you know that Miami has a native sunflower species? Its roughly three-inch-diameter flowers resemble miniature versions of its giant cousin. The east coast dune sunflower lives in beach dunes and coastal strands. Though it is popular in native wildflower gardens, be careful when planting it. Southwest Florida has a distinct subspecies, the west coast dune sunflower, that is technically not native to Miami, and the accidental mixing of the two subspecies has created populations of hybrid sunflowers that otherwise would not exist in nature. Planting the west coast subspecies in the garden or in restoration projects could compromise the conservation of our own native as the natural population is replaced by the hybrid.

Eastern Prickly Pear

Opuntia humifusa

NATIVE

WHERE TO FIND THEM: Camino 305 Field Trips 3, 7, 9, 11, 12, 17, 18, 20, and 23

Though cactuses are typically associated with dry deserts, they are also found in a variety of tropical and subtropical ecosystems. Miami-Dade County, for example, is home to five native species of cactus. Of these, the endemic semaphore (*Consolea corallicola*) and Caribbean apple (*Harrisia fragrans*) cactuses are exceedingly rare. The most common of the bunch is the eastern prickly pear, distinguished by their circular, flat pads and found in sandy coastal areas, grassy prairies, and pinelands. With limited availability in plant nurseries and the fact that most people avoid planting spiny species, it is usually only the most avid enthusiasts who incorporate our native cactuses in their home landscapes. But planting eastern prickly pear is encouraged, as the nectar and pollen in their yellow blooms supports native bees and bats, while birds and tortoises enjoy munching on their red-colored fruits.

Fun Fact

Opuntia cactuses, including eastern prickly pear, are a staple in Central and South American cuisine; pads are called *nopales* and fruits *tunas*. All species of cactus except for the epiphytic mistletoe cactus (*Rhipsalis baccifera*) are native only to the Americas.

Green Buttonwood

Conocarpus erectus

`NATIVE`

WHERE TO FIND THEM: Camino 305 Field Trips 1, 2, 7, 15–18, and 21–25

This ubiquitous coastal tree is known as a mangrove-associated species, often growing just upland of mangrove forests, on land that is a few inches higher than the high tide line. They belong to the same plant family as the white mangrove, but they don't have the biological characteristics to be classified as a true

Fun Fact

In the Florida Keys, there is a special silver variety of buttonwood with thin tufts of woolly hair on its leaves. These hairs likely evolved to give the tree extra protection from salt spray.

mangrove. Buttonwoods have oval-shaped leaves that end in a pointed tip. A very common tree today in natural and urban areas, wild-harvested buttonwood once supported a strong South Florida charcoal industry.

Jamaica Dogwood

Piscidia piscipula

NATIVE

WHERE TO FIND THEM: Camino 305 Field Trips 2, 3, 5–8, 16–18, and 20–25

Jamaica dogwood grows in coastal upland forests and is identifiable by its compound, gray-green leaves. In addition to serving as a host plant for Miami's smallest butterfly, the cassius blue (*Leptotes cassius*) and hammock skipper butterfly (*Polyganus leo*), its most interesting feature might be its historical ethnobotanical use. Centuries ago, the Calusas and Tequestas would collect the tree's leaves and bark and unload them into still, shallow pools of water. Jamaica dogwood contains a compound called rotenone that is potently toxic to fish. It works by halting cellular respiration—the process cells use to make energy—stunning or killing them for easy capture. The individual who first figured out how to do this is unknown, but the technique is quite ingenious and it earns the tree a second common name: Florida fishpoison tree. Don't get any ideas of trying this fishing method yourself. Though the practice was sustainable in the past, it is an indiscriminate, mass-fishing strategy and is now outlawed in Florida. Besides, without training, it probably isn't the safest thing to eat fish inoculated with poison.

Manchineel

Hippomane mancinella

`NATIVE` `ENDANGERED`

WHERE TO FIND THEM: Camino 305 Field Trips 24 and 25

In 1521, Juan Ponce de León was shot in the thigh by an arrow launched by a Calusa warrior. Fleeing south to Cuba, he died three days later from the wound. Historians believe the arrow may have been tipped with sap from the manchineel tree, which is widely regarded as the most poisonous tree on the planet. Sometimes, small details dictate the course of history.

It grows alongside beaches and interspersed with mangroves, and hopefully you'll never have the misfortune to discover its toxicity firsthand. Seeking shelter from the rain beneath its canopy is a bad idea, as even the minute amounts of sap that dissolve into the falling water can cause severe skin burns. Eating the seemingly innocuous fruit is an even worse mistake. Accounts from those who have accidentally taken a bite describe the initial taste as sweet, but shortly thereafter, a strong peppery sensation takes over, causing severe throat irritation and closing airways. Its nickname, *manzanilla de la muerte* or "little apple of death," communicates what several more bites might do. Luckily, these kinds of mishaps don't happen very often, as the species has become uncommon in Florida. Remaining trees in frequently visited areas are usually marked with clear signs cautioning people to stay away.

Mangroves

Mangrove forests are one of South Florida's most important ecosystem. As hubs for biodiversity, efficient carbon sinks, and an important line of defense against damage caused by storm surge and sea level rise, mangroves have much to offer. For these ecosystem services, mangroves receive protection under state law. Even on private property, it's illegal to so much as trim a mangrove tree without a permit. Mangrove restoration will play a big role in making Miami more resilient to the effects of climate change, so you might want to familiarize yourself with these trees. Lucky for you, they are easy to get to know—compared to the dozens of species found in other forest types, there are only three species of true mangroves native to Miami: red, black, and white.

▲ Red Mangrove

 Fun fact

Red mangroves are salt excluders, meaning they can tolerate a high saline environment by keeping salt out of their roots. They can filter out up to 90 percent of the salt found in seawater. You may notice several yellowing leaves on a red mangrove. A common myth says these are sacrificial leaves that concentrate salt, allowing the rest of the plant to thrive, but, in fact, these are just typical dying leaves, same as you might find on any other plant.

▲ Black Mangrove

▲ White Mangrove

Red Mangrove

Rhizophora mangle

NATIVE

WHERE TO FIND THEM: Camino 305 Field Trips 1, 2, 7, 15–18, and 21–25

With long arching roots emanating from its trunk, the red mangrove is the most distinctive and well-known of our three native species. Those arching roots, called prop roots, stabilize the mangrove in the water, protecting it from heavy waves. This ability to diminish incoming wave energy makes red mangrove forests effective buffer zones for hurricane storm surges. The many small cavities created by interlacing red mangrove roots are also prime shelters for smaller fish, allowing them to hide from larger predators who cannot maneuver through them as easily. Many species of oceanic fish make their way toward mangrove forests to lay their eggs, knowing this environment is suited for juveniles and will provide increased chances for survival to adulthood. For that reason, mangrove forests are often called fish nurseries.

Black Mangrove

Avicennia germinans

NATIVE

WHERE TO FIND THEM: Camino 305 Field Trips 1, 2, 7, 15–18, and 21–25

Growing in areas where water is a bit shallower, black mangroves are the second most recognizable mangrove species. Their first identifying feature is their oval-shaped leaves, which are light green on top and silvery-green below. The bottom of the leaf also feels slightly velvety. This tree's bark is often dark gray. Like red mangroves, black mangroves also have a specially adapted root system, but rather than arching prop roots, they have what are called pneumatophores. These are vertical, finger-like projections that poke up from the soil by the dozen around the base of the tree. Their purpose is similar to that of the red mangrove prop roots in that they provide stability in this dynamic marine environment. They also help aerate the soil, providing much needed oxygen to the tree's root system. If you see pneumatophores poking up, you're bound to find a black mangrove tree nearby.

White Mangrove

Laguncularia racemosa

NATIVE

WHERE TO FIND THEM: Camino 305 Field Trips 1, 2, 7, 15–18, and 21–25

The last of the three mangrove species, the white mangrove is the trickiest of the three to readily recognize. Unlike the other two mangrove species, the white mangrove doesn't usually exhibit specialized root structures (though in certain cases where the tree is particularly stressed, it may develop pneumatophores). Generally, it looks like any other tree, just growing closer to the saltwater. The best way to identify a white mangrove is by its almost circular leaves—at the end is a little indentation that is characteristic to the species. Its "fruits" (actually embryonic roots called propagules) hang at the end of branches and resemble green, shriveled almonds, and its flowers are greenish white.

Ocean Blue Morning Glory

Ipomoea indica

NATIVE

WHERE TO FIND THEM: All Camino 305 Field Trips

Some native species challenge the narrative that native plants are good in all contexts. Ocean blue morning glory, a close relative of

sweet potato, is one example. A beautiful vine, it grows heavy curtains of heart-shaped leaves adorned by phonograph-shaped indigo and magenta flowers. The curtains are composed of many twining, fast-growing stems that snag and swirl around the branches of other plants. Their fast growth rate and dense foliage allows them to enshroud entire trees and blanket large swaths of land, overwhelming and compromising plants installed in restoration sites. Though it's just as important as any other native plant—we would hate to lose this beautiful azure wildflower—there is a lesson to be learned here about balance and preventing any one plant (native or invasive) from negatively affecting the health of others. When ocean blue morning glory grows too aggressively, human management makes sense, and the same holds for many other native species that grow and disperse swiftly.

Saw Palmetto

Serenoa repens

NATIVE

WHERE TO FIND THEM: All Camino 305 Field Trips

Found in a wide variety of ecosystems, this ubiquitous, slow-growing palm is named for its serrated leaf stem (botanically called a *petiole*)—we advise caution when walking among the rough fronds. Saw palmettos are a common understory element of South Florida's pine rocklands, providing lots of food for wildlife. Their olive-sized fruits are enjoyed by bears, raccoons, opossums, deer, and birds, and the flowers provide ample nectar for pollinators. Saw palmetto flowers are considered

the most reliable source of nectar of any of Florida's native plants, making them incredibly important to their ecosystems. Saw palmetto fruits are also harvested by people for their purported effectiveness in promoting prostate health in men. Overharvesting fruits from natural areas has led to decreased availability for wildlife, so although saw palmetto is not a threatened or endangered species, it is designated as commercially exploited, meaning hefty fines or even jail time can await anyone collecting saw palmetto fruits from the wild.

Scaevolas

Beach Naupaka

Scaevola taccada

`INVASIVE`

Inkberry

Scaevola plumieri

`NATIVE` `THREATENED`

WHERE TO FIND THEM: Camino 305 Field Trips 1, 2, 4, 16–18, and 22–25

▲ Beach Naupaka

To be effective stewards of the world, it's important that we have a solid understanding of ecosystems and the species we are tasked with protecting. Without such knowledge, humans may accidentally alter an ecosystem. Unfortunately, sometimes knowledge is only obtained through egregious error. Land managers introduced beach naupaka, a native of Hawaii, to our state in the 1980s because they believed its wide and densely foliaged growth habit would make it a great coastal stabilizer. And while it does arguably help with coastal erosion control, it was a little too effective, quickly spreading uncontrollably along beach dunes and coastal uplands and supplanting large swaths of these rare native habitats. Though intentions might be good, the risks associated with introducing non-native plants to achieve land management goals far outweigh the potential benefits.

But not all scaevolas are created equal! Although beach naupaka has had devastating impacts in South Florida, inkberry (Florida's

▲ Inkberry

native counterpart), is beneficial because it has a lower growth habit (on average about three feet high). This slower and lower growth rate means it does not take over large areas. Through the extensive loss of coastal habitat in favor of development and fierce competition with invasive species, it is now listed as a threatened species in the state. A key feature to look out for is the color of the plants' fruits. Whereas inkberry's fruit is inky black, beach naupaka's fruit is snowy white. Inkberry also has smaller and more succulent leaves, while beach naupaka's leaves are longer and somewhat floppy, often a brighter green. Thankfully, inkberry is now available in several South Florida native nurseries, and its use in landscaping (particularly coastal landscaping) gives the species a boost.

Sea Lavender

Heliotropium gnaphalodes

`NATIVE` `ENDANGERED`

WHERE TO FIND THEM: Camino 305 Field Trips 1, 2, 15–18, 23, and 24

Our native sea lavender, which grows in rounded domes of silver, is named for the similarity of its elongated leaves to those of true lavender. But as the two are not related, sea lavender doesn't have that iconic, relaxing scent. Like many other dune and coastal strand species, sea lavender is state-endangered thanks to our tendency to develop natural land rather than preserve it. This plant usually grows interspersed among sea oats on beach dunes, punctuating the sea of green with silver. Rarely, some beach dunes, like the ones on Long Beach in the Keys, have little to no sea oats at all and are predominantly sea lavender.

Fun Fact

Sea lavender is a member of the family Boraginaceae, whose nectar has chemical compounds necessary for certain species of butterfly to make pheromones used in mating. If you live in a coastal home, this shrub will add beauty and hefty conservation value to your land.

Sea Oats

Uniola paniculata

NATIVE

WHERE TO FIND THEM: Camino 305 Field Trips 1, 2, 16–18, and 24

Sea oats are a dominant coastal species that grows on beach dunes. A tall, clumping grass, they have long, flat leaf blades and seed panicles that look very similar to those of true oats, making them easy to identify. They are incredibly important in Florida for a number of reasons. To start, they span most of the state's coastline, forming the basis of the beach eco-system. But it's underground where they have their greatest impact. Sea oats cast expansive and complex root systems, which extend several feet into the sand. These roots anchor the sand in place, offering grade-A coastal pro-tection. Damage from wind and storm surges is dramatically reduced in areas with a healthy amount of sea oats, an essential boost for Miami's climate change resiliency efforts. Simi-lar to mangroves, sea oats are not classified as threatened or endangered but are protected by state law because of the ecosystem support they provide. It is illegal to trample, harm, or uproot a sea oat. They protect us, so it's only fair we protect them.

Conservation Connection

Sand dunes are a critically impor-tant piece of green infrastructure that not only protect our city from storms and sea level rise but also store carbon in their tissues. The Phillip and Patricia Frost Museum of Science launched the Museum Volunteers for the Environment (MUVE) program in 2007 as a way to engage Miami residents in building coastal resilience through natural solutions. Volunteers replace inva-sive plants with native vegetation such as mangroves and sea oats and create living legacies of natural hab-itats on public lands they can visit and take pride in. MUVE volunteers have restored acres of native habi-tat, showing that green infrastruc-ture is not only more cost effective than building sea walls but engages scores of people in the process.

Seagrape

Coccoloba uvifera

NATIVE

WHERE TO FIND THEM: Camino 305 Field Trips 1, 2, 6–8, 15–18, and 21–25

It's hard to stroll down Miami's coastlines without finding seagrapes growing plentifully. Their uniquely large, kidney-shaped leaves make them one of the most recognizable trees in South Florida. While most seagrape leaves remain green year-round, some have reddish or orangish coloring that becomes most pronounced in fall, offering South Floridians the rare opportunity to experience the autumn foliage typically associated with the season. Though their natural range is limited to coastal uplands, seagrapes are popular throughout Miami as specimen trees or large hedges. From there, they have crept into inland natural areas. Most seagrapes are between ten and thirty feet tall, though some old trees—typically those planted away from the burning coastal salt breeze—have reached a magnificent stature of more than sixty feet high and about as wide. If you want to witness one of these statuesque seagrape trees firsthand, visit the Miami Beach Botanical Garden and seek their century-old specimen.

Seagrasses

Manatee Grass

Syringodium filiforme

`NATIVE`

Turtle Grass

Thalassia testudinum

`NATIVE`

WHERE TO FIND THEM: Camino 305 Field Trips 1, 2, 16–18, 23, and 25

Seagrasses can be an underappreciated component of South Florida's marine ecosystem. But, if you're fond of locally caught fish, you should be invested in protecting them—it's almost a certainty that the fish on your plate spent a portion of its life in the seagrass beds of shallow bays and estuary inlets.

Though they appear to be a kind of green algae, seagrasses are plants. They flower underwater and require pollination just like plants on land. To that goal, they have a nifty strategy. Some terrestrial plants use a technique called wind pollination, meaning pollen is broadcast into the air at the mercy of the wind in the hope that it will land on a female flower. Seagrasses employ a similar technique but with water currents. Seagrasses are also an important carbon sink—trapping large amounts of atmospheric carbon in their leaves and roots—which makes restoring and protecting them a great climate-mitigation strategy.

The two most common species of seagrass in Miami are manatee grass and turtle grass. Manatee grass is thin and cylindrical, whereas turtle grass is flat. And in case you're wondering, yes, turtles and manatees do love to eat seagrass. It is actually the main food source for manatees. Hard to believe that such massive animals can get as large as they do from munching on low-calorie vegetation.

▲ Manatee Grass

▲ Turtle Grass

 Fun Fact

One trick to easily identify seagrasses is to compare their shapes to different types of pasta. Manatee grass looks similar to spaghetti, and turtle grass looks like it would be served in a dish of fettuccine alfredo. Miami's third most common seagrass, shoal grass, is very thin, reminiscent of flattened angel hair pasta.

Conservation Connection

Since 2008, the Ocean Foundation has undertaken several coastal enhancement projects while promoting the concept of blue carbon, which is the capacity of ecosystems like seagrasses, tidal marshes, and mangroves to take up and trap large quantities of carbon in both the plants themselves and the sediment below. Coastal habitats have been proven considerably better at storing carbon than terrestrial forests. They store carbon-rich dead tissue in their underlying peat structures and also photosynthesize at a high rate, converting more carbon into roots, leaves, and stems. Through the Ocean Foundation's SeaGrass Grow program, individuals and businesses can calculate the carbon footprint of their home, workplace, or travel and offset it by restoring and protecting seagrass. Individuals can donate to this program and be assured that blue carbon sources will be restored and protected in perpetuity.

Seaside Mahoe

Thespesia populnea

`INVASIVE`

WHERE TO FIND THEM: Camino 305 Field Trips 1–3, 6–8, 16–18, 20, and 22–25

The malignantly invasive seaside mahoe has a similar origin story to Brazilian pepper. People liked the way it looked, they planted it as an ornamental specimen tree, and it escaped cultivation and began encroaching upon our coastal ecosystems. The tree forms monocultures along the edges of mangrove swamps, overrunning the white mangroves and green buttonwoods that would usually be

 Fun Fact:
Though seaside mahoe doesn't show much love to Miami (despite a canopy full of hearts) and should not be planted here, it is revered in its native Pacific range, where it is significant in religious ceremonies and stories.

prevalent there and compromising the health of the habitat. Mangroves support high biodiversity, have a remarkable ability to sequester atmospheric carbon, and are effective erosion controls. Seaside mahoe does not have those benefits, so the consequences of it replacing mangroves are particularly deleterious. It is quite easily identified by its heart-shaped leaves, as it's one of the few tree species in South Florida with this characteristic. Its light-yellow flowers mature into leathery, capsular fruits, each with several seeds and the potential to make several more trees.

Wild Lime

Zanthoxylum fagara

NATIVE

WHERE TO FIND THEM: Camino 305 Field Trips 2, 3, 5–7, 13, 15–18, 20, and 22–25

Capable of both evoking nostalgic memories and inflicting a painful bite, the wild lime tree cannot seem to decide whether it wants to be inviting or defensive. If you find one, crush one of its leaves and hold it up to your nose. Do you recognize that smell? Most people compare the aroma to lime fruits, but we think it most closely resembles Froot Loops cereal, a childhood favorite. This is especially true for the tender new leaves. Though the leaves will draw you in, one prick from the plant's extremely sharp, talon-like spines will repel you back quickly. The curved shape of these spines makes them good at grasping onto clothing. If you get caught, stay still and calmly try to find where you're snagged. If you thrash around too much, you may become more entangled or rip an embarrassing hole in your clothing. But don't let the spines discourage you from planting this tree at home! Wild lime should be included in every butterfly lover's garden, as they serve as a host plant for the kite-like giant swallowtail, North America's largest butterfly.

COMMONLY USED ACRONYMS

ESA (Endangered Species Act of 1973) a key legislation for both domestic and international conservation aiming to provide a framework to conserve and protect endangered and threatened species and their habitats

FWC (Florida Fish and Wildlife Conservation Commission) a Florida government agency founded in 1999 and based out of Tallahassee that manages, regulates, and enforces the state's fish and wildlife resources and related laws

FWS (US Fish and Wildlife Service) a government agency dedicated to conservation, protection, and enhancement of fish, wildlife and plants, and their habitats

IUCN (International Union for Conservation of Nature) an international organization working in the field of nature conservation and sustainable use of natural resources, including research, data analysis, data gathering, field projects, advocacy, and education

MSA (Magnuson–Stevens Fishery Conservation and Management Act) the primary law governing marine fisheries management in US federal waters

MMPA (Marine Mammal Protection Act) legislation enacted on October 21, 1972, that states all marine mammals are protected, prohibiting (with certain exceptions) the take of marine mammals in US waters and by US citizens on the high seas, specifically the importation of marine mammals and marine mammal products into the United States

NMFS (National Marine Fisheries Service) an agency within the National Oceanic and Atmospheric Administration (NOAA) responsible for management, conservation, and protection of the nation's marine resources

NPS (National Park Service) preserves the natural and cultural resources and values of the National Park System for the enjoyment, education, and inspiration of this and future generations

PATRIC (Python Action Team Removing Invasive Constrictors) FWC's initiative that engages qualified individuals with non-native constrictor control efforts

Trap Neuter Release (TNR) safe, effective, and humane programs that target community cat populations to improve the lives of cats and address overpopulation concerns

◄ An invasive, juvenile green iguana makes its way up a native sabal palm, Florida's state tree, in Crandon Park.

ACKNOWLEDGEMENTS

Between all us authors, we have an uncountable number of people to thank for this book becoming a reality. From the constant support of family, to the never-ending affirmations of friends and colleagues, we are eternally grateful for everyone's help throughout this process. The photography alone is a testament to the support we received—a majority of the photographs within this guide were taken by friends and local photographers. This book is the result of four friends coming together to savor a once-in-a-lifetime opportunity to tell a fresh story about the city, and we hope our work will be loved by any nature enthusiasts living in or visiting Miami. We'd like to thank everyone who was either directly involved in this process or provided a shoulder to lean on when we needed it most.

◄ Key Deer says
thank you for
joining us through
Wild Miami!

RESOURCES

Animal and Plant Health Inspection Service of the United States Department of Agriculture maintains a useful tool to help understand how nature and humans can cooperate, including data sources and resources on animal and plant health, common pests and diseases, animal welfare, biotechnology, wildlife damage management, and global trade.

Animalia is an open-access, online animal encyclopedia including detailed taxonomic and ecological information for more than 1,800 species, focusing on mammals, birds, and reptiles.

Audubon Society of America is perhaps the most well-known organization advocating for bird conservation and public education, with Miami having its own chapter called the Tropical Audubon Society, founded in 1947.

Cornell Laboratory of Ornithology – All About Birds is not only an online bird identification tool but also has free articles including recent ornithological news stories, birdwatching tips, feeding guides, live camera feeds of wild birds, and a range of university-level courses on a variety of topics.

Dallas World Aquarium in Texas focuses on animal welfare and conservation and maintains a useful website that takes visitors on a virtual journey through the ocean and rainforests.

Florida Atlantic University is a public university based in Boca Raton that hosts an Avian Ecology Lab focused on questions related to wetland birds and the aquatic ecosystems on which they depend, specifically the management needs in the Everglades.

FloridasCoralReef.org is run by the Florida Department of Environmental Protection and is dedicated to the importance of Florida's Coral Reef, emphasizing its impact on our South Florida ecosystems, biological diversity, tourism, and economy while highlighting the continued efforts of organizations and partners aiming to preserve and restore it.

Florida Museum sits on the University of Florida campus in Gainesville and focuses on understanding, preserving, and interpreting biological diversity and cultural heritage, while acting as an engaging and impactful hub where the public can learn and use science across a rich array of scientific fields.

Florida Natural Areas Inventory (FNAI) is part of the Florida Resources and Environmental Analysis Center at Florida State University, with an objective of maintaining a database of the state's rare plants and animals as well as conducting research that helps spur effective land management and conservation efforts.

Florida Springs Institute is a non-profit organization that tries to foster public education and effective conservation strategies for these iconic but fragile bodies of water.

Florida State University Coastal and Marine Laboratory is a marine lab at St. Theresa that focuses on conducting innovative, pioneering, interdisciplinary research on coastal and marine ecosystems and involving the local community in environmental advocacy.

Geckoweb is a user-friendly website operated by Finding Species, which is a biodiversity information clearinghouse, and the United States Geological Survey; it provides information related to gecko species throughout the country, both native and invasive.

JSTOR is a digital library of academic journals and books; although access requires a subscription, most public libraries and institutions have one that you can use.

Lander University is a regional, four-year university based in Greenwood, South Carolina, with an environmental science program and associated information related to biology, geology, physics, and current environmental challenges.

National Geographic Field Guide to the Birds of North America was first published in 2006 and offers an in-depth look at the identifying features, ranges, and ecology of all bird species found within North America; the most recent edition was published in 2017.

National Oceanic and Atmospheric Administration (NOAA) is a federal agency run out of the US Department of Commerce, which governs and funds marine research focused on a wide variety of topics associated with weather and fisheries. The fisheries department is a trusted government authority responsible for the stewardship of the nation's ocean resources and their habitat through sound science and an ecosystem-based approach to management.

Oceana is an international nonprofit organization working exclusively to protect and restore oceans on a global scale through specific, science-based policy campaigns and goals.

Reef Fish Identification is considered the holy grail of fish identification books written by Paul Human and Ned DeLoach. A must-have for diving, this guide contains photographs, taxonomy, and distribution information for nearly 700 marine species in South Florida and the Caribbean.

Rescue a Reef is the University of Miami Rosenstiel School's coral conservation program, designed to build community and coastal resilience through coral reef research, restoration, citizen science, public awareness, and educational outreach. Their research lab uses strong, science-based techniques to grow threatened coral species in land and offshore nurseries as a sustainable source of healthy coral colonies for use in active reef restoration.

Savannah River Ecology Laboratory (SREL) is a research lab at the University of Georgia whose mission is to "provide an independent evaluation of the impact of Savannah River Site's operations on the environment to the public and to the Department of Energy."

Smithsonian Tropical Research Institute is located in Panama City, Panama, with a focus on increasing and sharing knowledge about the past, present, and future of tropical ecosystems and their relevance to human welfare on terrestrial and marine species and habitats. Its online resources have species descriptions, lively articles about biodiversity, and science databases.

South Florida Sponges: A Guide to Identification is an online identification guide maintained by the Department of Computer and Information Sciences at the University of Alabama at Birmingham as part of the Porifera Tree of Life (PorToL), this resource offers practical identifications of the shallow-water marine sponges of southern Florida and surrounding waters, including in situ color photographs, descriptions, and key features needed for proper identification.

Texas Marine Species is an online identification guide to marine organisms of Texas for both biology technicians and the public, specifically the Marine Species Identification Project, which is an interactive, web-based collection of detailed photographs and information on marine species found off the Texas coast.

United States Department of Agriculture – Aquatic Invasives provides information about the National Invasive Species Information Center (NISIC), specifically mentioning marine invasive species and their impact on local ecosystems.

United States Geological Service, Nonindigenous Aquatic Species Program (NAS) is a national program collecting and analyzing data on invasive aquatic species sightings, often organizing data to be accessible for both the public and land managers.

University of California Museum of Paleontology (UCMP), located on the UC Berkeley campus focuses on investigating and promoting the understanding of the history of life and the diversity of the Earth's biota through research and education.

University of Florida-Gardening Solutions is a website run by the University of Florida Institute of Food and Agricultural Sciences, which provides tips on what types of species (native and non-native) to plant based on your area.

University of Florida Wildlife Ecology and Conservation – Johnson Lab conducts research on invasive species, with a focus on reptiles, amphibians, and birds.

University of Miami (UM) is a private research university located in Coral Gables and Miami's oldest institute of higher learning; it maintains a vast online database covering historical archives and marine science.

University of Rhode Island is prominent within the marine science field, being responsible for countless publications across multiple topics of research, including fisheries and population dynamics.

University of West Indies, based in Jamaica, is responsible for multiple publications related to marine species found in South Florida and the Caribbean.

US Fish and Wildlife Service is a federal agency dedicated to the management of fish, wildlife and habitats; their website contains important information about endangered species, the programs intended to protect them, and national wildlife refuges.

PHOTO AND ILLUSTRATION CREDITS

All illustrations by Kiko Rodriguez

Broward County Library Digital Archives, Photographer G.W.T., ca. 1888, 19 bottom

Evan K. D'Alessandro Ph.D., 4, 98, 129, 133 top, 134, 150, 151 top, 155, 163 bottom, 185, 187 left, 187 top, 196 bottom, 253, 265 bottom, 279, 284, 288, 289, 292 top, 303, 305, 305 top, 306 bottom, 310 bottom, 312, 313 bottom, 314, 319 top, 324, 324 top, 330, 342, 343 top, 343 bottom, 362

David Dantzler, 142, 144, 149, 181

Brian Diaz, 30, 37, 39, 40, 42, 44, 46, 47, 49, 50, 53, 57, 67, 68, 71, 77, 78, 80, 81, 86, 87, 90, 91, 92, 95, 96, 97, 100, 101, 139, 168 bottom, 191 top, 208 top, 210, 211 bottom, 212, 213, 215 top, 215 bottom, 216 bottom, 217, 218, 220 top, 212, 222, 223, 224, 225, 226, 227, 228, 229 top, 271 top, 272, 273, 274, 287, 341 bottom, 344, 345, 346, 347, 348, 350, 351, 353, 354, 356, 357 top, 358, 359

Everglades: River of Grass, Third Edition, by Marjory Stoneman Douglas, Afterward by Michael Grunwald, published by Pineapple Press, copyright Marjory Stoneman Douglas, 1986., 22

Reclus Elisee (1873) Ocean Atmosphere and Life, Being the Second Series of a Descriptive History of the Life of the Globe, New York City, NY: Harper and Brothers, Publishers, 16

Dean Grubbs, 321

Shannon C. Jones, 64, 65, 110, 110–111, 114

Library of Congress Online Catalog, 15 top

Ron Magill, 73, 74

Barry Mansell, Nature Picture Library, 160 bottom

Rosemarie Moore, 135, 163 top, 240

Thomas J. Morrell, 55, 158, 336 top

Edward H. Pritchard, 192 bottom, 208 bottom, 267, 269 top, 275 top, 286, 355, 357 bottom, 360

Zach Ransom, 121, 146, 276, 278, 302 bottom, 313 top, 318 top, 319 bottom, 324 bottom, 325, 327

Nicolas Rivas, 62 bottom, 170 bottom, 183, 201, 231, 242 top, 244, 277, 292 bottom, 296 bottom

University of Florida, Napoleon B. Broward portrait, 19 top

University of Miami Library Special Collections, digital ID asm00150004940001001, 21

Olivia M. Williamson, 7 top, 124 right, 128, 230, 241, 246 bottom, 249 top, 249 bottom, 255 bottom, 282, 302, 309, 310 top, 315, 316 top, 316 bottom, 318 bottom, 322, 326 top, 328, 329, 333, 335, 336 bottom, 338, 339, 340, 341 top

Benjamin Young, 7 bottom, 83, 132, 151 bottom, 153 top, 165 bottom, 169, 170 top, 171 top, 172 top, 175, 176, 179, 178 top, 178 bottom, 179, 180, 187 bottom, 239, 242 bottom, 245 bottom, 246 top, 247 top, 250 top, 251, 291 top, 291 bottom, 293 bottom, 294, 295

Alamy

agefotostock, 304 bottom

All Canada Photos, 235 bottom, 285

Arto Hakola, 192 bottom

Bryan Reynolds, 254

Charles Melton, 193 bottom

Florida Images, 264 top

George Grall, 209 top, 265 top

Nature Picture Library, 243, 262 top, 271 bottom

Pictures Now, 17

Roberto Nistri, 255 top

Flickr

Becky Matsubara, 168 top

Distinguished Reflections, 153

Don Faulkner, 177

Everglades National Park, 103

Judy Gallagher, 154 bottom, 184 top, 184 bottom, 252 bottom

NOAA Photo Library, 300

Rushen, 159 bottom

University of Florida/Institute of Food and Agriculture Sources, 190 top

USFWS/Mary Peterson, 172

iStock

DerrenMeadwell, 133 bottom left

DMVPhotography, 211 top

FtLaudGirl, 133 bottom right

Kirk Hewlett, 132 bottom

MorelSO, 14

Shutterstock

ABEMOS, 15 bottom

Al McGlashan, 311

alybaba, 275 bottom

Anton Balazh, 13

Armin Rose, 195 bottom right

ARNON SUDEE, 264 bottom

Arunee Rodloy, 260 bottom

atiger, 214

Bappa Pabitra, 250 bottom

Barnaby Chambers, 195 top

boban_nz, 258 top

Brent Barnes, 124 left, 138

Cathy Keifer, 194 bottom

Charlotte Bleijenberg, 257

Chase D'animulis, 216 top

Cosmin Manci, 197 top

Danita Delimont, 269 bottom

David Havel, 159 top

DesiDrewPhotography, 113

dossyl, 252 top

Elliot Hurwitt, 247 bottom

Elliotte Rusty Harold, 182 bottom, 293 top, 298

FashionStock.com, 26

Felix Mizioznikov, 29, 117

Fiona M. Donnelly, 189 bottom

Focused Adventures, 326 bottom

FotoRequest, 166

George Chernilevsky, 260 top

Gerald A. DeBoer, 297

Hernando Sorzano, 30

Holly Kuchera, 148, 234 bottom

Im Bellentani, 123

IrinaK, 199

Jack Nevitt, 84

Jarous, 337

Jay Ondreicka, 193 top, 198 bottom

Jesus Cobaleda, 147

Johanna Veldstra, 157 bottom

John P Ruggeri, 245 top

Joseph Thomas Photography, 62

Kaesler Media, 219

Karuna Eberi, 349

Katarina Christenson, 202 bottom

Kelly vanDelien, 119

Ken Schulze, 207

Kristi Blokhin, 27

littlenySTOCK, 23

Liz Weber, 235 top

LorraineHudgins, 164

Lost Mountain Studio, 107

M Rose, 236

Manfred Ruckszio, 229 bottom

Melinda Fawver, 268

meunierd, 61

Mia2you, 75

Miroslav Halama, 256

MJANaturePics, 202 top

M-Production, 258 bottom

Mr F, 162
Olga Shum, 195 bottom left
Ovidiu Hrubaru, 108
Patricia K. Campbell, 160
peter jesche, 237 bottom
Peter Leahy, 320, 323
Philip Bird LRPS CPAGE, 167 bottom
pixelworlds, 188
psmphotography, 157 top
r_silver, 266
Reisegraf.ch, 152
Rob Christiaans, 174
Roberto Pascual Gomez, 220 bottom
Rodri75, 204 top
Rosamar, 290
Rostislav Stefanek, 259
Russell Marshall, 182 top, 202 middle
Shawn Hempel, 186
Silent Shoot, 196 top
skippy666, 206 bottom
Steve Bower, 143, 148 bottom, 190
    bottom, 205
Steve Byland, 173

Sunet Suesakunkhrit, 209 bottom
SURAJKMALIPhotography, 193 top
SWF 1, 296 top
Tatiana Kilimnik, 60
Thomas Barrat, 331 bottom
Tim Abeln, 194 top
Tomasz Klejdysz, 206 top
Tory Kallman, 281
Vadim ZH, 200
vagabond54, 145, 234 top
vbalson, 204 bottom
Vladimir Wrangel, 133 middle right, 305
    bottom
wildestanimal, 301 top
William Cushman, 189 top
William Silver, 232–233
yhelfman, 161

Wikimedia Commons
Daderot, 104
Daniel Di Palma, 58
DickDaniels, 165 top
Dunpharlain, 299

Ebyabe, 14–15
Enwebb, 137
Everglades NPS, 141, 331 top
Geoff Gallice, 198 top
James St. John, 167 top, 304 top, 334
Jeanloujustine, 237 middle
Jeffrey Weston Lotz, Florida Department
    of Agriculture, 197 bottom
John James Audubon, Birds of
    America, 248
LittleOrphanDani, 116
Mariofan13, 238
Munkinator, 262 bottom
New York Zoological Society, 280
Pallowick, 120
The High Fin Sperm Whale, 237 top
Tony Hisgett, 317
US Marine Corps, National Archive and
    Records Administration, 18
USFWS/Ann Froschauer, 136
Vassil, 261, 263
Will Thomas, 306 top

INDEX

About the Authors

Shannon C. Jones

Thomas J. Morrell is a fishery biologist contractor for the National Oceanic and Atmospheric Administration (NOAA) at the Southeast Fisheries Science Center in Miami, Florida. Having worked with multiple programs related to or focused on fisheries management, biological sampling, and data management, he has a passion for ensuring fisheries populations and oceanic trends are closely monitored for future generations. As a cofounder of the local nonprofit MORAES (Marine Order for Research and Action through Environmental Stewardship), he has focused both his professional career and personal life on environmental advocacy, hoping to provide others with opportunities to follow their passions. From volunteering with marine mammal strandings through MARS (Marine Animal Rescue Society), to acting as a lead marine safety instructor for NOAA, to becoming a certified python wrangler, he continues to learn and gain experience in all aspects of environmental science.

Thomas J. Morrell

Shannon C. Jones's career is focused on marine conservation and science education, through which she engages community members in philanthropic activities surrounding the ocean and marine life. As the conservation programs manager at the Phillip and Patricia Frost Museum of Science, she runs a citizen-science based habitat restoration program and Museum Volunteers for the Environment (MUVE), and also assists with managing innovative coral reef restoration efforts. A cofounder of the Marine Order for Research and Action through Environmental Stewardship (MORAES), Shannon previously ran the education department at Miami Seaquarium, designing and executing STEAM and conservation curriculum that reached over 8,000 students annually. She is an advanced Florida Master Naturalist Land Steward and a member of Catalyst Miami's Community Leadership on the Environment, Advocacy, and Resilience (CLEAR).

Shannon C. Jones

Brian Diaz was born and raised in Hialeah to parents who emigrated from Cuba, and he grew up with a deep-seated appreciation, curiosity, and respect for the natural world that would follow him through his life. Brian's mission is to take the lessons of conservation wherever he goes, inspiring others to take up their responsibility as environmental stewards. From 2017 to 2021, he worked as the coordinator for the Phillip and Patricia Frost Museum of Science program Museum Volunteers for the Environment (MUVE), where he helped lead volunteer-based initiatives to restore natural habitats at Virginia Key. Brian is now an interpretive naturalist with Miami-Dade County. Particularly passionate about plants and their foundational role in healthy ecosystems, he also serves on the board for TREEmendous Miami and is the current president of the Dade Chapter of the Florida Native Plant Society.

Véronique Koch

Fernando M. Bretos was born in Colombia to Cuban parents and raised in Sydney, Australia, and Miami. He is a conservation scientist who focuses on the restoration and protection of subtropical coastal and marine habitats and the study and conservation of marine migratory species and rare corals. As program officer at the Ocean Foundation, he oversees blue carbon projects in the western Caribbean and Gulf of Mexico and directs an international marine protected area network called RedGolfo. The international research expeditions he has led include a 1999 cruise to Navassa, an uninhabited island between Jamaica and Haiti, which led to the island's full protection as a US National Wildlife Refuge. He is the founder of the Phillip and Patricia Frost Museum of Science program Museum Volunteers for the Environment (MUVE), an Audubon and Kinship Conservation Fellow, and a National Geographic Society Explorer.